Learning Frameworks

Student Development

SAN ANTONIO COLLEGE

XanEdu

Printed in the United States of America

ISBN 13: 978-1-71147-187-7

Cover Image: © Adobe Stock Leigh Prather

Acknowledgements

Chapter 1

Contents of this chapter are from *College Success*, textbook content produced by OpenStax and licensed under a Creative Commons Attribution 4.0 International License (CC BY 4.0).

Chapter 2

Contents of this chapter are from *College Success*, textbook content produced by OpenStax and licensed under a Creative Commons Attribution 4.0 International License (CC BY 4.0).

Chapter 3

Contents of this chapter are from two titles: *College Success* and *Organizational Behavior*, textbook content produced by OpenStax and licensed under a Creative Commons Attribution 4.0 International License (CC BY 4.0).

Chapter 4

Contents of this chapter are from *College Success*, textbook content produced by OpenStax and licensed under a Creative Commons Attribution 4.0 International License (CC BY 4.0).

Chapter 5

Contents of this chapter are from *College Success* and *Psychology 2e*, textbook content produced by OpenStax and licensed under a Creative Commons Attribution 4.0 International License (CC BY 4.0). Additional OER sources are listed at the end of the chapter.

Chapter 6

Contents of this chapter are from *College Success* and *Psychology 2e*, textbook content produced by OpenStax and licensed under a Creative Commons Attribution 4.0 International License (CC BY 4.0).

Chapter 7

Contents of this chapter are from *College Success*, textbook content produced by OpenStax and licensed under a Creative Commons Attribution 4.0 International License (CC BY 4.0).

Appendix 7

Klatt, J., & Ray, R. (2014). "Student academic outcomes after completing a first-year seminar." *Nacta Journal*, 58(4), 288–2. Copyright © 2014 North American Colleges and Teachers of Agriculture (NACTA). Used With Permission.

Appendix 8

Duckworth, A. L., & Seligman, M. E. P. (2005). "Self-discipline outdoes IQ in predicting academic performance of adolescents." *Psychological Science*, 16(12), 939–944. Copyright © 2005 by SAGE Publications, Inc.; permission conveyed through Copyright Clearance Center, Inc.

Appendix 9

Kawyannejad, R., Mirzaei, M., Valinejadi, A., Hemmatpour, B., Karimpour, H. A., AminiSaman, J., Ezzati, E., Vaziri, S., Safaeepour, M., & Mohammadi, S. (2019). "General health of students of medical sciences and its relation to sleep quality, cell phone overuse, social networks and internet addiction." *Biopsychosocial Medicine*, 13. https://doi.org/10.1186/s13030-019-0150-7. This article is distributed under the terms of the Creative Commons Attribution 4.0 International License (http://creativecommons.org/licenses/by/4.0/).

XanEdu
17177 Laurel Park Drive
Suite 233
Livonia, MI 48152
800-562-2147
www.xanedu.com

Contents

Chapter 1 Exploring College

Figure 1.1

Chapter Outline

1.1 Why college and this course?

1.2 The First Year of College Will Be an Experience

1.3 College Culture and Expectations

1.4 Personal and Campus Safety

1.5 How can this course and this book help?

Student Survey

Welcome to San Antonio College! This course will help you gain the skills, behaviors, and attitudes needed to meet your academic goals. Your instructor is passionate about helping first-semester students be successful as they begin their college journeys. Let's start with a quick survey to see how you are feeling about your ability to meet the expectations of college.

How do you feel about your ability to meet the expectations of college? Rank the following questions on a scale of 1 to 4, with 1 meaning "least like me" and 4 meaning "most like me."

1. ____ I am fully aware of the expectations of college and how to meet them.
2. ____ I know why I am in college and have clear goals that I want to achieve.
3. ____ I know what is important to me and how college fits into my life mission.

4. ____ Most of the time, I take responsibility for learning new and challenging concepts.
5. ____ I feel comfortable working with faculty, advisors, and classmates to accomplish my goals.

Don't be concerned with the results. If your score is low, you will most likely gain even more from this book.

Chapter Outcomes

In this chapter, you will learn about what you can do to get ready for college. By the time you complete this chapter, you should be able to do the following:

- Recognize the purpose and value of college.
- Articulate personal mission statement.
- Describe the transitional experience of the first year of college.
- Discuss how to handle college culture and expectations.
- Identify resources on campus for supporting your college success.
- Get acquainted with college polices and safety procedures.

Introduction

Reggie	Marisol
Reggie has, after much thought and with a high level of family support, decided to enroll in college. It has been a dream in the making, as he was unable to attend immediately after high school graduation. Instead, he worked for several years in his family's business, got married, had a son, and then decided that he didn't want to spend the rest of his life regretting that he didn't get a chance to follow his dreams of becoming a teacher. Because it has been almost a decade since he sat in a classroom, he is worried about how he will fit in as an adult learner returning to college. Will his classmates think he is too old? Will his professors think he is not ready for the challenges of college work? Will his family get tired of his long nights at the library and his new priorities? There is so much Reggie is unsure of, yet he knows it's a step in the right direction.	It has been only three months since Marisol graduated from high school. She graduated in the top 10 percent of her class, and she earned college credit while in high school. She feels academically prepared, and she has a good sense of what degree she wants to earn. Since Marisol was 5 years old, she's wanted to be an engineer because she loved building things in the backyard with her father's tools. He always encouraged her to follow her dreams, and her whole family was supportive of her hobbies and interests. However, Marisol is concerned that her choice of major will keep her from dance, creative writing, and other passions. Furthermore, Marisol doesn't know anyone at this college. Will she be able to find new friends quickly? Will her engineering classes crush her or motivate her to complete college? Will she be able to explore other interests? Marisol has a lot on her mind, but she aims to face these challenges head-on.

While Reggie and Marisol have had different experiences and certainly have different motivations for enrolling in college, they have quite a bit in common. They are both committed to this new chapter in their lives, and they are both connected to their families in ways that can influence their commitment to this pursuit. What they don't know just yet—because they haven't started their classes—is that they will have even more in common as they move through each term, focus on a major, and plan for life after graduation. And they have a lot in common with you because you are in a similar position—starting the next chapter of the rest of your life.

In this chapter, you will first learn more about identifying the reason you are in college and get clarity on what your life mission is. This is an important first step because knowing your *why* and your *purpose* will keep you motivated. Next, the chapter will cover the transitions you may experience as a new college student. Then, the chapter will focus on how you can acclimate to the culture and meet the expectations—all of which will make the transition to a full-fledged college student easier. Finally, the chapter will provide you with strategies for overcoming the challenges that you may face by providing information about how to find and access resources and stay safe.

1.1 Why College?

Questions to consider:

- Why are you in college?
- What is most important to you in life?
- What are the rewards and value of a college degree?
- Why this course?

You just read the profiles of two students, Reggie and Marisol, but now we turn to who you are and why you are in college. Starting this chapter with *you*, the student, seems to make perfect sense. Like Reggie and Marisol, you are probably full of emotions as you begin this journey toward a degree and the fulfillment of a dream. Are you excited about meeting new people and *finally* getting to take classes that interest you? Are you nervous about how you are going to handle your courses and all the other activities that come along with being a college student? Are you thrilled to be making important decisions about your future? Are you worried about making the right choice when deciding on a major or a career? All these thoughts, even if contradictory at times, are normal. And you may be experiencing several of them at the same time.

Figure 1.2 Decision-making about college and our future can be challenging, but with self-analysis and support, you can feel more confident and make the best choices.

Why Are You in College?

We know that college is not mandatory—like kindergarten through 12th grade is—and it is not free. You have made a *choice* to commit several years of hard work to earn a degree or credential. In some cases, you may have had to work really hard to get here by getting good grades in high school and earning money to pay for tuition and fees and other expenses. Now you have more at stake and a clearer path to achieving your goals, but you still need to be able to answer the question.

To help answer this question, consider the following questioning technique called "The Five Whys" that was originally created by Sakichi Toyoda, a Japanese inventor, whose strategy was used by the Toyota Motor Company to find the underlying cause of a problem. While your decision to go to college is not a problem, the exercise is helpful to uncover your underlying purpose for enrolling in college.

The process starts with a "Why" question that you want to know the answer to. Then, the next four "Why" questions use a portion of the previous answer to help you dig further into the answer to the original question. Here is an example of "The Five Whys," with the first question as "Why are you in college?" The answers and their connection to the next "Why" question have been underlined below so you can see how the process works.

While the example is one from a student who knows what she wants to major in, this process does not require that you have a specific degree or career in mind. In fact, if you are undecided, then you can explore the "why" of your indecision. Is it because you have lots of choices, or is it because you are not sure what you really want out of college?

The Five Whys in Action	
Why are you in college?	I am in college to *earn a degree in speech pathology.*
Why do you want to *earn a degree in speech pathology?*	I want to be able to *help people who have trouble speaking.*
Why do you want to *help people who have trouble speaking?*	I believe that *people who have trouble speaking deserve a life they want.*
Why do you feel it is important that *people who have trouble speaking deserve a life they want?*	I feel they often *have needs that are overlooked and do not get treated equally.*
Why do you want to use your *voice to help these people live a life they deserve?*	I feel it is my purpose to *help others achieve their full potential despite having physical challenges.*

Do you see how this student went beyond a standard answer about the degree that she wants to earn to connecting her degree to an overall purpose that she has to help others in a specific way? Had she not been instructed to delve a little deeper with each answer, it is likely that she would not have so quickly articulated that deeper purpose. And that understanding of "why" you are in college—beyond the degree you want or the job you envision after graduation—is key to staying motivated through what will most likely be some challenging times.

How else does knowing your "why" or your deeper reason for being in college help you? According to Angela Duckworth (2016), a researcher on *grit*—what it takes for us to dig in deep when faced with adversity and continue to work toward our goal—knowing your purpose can be the booster to grit that can help you succeed.[1] Other research has found that people who have a strong sense of purpose are less likely to experience stress and anxiety (Burrow, 2013)[2] and more likely to be satisfied in their jobs (Weir, 2013).[3] Therefore, being able to answer the question "Why are you in college?" not only satisfies the person asking, but it also has direct benefits to your overall well-being.

Activity 1.1

Try "The Five Whys" yourself in the table below to help you get a better sense of your purpose and to give you a worthy answer for anyone who asks you "Why are you in college?"

The Five Whys: Your Turn

Why are you in college?	I am in college to . . .
Why do you . . .	I . . .
Why do you . . .	I . . .
Why do you . . .	I . . .
Why do you . . .	I . . .

What Are the Rewards and Value of a College Degree?

Once you have explored your "why" for enrolling in college, it may be worth reviewing what we know about the value of a college degree. There is no doubt you know people who have succeeded in a career without going to college. Famous examples of college dropouts include Bill Gates (the cofounder and CEO of Microsoft) and Rachel Ray (chef, TV personality, cookbook author, and entrepreneur). These are two well-known, smart, talented people who have had tremendous success on a global scale. They are also not the typical profile of a student who doesn't finish a degree. For many students, especially those who are first-generation college students, a college degree helps them follow a career pathway and create a life that would not have been possible without the credential. Even in this time of rapid change in all kinds of fields, including technology and education, a college degree is still worth it for many people.

Consider the following chart that shows an average of lifetime earnings per level of education. As you can see, the more education you receive, the greater the increase in your average lifetime earnings. Even though a degree costs a considerable amount of money on the front end, if you think about it as an investment in your future, you can see that college graduates receive a substantial return on their investment. To put it into more concrete terms, let's say you spend $100,000 for a four-year degree (*Don't faint! That is the average sticker cost of a four-year degree at a public university if you include tuition, fees, room, and board*). The return on investment (ROI) over a lifetime is 1,500%! You don't have to be a financial wizard to recognize that 1,500% return is fantastic.

1 Duckworth, A. (2016). *Grit: The Power and Passion of Perseverance.* NY: Simon & Schuster.

2 Burrow, A. L. and Hill, P. L. (2013). Derailed by diversity? Purpose buffers the relationship between ethnic composition on trains and passenger negative mood. *Personality and Psychology Bulletin*, 39 (12), 1610–1619. https://doi.org/10.1177/0146167213499377.

3 Weir, K. (2013). More than job satisfaction: Psychologists are discovering what makes work meaninful—and how to create value in any job. *American Psychological Association*, 44 (11), 39.

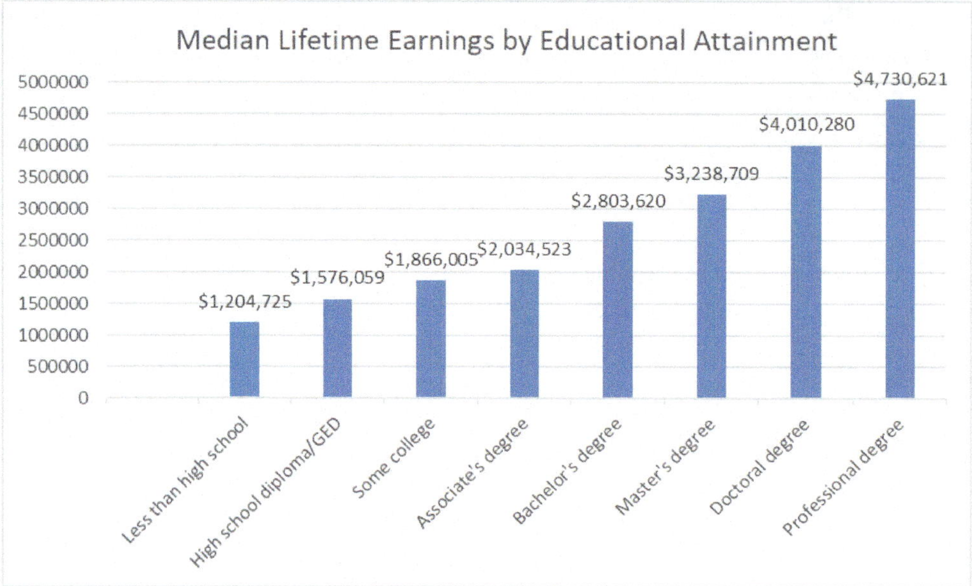

Figure 1.3 Education and Lifetime Earnings

Every education level brings with it potential for greater lifetime earnings. These are simply averages and may not apply to all career types and individuals. For clarity, the "professional degree," attaining the highest earnings, refers to degrees such as those given to doctors or lawyers.

Source: Georgetown University Center on Education and the Workforce analysis of the U.S. Census Bureau, American Community Survey (ACS), 2009–2019.

Note: The figure is based on data for 25- to 64-year-olds working full-time, full-year.

Making more money over time is not the only benefit you can earn from completing a college degree. College graduates are also more likely to experience the following:

- **Greater job satisfaction.** That's right! College graduates are more likely to get a job that they like or to find that their job is more enjoyable than not.
- **Better job stability.** Employees with college degrees are more likely to find and keep a job, which is comforting news in times of economic uncertainty.
- **Improved health and wellness.** College graduates are less likely to smoke and more likely to exercise and maintain a healthy weight.
- **Better outcomes for the next generation.** One of the best benefits of a college degree is that it can have positive influences for the graduate's immediate family and the next generations.

One last thing: There is some debate as to whether a college degree is needed to land a job, and there are certainly jobs that you can get without a college degree. However, there are many reasons that a college degree can give you an edge in the job market. Here are just a few reasons that graduating with a degree is still valuable:

- More and more entry-level jobs will require a college degree. According to Georgetown University's Center on Education and the Workforce, in 2020, 35% of jobs will require a college degree.[4]

---

4 Carnevale, A. P., Smith, N., and Strohl, J. (2013). Recover: Job growth and education requirements through 2020. Georgetown University's Center on Education and the Workforce. Retrieved from https://cew.georgetown.edu/cew-reports/recovery-job-growth-and-education-requirements-through-2020/.

- A credential from a college or university still provides assurance that a student has mastered the material. Would you trust a doctor who never went to medical school to do open-heart surgery on a close relative? No, we didn't think so.
- College provides an opportunity to develop much-needed soft skills. In this course, there are specific student learning outcomes that you will be learning. In addition to these outcomes, you will be gaining marketable skills. By the time you leave San Antonio College, you should have attained these eight marketable skills that employers say they want their new hires to possess.
  - Critical Thinking
  - Teamwork
  - Social Responsibility
  - Personal Responsibility
  - Leadership
  - Performance
  - Communication
  - Empirical and Quantitative Skills

The chart below shows what you will be learning in this class, the assignments you will complete to demonstrate your learning, and the marketable skills you will be gaining.

Table 1.1 Course Learning Outcomes, Marketable Skills Gained, and Assessment Assignments

Learning Outcome	Marketable Skills Gained	Assessment
1. Students will explore, identify and apply psychological theories of learning, cognition and motivation.	**Critical Thinking** - Analysis: Students will identify, classify or challenge components of an argument/problem.	Chapter 5 Exam
2. Students will identify and apply effective learning strategies.	**Critical Thinking** - Analysis: Students will identify, classify or challenge components of an argument/problem.	Chapter 6 Exam
3. Students will evaluate and implement academic and interpersonal skills needed to achieve college, career and personal goals.	**Personal Responsibility** - Self-awareness: Students will articulate their own core beliefs and describe their source. **Critical Thinking** - Synthesis: Students will combine and organize evidence to demonstrate a greater depth of understanding of an argument/problem.	Career Research Project/Paper
4. Students will explore a variety of leadership models and theories.	**Teamwork** - Cooperation: Students will collaborate with others by integrating individual contributions into a team task to achieve a successful outcome. **Leadership** - Vision: Students will craft a vision for their group or organization and develop a strategic plan to achieve that vision.	Leadership Group Assignment
5. Students will build information literacy skills by applying a variety of resources, including library tools, to find, analyze and use high-quality information.	**Critical Thinking** - Analysis: Students will identify, classify or challenge components of an argument/problem.	Peer-reviewed Journal Article Summary

There are few occasions that will provide you the opportunity to develop all of these skills in a low-stakes environment (i.e., without the fear of being fired!). You will learn all of this *and* more in your classes. Seems like a great opportunity, doesn't it? If you find yourself asking the question "What does *this* course have to do with my major?" or "Why do I have to take *that*?" challenge yourself to learn more about the course and look for connections between the content and your larger educational, career and life goals.

Analysis Question

In what ways will earning a college degree be valuable to you now and in the future? Be sure to describe the financial, career and personal benefits to earning a college degree.

Mission and Purpose

This section challenges you to really think about the *why*. Why did you decide to attend college? Why is it important to you? What is your purpose in life? How do you want to be remembered?

We all have life goals or objectives—some are clearer than others, but they are there. You may think of your objectives in terms of finances (to hold a job that allows you to be financially independent, for example), or perhaps your goals are more personal (to be married and have a family). They might be specific (pay off my student loans within three years of leaving college) or very general (to do good). Regardless of what they may be, they are all important because they influence the decisions you are making today about your future.

Understanding what motivates your goals and aspirations is essential because you are then better able to prioritize your thoughts about the future and identify new options that you may not have thought of before that will bring you fulfillment. Beware of accepting dreams others may have for you as your own ("I want to finish college to make my parents proud" or "I want to complete my associate's degree because my boyfriend says I can get a better job"). These are not necessarily bad dreams to pursue, but they will lead to genuine fulfillment only if they are *your* dreams.

Activity 1.2 My Dream Machine

In the table that follows, list the four or five most important dreams you have for your future. Include your personal, professional, and economic goals. Now take some time to think about *why* these dreams are important to *you*. What do they tell you about what is important to you? How are they linked to each other?

My dreams for the future	Why they are important to me

Since you were a child and first definitively stated, "When I grow up I want to be a ______________," you have been making decisions in order to fulfill your dreams. Most likely you are in college today as a step toward fulfilling a lifetime goal. But very few of us are still passionate about our childhood dream. As we grew up, we discovered new options; were influenced by people we met; or perhaps even learned that being a fireman, nurse, circus clown, pro baseball player, or princess is not all we thought it might be. Your evolving life dreams may continue even today and should be embraced. But for most people, the motivators behind the dreams—the answers to "Why they are important to me" in Activity 1.2—change very little over time. If as a child you wanted to be a princess so your kingdom would have a kind ruler, today you may want to be a teacher to help children learn—and both of these dreams, at their core, are motivated by the desire to help others.

Activity 1.3 Mission Statement

Take a close look at your "importance" statements in Activity 3.1. What do they tell you about the direction you want to take in your life? What are your priorities? Will some dreams need to be put on the back burner while you pursue others? Using your dream statements as a guide, write a three to five sentence mission for yourself. You should refer to it a few times a year and ask yourself, "Am I living up to my mission?" and "Am I taking the right steps toward this mission?" You may also want to fine-tune it as you progress.

Why this Course?

Now that you have considered why you are in college and why a college degree may be valuable to you, it's time to focus on why you are taking this course and reading this book. You are taking this course because San Antonio College believes that it will *help you succeed in college and beyond*. Likewise, the reason your professor has assigned this book is because it has been designed to give you the best information about how to make your transition to college smoother. We know that students who complete a first-year seminar course have higher grades, take more advantage of resources and get more involved than students who do not. If you are not convinced just yet of the value of this course and its content, consider the following questions that you will be encouraged to answer as you learn about how to succeed in college:

- What will college expect of me in terms of skills, habits, and behaviors? How can I develop them to ensure that I am successful?
- What do I need to know about navigating the process of completing a college degree?
- How do I improve the foundational academic skills needed to be successful in college classes?
- How can I ensure that I develop worthy long-term goals and how best can I meet those goals?

These questions are designed to assist you in the transition from high school or the workforce, to the new world of college. And this won't be the last monumental transition that you will experience. For example, you will experience a new job more than once in your life, and you may experience the excitement and challenge of moving to a new house or a new city. You can be assured that transitions will require that you identify what you need to get through them and that you will experience some discomfort along the way. It wouldn't be such a great accomplishment without a little uncertainty, doubt and self-questioning. To help you, the next section speaks specifically of transitions for the purpose of making your next steps smoother.

1.2 The First Year of College Will Be an Experience

Questions to consider:

1. How will you adjust to college?
2. What are the common college experiences you will have?

Adjustments to College Are Inevitable

College not only will expand your mind, but it may also make you a little uncomfortable, challenge your identity, and at times, make you doubt your abilities. It is hard to truly learn anything without getting messy. This is what education does: it transforms us. For that to happen, we will need to be open to the transformation and allow the changes to occur. *Flexibility*, *transition*, and *change* are all words that describe what you will experience. Laurie Hazard and Stephanie Carter (2018)[5] use the word *adjustment*. Hazard and Carter (2018) believe there are six adjustment areas that first-year college students experience: academic, cultural, emotional, financial, intellectual, and social. Of course, you won't go through these adjustments all at once or even in just the first year. Some will take time, while others may not even feel like much of a transition. Let's look at them in brief as a way of preparing for the road ahead:

- *Academic adjustment*. No surprises here. You will most likely—depending on your own academic background—be faced with the increased demands of learning in college. This could mean that you need to spend more time "learning to learn" and using those strategies to master the material.
- *Cultural adjustment*. You also will most likely experience a cultural adjustment just by being in college because most campuses have their own language and customs (*syllabus*, *registrar*, and *office hours*, for example). You may also experience a cultural adjustment because of the diversity that you will encounter. Most likely, the people on your college campus will be different than the people at your high school—or at your workplace.
- *Emotional adjustment*. Remember the range of emotions presented at the beginning of the chapter? Those will likely be present in some form throughout your first weeks in college and at stressful times during the semester. Knowing that you may have good days and bad—and that you can bounce back from the more stressful days—will help you find healthy ways of adjusting emotionally.
- *Financial adjustment*. Most students understand the investment they are making in their future by going to college. Even if you have all your expenses covered, there is still an adjustment to a new way of thinking about what college costs and how to pay for it. You may find that you think twice about spending money on entertainment or that you have improved your skills in finding discounted course supplies.
- *Intellectual adjustment*. Experiencing an intellectual "a-ha!" moment is one of the most rewarding parts of college, right up there with moving across the graduation stage with a degree in hand. Prepare to be surprised when you stumble across a fascinating subject or find that a class discussion changes your life. At the very least, through your academic work, you will learn to think differently about the world around you and your place in it.

---

5 Hazard, L., and Carter, S. (2018). A framework for helping families understand the college transition. *E-Source for College Transitions*, 16(1), 13–15.

- *Social adjustment.* A new place often equals new people. In college, those new relationships can have even more meaning. Getting to know professors not only can help you learn more in your classes, but it can also help you figure out what career pathway you want to take and how to get desired internships and jobs. Learning to reduce conflicts during group work or when living with others helps build essential workplace and life skills.

The table "Six Areas of Adjustment for First-Year College Students" provides a succinct definition for each of the areas as well as examples of how you can demonstrate that you have adjusted. Think about what you have done so far to navigate these transitions, in addition to other things you can do to make your college experience a successful one.

Table 1.2 Six Areas of Adjustment for First-Year College Students

	Academic	Cultural	Emotional	Financial	Intellectual	Social
What is it?	Students will take a more active role in their learning than in high school and have the ability to meet the increasing demands of change.	Students will interact with others of various cultures, religious beliefs, sexual identities and orientations, ages, and abilities.	Students will need to be prepared for the stressors of college and develop habits and behaviors to cope with these changes.	Students will need to demonstrate basic financial literacy, an understanding of the cost of college, and methods of paying for those costs.	Students will have the opportunity to join an academic community that includes classmates, faculty, support personnel, and administrators	Students will be faced with shifts in their relationships, finding a new peer group, and handling the pressure of fitting in.
Students exhibit it when they:	• Take an active role in learning. • Attain college-level learning strategies. • Make adjustments to learning strategies as needed.	• Accept and welcome differences in others. • Recognize the inclusion of their own cultural identity. • Seek opportunities to explore other cultures.	• Readily handle the stressors of college life. • Develop emotional coping strategies. • Seek support from campus resources.	• Manage money independently. • Recognize the costs of college. • Explore job and aid opportunities.	• Engage in intellectual discussions. • Are open to new ideas, subject areas, and career choices. • Integrate new ideas into belief systems.	• Join a club or organization. • Form supportive, healthy relationship. • Understand the impact of peer pressure. • Manage conflict in relationship.

Based on work by Laurie Hazard, Ed.D. and Stephanie Carter, M.A.

Analysis Question

Which of the six areas of adjustment do you think will be the least challenging for you, and which do you think will be most challenging? What can you do now to prepare for the more challenging transitions?

1.3 College Culture and Expectations

Questions to consider:

- What language and customs do you need to know to succeed in college?
- What is your responsibility for learning in college?
- What resources will you use to meet these expectations?
- What are the common challenges in the first year?

College Has Its Own Language and Customs

Going to college—even if you are not far from home—is a cultural experience. It comes with its own language and customs, some of which can be confusing or confounding at first. Just like traveling to a foreign country, it is best if you prepare by learning what words mean and what you are expected to say and do in certain situations.

Let's first start with the language you may encounter. In most cases, there will be words that you have heard before, but they may have different meanings in a college setting. Take, for instance, "office hours." If you are not in college, you would think that it means the hours of a day that an office is open. If it is your dentist's office, it may mean Monday through Friday from 8 a.m. to 5 p.m. In college, "office hours" can refer to the specific hours a professor is in her office to meet with students, and those hours may be only a few each day: for example, Mondays and Wednesdays from 1 p.m. until 3 p.m.

"Syllabus" is another word that you may not have encountered, but it is one you will soon know very well. A syllabus is often called the "contract of the course" because it contains information about what to expect—from the professor and the student. It is meant to be a roadmap for succeeding in the class. Understanding that office hours are for you to ask your professor questions and the syllabus is the guide for what you will be doing in the class can make a big difference in your transition to college. The table on Common College Terms, has a brief list of other words that you will want to know when you hear them on campus.

You will discover that there are many differences between high school and college. Some of the differences are included in the table below. If your most recent experience has been the world of work or the military, you may find that there are other noticeable differences between those experiences and college.

Table 1.3 Common College Terms, What They Mean, and Why You Need to Know

Term	What It Means	Why You Need to Know
Attendance policy	A policy that describes the attendance and absence expectations for a class	Professors will have different attendance expectations. Read your syllabus to determine which ones penalize you if you miss too many classes.
Final exam	A comprehensive assessment that is given at the end of a term	If your class has a final exam, you will want to prepare for it well in advance by reading assigned material, taking good notes, reviewing previous tests and assignments, and studying.
Learning	The process of acquiring knowledge	In college, most learning happens *outside* the classroom. Your professor will only cover the main ideas or the most challenging material in class. The rest of the learning will happen on your own.
Student Office Hours	Specific hours the professor is in the office to meet with students	Visiting your professor during office hours is a good way to get questions answered and to build rapport.
Plagiarism	Using someone's words, images, or ideas as your own, without proper attribution	Plagiarism carries much more serious consequences in college, so it is best to speak to your professor about how to avoid it and review your student handbook's policy.
Study	The process of using learning strategies to understand and recall information	Studying in college may look different than studying in high school in that it may take more effort and more time to learn more complex material.
Syllabus	The contract of a course that provides information about course expectations and policies	The syllabus will provide valuable information that your professor will assume you have read and understood. Refer to it first when you have a question about the course.
Smart Start	Students need to be active and/or present during the first few days of class	Students who are not present on the first day of a face-to-face class or who are not active during the first three days of an online class can be dropped from the course.
Census Date	Date college certifies enrollment to the state	Dropping a course after this date will results in a Withdrawal on your transcript and may have financial aid implications.
Last Date to Withdraw	Last day you can withdraw from a course	After this date, you will receive a grade in the course.
3-peat Rule	Third attempt charge	Upon taking the same course a third time, you will be charged out-of-state tuition.
6-drop Rule	Can only drop 6 courses while pursuing your undergraduate degree	After dropping 6 college-level courses, you will no longer be able to drop and will get a grade on your transcript for all future courses attempted.
Pre-requisite	Course needed before you can register for a higher-level course	It is important to understand the order in which courses must be taken when registering for classes.
Core Curriculum	General education courses required at Texas public institutions	Completing the 42 credit hours of core classes makes you "core complete" and these hours are transferable to any Texas public college or university.
Academic Standing	Indicates if you are meeting college grade expectations	Students with a 2.0 GPA are in good academic standing. Continued semesters under a 2.0 GPA can lead to dismissal from the college.
Satisfactory Academic Progress	Progress towards degree	To maintain financial aid, students must have a 2.0 GPA and successfully complete at least 67% of the courses they attempt.
GPA	Grade Point Average	The average of all your grades impacts your ability to remain in college, get financial aid, and transfer to universities.

Table 1.4 Differences Between High School and College

	High School	College	Why You Need to Know the Difference
Grades	Grades are made up of frequent tests and homework, and you may be able to bring up a low initial grade by completing smaller assignments and bonuses.	Grades are often made up of fewer assignments, and initial low grades may keep you from earning high course grades at the end of the semester.	You will need to be prepared to earn high grades on all assignments because you may not have the opportunity to make up for lost ground.
Learning	Learning is often done in class with the teacher guiding the process, offering multiple ways to learn material and frequent quizzes to ensure that learning is occurring.	Learning happens mostly outside of class and on your own. Faculty are responsible for assigning material and covering the most essential ideas; you are responsible for tracking and monitoring your learning progress.	You will need to practice effective learning strategies on your own to ensure that you are mastering material at the appropriate pace.
Getting Help	Your teachers, parents, and a counselor are responsible for identifying your need for help and for creating a plan for you to get help with coursework if you need it. Extra assistance is usually reserved for students who have an official diagnosis or need.	You will most likely need help to complete all your courses successfully even if you did not need extra help in high school. You will be responsible for identifying that you need it, accessing the resources and using them.	Because the responsibility is on you, not parents or teachers, to get the help you need, you will want to be aware of when you may be struggling to learn material. You then will need to know *where* the support can be accessed on campus or where you can access support online.
Tests and Exams	Tests cover small amounts of material and study guides are common to help you focus on what you need to study. If you paid attention in class, you should be able to answer all the questions.	Tests are fewer and cover more material than in high school. If you read all the assigned material, took good notes in class, and spent time practicing effective study techniques, you should be able to answer all the questions.	This change in how much material and the depth of which you need to know the material is a shock for some students. This may mean you need to change your strategies dramatically to get the same results.

Some of What You Will Learn Is "Hidden"

Many of the college expectations that have been outlined so far may not be considered common knowledge, which is one reason that so many colleges and universities have classes that help students learn what they need to know to succeed. The term, which was coined by sociologists,[6] describes unspoken, unwritten, or unacknowledged (hence, *hidden*) rules that students are expected to follow that can affect their learning. To illustrate the concept, consider the situation in the following activity.

6 P. P. Bilbao, P. I. Lucido, T. C. Iringan, and R. B. Javier. (2008). *Curriculum Development*.

Activity 1.4

Situation: Your history syllabus indicates that on Tuesday your professor is lecturing on the chapter that covers the stock market crash of 1929. This information sounds pretty straightforward. Your professor lectures on a topic and you will be there to hear it. However, there are some unwritten rules or hidden curriculum that are not likely to be communicated. Can you guess what they may be? Take a moment to write at least one potential unwritten rule for each question.

What is an unwritten rule about what you should be doing before attending class?

____

What is an unwritten rule about what you should be doing in class?

____

What is an unwritten rule about what you should be doing after class?

____

What is an unwritten rule if you are not able to attend class?

____

Some of your answers could have included the following:

Before class: Read the assigned chapter, take notes and record any questions you have about the reading.

During class: Take detailed notes, ask critical thinking or clarifying questions, avoid distractions, bring your book and your reading notes.

After class: Reorganize your notes in relation to your other notes, start the studying process by testing yourself on the material, make an appointment with your professor if you are not clear on a concept.

Absent: Communicate with the professor, get notes from a classmate, make sure you did not miss anything important in your notes.

The expectations before, during and after class, as well as what you should do if you miss class, are often unspoken because many professors assume you already know and do these things or because they feel you should figure them out on your own. Nonetheless, some students struggle at first because they don't know about these habits, behaviors, and strategies. But once they learn them, they can meet them with ease.

Learning Is Your Responsibility

As you may now realize by reviewing the differences between high school and college, learning in college is your responsibility. Before you read about the how and why of being responsible for your own learning, complete the Activity below.

Activity 1.5

For each statement, circle the number that best represents you, with 1 indicating that the statement is least like you, and 5 indicating that the statement is most like you.

Most of the time, I can motivate myself to complete tasks even if they are boring or challenging.	1	2	3	4	5
I regularly work hard when I need to complete a task no matter how small or big the task may be.	1	2	3	4	5
I use different strategies to manage my time effectively and minimize procrastination to complete tasks.	1	2	3	4	5
I regularly track my progress completing work and the quality of work I produce.	1	2	3	4	5
I believe how much I learn and how well I learn is my responsibility.	1	2	3	4	5

Were you able to mark mostly 4s and 5s? If you were able to mark at least one 4 or 5, then you are well on your way to taking responsibility for your own learning. Let's break down each statement in the components of the ownership of learning:

- **Motivation.** Being able to stay motivated while studying and balancing all you have to do in your classes will be important for meeting the rest of the components.
- **Deliberate, focused effort.** Taking ownership of learning will hinge on the effort that you put into the work. Because most learning in college will take place outside of the classroom, you will need determination to get the work done. And there will be times that the work will be challenging and maybe even boring, but finding a way to get through it when it is not exciting will pay in the long run.
- **Time and task management.** You will learn more about strategies for managing your time and the tasks of college in a later chapter, but without the ability to control your calendar, it will be difficult to block out the time to study.
- **Progress tracking.** A commitment to learning must include monitoring your learning, knowing not only what you have completed (*this is where a good time management strategy can help you track your tasks*), but also the quality of the work you have done.

Taking responsibility for your learning will take some time if you are not used to being in the driver's seat. However, if you have any difficulty making this adjustment, you can and should reach out for help along the way.

Don't Do It Alone

Think about our earlier descriptions of two students, Reggie and Marisol. What if they found that the first few weeks were a little harder than they had anticipated? Should they have given up and dropped out? Or should they have talked to someone about their struggles? Here is a secret about college success that not many people know: successful students seek help. They use resources. And they do that as often as necessary to get what they need. Your professors and advisors will expect the same from you, and San Antonio College has all kinds of offices, staff, and programs that are designed to help. This bears calling out again: *you need to use those resources*. These are called "help-seeking behaviors," and along with self-advocacy, which is speaking up for your needs, they are essential to your success. As you get more comfortable adjusting to life in college, you will find that asking for help is easier. In fact, you may become really good at it by the time you graduate, just in time for you to ask for help finding a job! Review the table on Issues, Campus Resources, and Potential Outcomes for a few examples of times you may need to ask for help. Make sure to download the Alamo Colleges District app on your phone so that you will have at your fingertips information on all the resources SAC offers to students.

Table 1.5 Issues, Campus Resources, and Potential Outcomes

Type	Issue	Campus Resource	Potential Outcome
Academic/ Intellectual	You are struggling to master the homework in one of your classes.	The Student Learning Assistance Center, Math Labs, Writing Center, Library, Disability Support Services, plus more.	A peer or professional tutor can walk you through the steps until you can do them on your own.
Health	You have felt extremely tired over the past two days and now you have a cough.	Wellness 360 Health Center	A licensed professional can examine you and provide care.
Social/Cultural	You haven't found a group to belong to. Your classmates seem to be going in different directions and your roommate has different interests.	Student organizations, interest groups, and cultural awareness months. Victory Center for Veterans	Becoming a member of a group on campus can help you make new friends, make connections for your career, and learn about other cultures. Visiting the Victory Center can help veterans and their dependents make the transition to college.
Financial	Your scholarship and student loan no longer cover your college expenses. You are not sure how to afford it next semester.	Financial Aid Office	A financial aid counselor can provide you with information about your options for meeting your college expenses.
Life Challenges	You are having trouble covering a utility bill, need food, or are having trouble managing an emotional situation.	Student Advocacy Center	You can get food, counseling, and case management assistance to overcome challenges to completing your education.

Figure 1.4 Creating a social network on campus can help with the adjustments to college

Common Challenges in the First Year

It seems fitting to follow up the expectations for the first year with a list of common challenges that college students encounter along the way to a degree. If you experience any—or even all—of these, the important point here is that you are not alone and that you can overcome them by using your resources. Many college students have felt like this before, and they have survived—even thrived—despite them because they were able to identify a strategy or resource that they could use to help themselves. At some point in your academic career, you may do one or more of the following:

- **Feel like an imposter.** There is actually a name for this condition: imposter syndrome. Students who feel like an imposter are worried that they don't belong, that someone will "expose them for being a fake." This feeling is pretty common for anyone who finds themselves in a new environment and is not sure if they have what it takes to succeed. Trust the professionals who work with first-year college students: you *do* have what it takes and you *will* succeed. Just give yourself time to get adjusted to everything.
- **Worry about making a mistake.** This concern often goes with the imposter syndrome. Students who worry about making a mistake don't like to answer questions in class, volunteer for a challenging assignment, and even ask for help from others. Instead of avoiding situations where you may fail, embrace the process of learning, which includes—is even dependent on—making mistakes. The more you practice courage in these situations and focus on what you are going to learn from failing, the more confident you become about your abilities.
- **Try to manage everything yourself.** Even superheroes need help from sidekicks and mere mortals. Trying to handle everything on your own every time an issue arises is a recipe for getting stressed out. There will be times when you are overwhelmed by all you have to do. This is when you will need to ask for and allow others to help you.
- **Ignore your mental and physical health needs.** If you feel you are on an emotional rollercoaster and you cannot find time to take care of yourself, then you have most likely ignored some part of your mental and physical well-being. What you need to do to stay healthy should be non-negotiable. In other words, your sleep, eating habits, exercise, and stress-reducing activities should be your highest priorities.

- **Forget to enjoy the experience.** Whether you are 18 years old or 48 years old starting back to college after taking a break to work and raise a family, be sure to take the time to remind yourself of the joy that learning can bring.

Policies and Procedures

Wondering when final exams are or what the prerequisites are for a course? Maybe you need to know what the tuition rate is or how long Spring Break is. Most of the information students need about all college policies, procedures, degrees and resources can be found in the San Antonio College Schedule/Catalog. Also included are the Student Code of Conduct and the Student Handbook which outlines behavior expectations for students and how to handle any problems that may arise. This document can be found on the SAC website (mysaccatalog.alamo.edu). Also, your instructor in this class will be going over much of this information throughout the semester so that you can be well-equipped with the information you need to smoothly continue your education.

1.4 Personal Campus Safety

Questions to consider:

- What makes a person safety conscious?
- How can you improve your personal safety?
- What are the safety procedures on campus?

Safety Consciousness

To be safety conscious means you have an awareness of potential hazards and an alertness to danger. Simply, you are conscious of being safe. This includes being smart about your physical surroundings and being careful with drug and alcohol use.

Personal Safety

For many students, their first year in college is also the first time they have lived away from home, or for commuting students, often the most time they have spent away from home. This new freedom can feel really exciting. College should be a time for fun, experimentation (in healthy ways), and growth. It's important to be smart about your safety and conscious that you don't put yourself in any high-risk situations. It's also important to know what to do if any problems arise. Here are some ways to remain safe while enjoying your college experience:

- **Speak up.**

  If you are worried about a friend's well-being, ask them if they are OK. If you see inappropriate behavior, let someone know. Get a campus employee involved if someone looks like they are in trouble or an activity looks like it is leading to trouble. In general, speak up if you notice something going on that concerns you.

Figure 1.5 Emergency phones and related systems are present on campus. Learn your system and note the locations of these devices as you travel. If you commute via public transportation, learn the safety procedures and devices available for those systems. (Credit: KOMO News/ Flickr/Attribution 2.0 Generic (CC-BY 2.0))

- **Protect your drink.**

  A risk at bars and at college campus parties is the use of date-rape drugs to assist sexual assaults. Date-rape drugs often have no color, smell, or taste, so you can't tell if you are being drugged. The drugs can make you weak and confused so you are unable to refuse sex or defend yourself. It is easy for anyone to slip a date-rape drug in your drink. Never leave your drink unattended, and never accept a drink from someone you do not trust.

- **Be alert and stay charged.**

  Always be aware of the people in your surrounding area. Notice anyone who looks out of place and avoid dark and unpopulated areas. Make sure to charge your cell phone before you go out for the evening.

- **Avoid walking alone at night and don't accept rides from strangers.**

  Going out with a group is the best way to make sure everyone gets home safely. In the event you find yourself alone at the end of the night, know ahead of time what safety escort services your school offers. Or use services like Uber and Lyft, and MAKE SURE you get in the car that matches the license plate on the app.

  It's also wise to install safety apps. These apps can automatically alert police and your emergency contacts in the event of an emergency. Always let your roommates and friends know your plans for the evening and when you expect to return.

- **Protect your belongings.**

  Make sure to lock your vehicle. Never leave your items unattended, even for a few minutes.

Safety On Campus

The Alamo College District Police Officers are available 24/7/365 to assist you. They are certified Texas Peace Officers. For non-emergency assistance, call 210-485-0099. Please direct all **emergencies to 210-485-0911**. These numbers should be saved in your phone.

The Alamo Colleges District Police Department is responsible for:

- Emergency services
- Criminal investigations
- Traffic enforcements/investigations
- Providing courtesy safety escorts
- Crime prevention
- Responding to call(s) for service
- Non-emergency request(s)
- Parking management
- Lost and Found
- Courtesy service if car won't start, locked out, flat tire, etc.
- Bike registration

SAC has blue-light phones with direct access to campus security. Take the time to find out where they are. The Campus Map in *Appendix 1* shows where the emergency phones are located.

While on campus, follow the campus safety procedures that are outlined in *Appendix 2*.

If You Are a Victim of a Crime

Most college students report feeling safe on campus. College administrators are fully committed to making your campus experience as safe as possible. If you are attacked, it is important to know what to do:

- **If possible, get to a safe place.** Move to a well-lit area to call for help.
- **Call 911** or have someone call 911 for you.
- **Follow the operator's instructions.** 911 operators will instruct you until police or paramedics arrive.
- **Contact a trusted friend or family member.** You will want emotional support and also somewhere to go after all the official procedures are complete.
- **Take time to heal.** If you are a victim of crime or assault, it can be traumatic. The healing process will take time. Check with counselors in the Advocacy Center about how they can help in your recovery.
- **Title IX.** Under Title IX legislation, sexual harassment and sexual violence are forms of gender discrimination and are prohibited. This includes off-campus incidents or incidents that involve people who are not students. If you experience a hostile environment, sexual harassment, or sexual assault, schools have a responsibility to stop the discrimination, prevent its recurrence, and address its effects. Schools also have a responsibility to protect people who report sexual harassment or assault from retaliation from other students, school administrators or faculty. The Campus Cares office on campus can aid if you have experienced any of these situations.

1.5 How Can This Book and This Course Help?

Questions to consider:

- How will you be able to develop your purpose?
- In what ways will you be able to create strategies for your success?
- What other resources can you use to help you succeed?

As Reggie and Marisol go through their college experiences and create a balance between their academic and personal lives, their stories, no doubt, will diverge. But you can be assured that each of them will demonstrate grit, the ability to stay focused on a goal over the long-term, along the way. As Duckworth (2016) has said, it takes passion and perseverance to be gritty. It also takes resilience or the ability to bounce back from adversity. The challenges you face will certainly stretch you, but if you have these three things—purpose, strategies, and resources—you will be more likely to bounce back, even become stronger in the process. This book has been designed with these things in mind.

Develop Your "Why"

This chapter began with the suggestion to explore why you are in college or more simply, what your purpose is. This course—and this book—will help you continue to refine your answer and create a map for your journey to fulfill your purpose. The features in this book that help you develop your purpose include the following:

- Student Survey Questions: Each chapter opens with several questions that provide you with a snapshot of how you feel about the chapter content. How does this feature help you develop purpose? It allows you to develop better self-awareness, which will in turn help you build an awareness of your purpose.
- Questions to Consider: At the start of each section, there will be a set of questions to ask yourself before you start reading. By asking these questions, your brain is primed to focus on what is most important.

Refine Your Strategies for Success

Purpose by itself may illuminate the pathway forward, but it will take strategies to help you complete your journey. Think of the strategies you will learn in this course as tools you will need along the way to completing your degree. The following features provide you with an opportunity to practice and refine strategies for success:

- Analysis/Application Questions: Any time you are asked to *apply* what you are learning in the chapters you are improving your skills. Look for them throughout and take some time to stop, think, and use the skill.
- Activities: As you read, you will also have the opportunity to interact with the content. They give you the chance to refine the strategies that will help you succeed in college.

Summary

This chapter introduces the transition to college by first asking "Why"? Understanding why you are in college, what your life purpose is, and what a college degree can do for you is the foundation of making a smooth transition. These transitional experiences are part of being in college. This chapter provides you with information about what to expect and how to handle the changes you will go through. Next, the chapter discusses college culture and how to understand the customs and language of higher education. These customs include college policies and how to stay safe on campus. The chapter ends with an introduction to resources provided throughout the textbook that can help you practice skills and dive deeper into the topics.

Chapter 2 Thinking, Research, and Academic Integrity

Figure 2.1 Students researching in the library

Chapter Outline

Student Survey

Are you confident in your skills of finding accurate information? Take this quick survey to figure it out, ranking questions on a scale of 1–4, 1 meaning "least like me" and 4 meaning "most like me." These questions will help you determine how the chapter concepts relate to you right now. As you are introduced to new concepts and practices, it can be informative to reflect on how your understanding changes over time. We'll revisit these questions at the end of the chapter to see whether your feelings have changed.

1. ______ I comprehend how to approach problem-solving.
2. ______ I have creative potential.
3. ______ I often think about how I'm learning.
4. ______ I know how to find and evaluate valid information.

Chapter Outcomes

In this chapter, you'll be introduced to different ways of thinking about how you think and use information. By the time you complete this chapter, you should be able to do the following:

- Describe thinking as a process and the reasons it is important.
- Articulate the process and importance of critical thinking.
- Describe the best approaches to problem-solving.
- Define information literacy for college students.
- Distinguish between different types of resources.
- Identify the parts of a peer reviewed journal article.
- Explain the meaning and importance of academic integrity.
- Recognize how citing your sources can help safeguard against plagiarism.

What Thinking Means

Thinking is one of those hard-to-pinpoint aspects of life we typically don't analyze much—like breathing or walking or sleeping. We constantly think. Becoming more attuned to how we think and what we do when we encounter new ideas is an excellent habit to pursue.

> "If you are going to do anything as much as you think, you might just as well learn about it and hone this skill."

You may have read quotes or inspirational slogans that claim you are what you think. What does that mean? Can you think yourself into a good mood? Can you think you have a million dollars in your pocket? Does that mean you are the next music sensation if you often sing at parties? Not necessarily, but consider Jose, for instance. He isn't a rock and roll star, but Jose spends a lot of his leisure time thinking about music, analyzing performances, memorizing his favorite musicians' characteristics, buying fan clothing, and even designing a creative means to explain his excitement for music to his friends through a homemade video. Jose certainly could allow his fascination to seep into other aspects of his life. Do you have a hobby or interest you spend a lot of time thinking about?

Many people go to great lengths to attend a concert by a favorite musician. They think creatively about how to save enough money for tickets; they think analytically about scheduling their other obligations to have time off work to attend or how to make up work in their college classes. This much planning involves a great deal of thinking, and not all about music. In the example about Jose, thinking directs the actions of the person doing the thinking. So, in fact, what we think does influence who we are and how we act. We have many resources available to be more effective thinkers. Learning about these resources gives us options.

2.1 Critical Thinking

Questions to consider:

- How can determining the situation help you think critically?
- How do you present informed, unbiased thinking?
- How can you identify information bias?
- What is the difference between factual arguments and opinions?

Critical thinking has become a buzz phrase in education and corporate environments in recent years. The definitions vary slightly, but most agree that thinking critically includes some form of judgement that thinkers generate after careful analysis of the perspectives, opinions, or experimental results present for a particular problem or situation. Before you wonder if you are even capable of critical thinking, consider that you think critically every day.

When you decide to make your lunch rather than just grabbing a bag of chips, you are thinking critically. You have to plan ahead, buy the food, possibly prepare it, arrange to carry the lunch with you. You may have various reasons for doing that—making healthier eating choices, saving money for an upcoming trip, or wanting more quiet time to unwind instead of waiting in a crowded lunch line. You are constantly weighing options, consulting data, gathering opinions, making choices, and then evaluating those decisions, which is a general definition of critical thinking.

Consider the following situations and how each one demands your thinking attention. Which do you find most demanding of critical thinking? Why?

1. Participating in extracurricular events
2. Watching competitive extracurricular events
3. Reading a novel for pleasure
4. Reading a textbook passage in science

Critical thinking forces you to determine the actual situation under question and to determine your thoughts and actions around that situation.

Determining the Situation

One component to keep in mind to guide your critical thinking is to determine the situation. What problem are you solving? When problems become complex and multifaceted, it is easy to be distracted by the simple parts that may not need as much thinking to resolve but also may not contribute as much to the ultimate problem resolution. What aspect of the situation truly needs your attention and your critical thinking?

Critical thinking differs according to the subject you are thinking about, and as such it can be difficult to pin down any sort of formula to make sure you are doing a good job of thinking critically in all situations. While you may need to adapt this list of critical thinking components, you can get started if you do the following:

- Question everything
- Conduct legitimate research

- Limit your assumptions
- Recognize your own biases
- Gather and weigh all options

Additionally, you must recognize that changes will occur and may alter your conclusions now and in the future. You may eventually have to revisit an issue you effectively resolved previously, and adapt to changing conditions. Knowing when to do that is another example of critical thinking. Informed flexibility, or knowing that parts of the plan may need to change and how those changes can work into the overall goal, is also a recognized element of thinking critically.

For example, early in the 20th century, many people considered cigarette smoking a relaxing social pastime that didn't have many negative consequences. Some people may still consider smoking a way to relax; however, years of medical research have proven with mounting evidence that smoking causes cancer and exacerbates numerous other medical conditions. Researchers asked questions about the impact of smoking on people's overall health, conducted regulated experiments, tracked smokers' reactions, and concluded that smoking did impact health. Over time, attitudes, evidence, and opinions change, and as a critical thinker, you must continue to research, synthesize newly discovered evidence, and adapt to that new information.

Figure 2.2 Information, attitudes, laws, and acceptance of smoking changed dramatically over time. More recently, vaping and related practices have rekindled debates and launched new research into safety. (Credit: Satish Krishnamurthy / Flickr / Attribution 2.0 Generic (CC-BY 2.0)

Approaches against Bias

Once you have all your information gathered and you have checked your sources for currency and validity, you need to direct your attention to how you are going to present your well-informed analysis. Be careful on this step to recognize your own possible biases. Facts are verifiable; opinions are beliefs without supporting evidence. Stating an opinion is just that. You could say "Blue is the best color," and that's your opinion. If you were to conduct research and find evidence to support this claim, you could say, "Researchers at Oxford University recognize that the use of blue paint in mental hospitals reduces heart rates by 25% and contributes to fewer angry outbursts from patients." This would be an informed analysis with credible evidence to support the claim.

Not everyone will accept your analysis, which can be frustrating. Most people resist change and have firm beliefs on both important issues and less significant preferences. It is important to recognize that everyone comes with and experiences unconscious biases. Human beings come into all situations with predispositions and beliefs that can affect our perceptions and decisions. A conscious or unconscious preconception or prejudice towards something, perhaps a person, or even a group is known as **bias**. A bias can be positive or negative. Bias in research causes distorted results which leads to incorrect conclusions being drawn and a misinterpretation of facts. For college students, awareness of bias in research is key, as bias naturally exists in all research, is difficult to eliminate, and can impact the interpretation of research findings.

With all the competing information surfacing online, on the news, and in general conversation, you can understand how confusing it can be to make any decisions. Look at all the reliable, valid sources that claim different approaches to be the best diet for healthy living: ketogenic, low-carb, vegan, vegetarian, high fat, raw foods, paleo, Mediterranean, etc. All you can do in this sort of situation is conduct your own serious research, check your sources, and write clearly and concisely to provide your analysis of the information for consideration. You cannot force others to accept your stance, but you can show your evidence in support of your thinking, being as persuasive as possible without lapsing into your own personal biases. Then the rest is up to the person reading or viewing your analysis.

Factual Arguments versus Opinions

Thinking and constructing analyses based on your thinking will bring you in contact with a great deal of information. Some of that information will be factual, and some will not. You need to be able to distinguish between facts and opinions so you know how to support your arguments. Begin with basic definitions:

- Fact: a statement that is true and backed up with evidence; facts can be verified through observation or research.
- Opinion: a statement someone holds to be true without supporting evidence; opinions express beliefs, assumptions, perceptions, or judgments.

Of course, the tricky part is that most people do not label statements as fact and opinion, so you need to be aware and recognize the difference as you go about honing your critical thinking skills.

You probably have heard the old saying "Everyone is entitled to their own opinions," which may be true, but conversely, not everyone is entitled to their own facts. Facts are true for everyone, not just those who want to believe in them. For example, mice are animals is a fact; mice make the best pets is an opinion.

Activity 2.1

Determine if the following statements are facts or opinions based on just the information provided here, referring to the basic definitions above. Some people consider scientific findings to be opinions even when they are convincingly backed by reputable evidence and experimentation. However, remember the definition of fact—verifiable by research or observation. Think about what other research you may have to conduct to make an informed decision.

- Oregon is a state in the United States. (How would this be proven?)
- Beef is made from cattle. (See current legislation concerning vegetarian "burgers.")
- Increased street lighting decreases criminal behavior. (What information would you need to validate this claim?)
- In 1952, Elizabeth became Queen of England. (What documents could validate this?)
- Oatmeal tastes plain. (What factors might play into this claim?)
- Acne is an embarrassing skin condition. (Who might verify this claim?)
- Kindergarten decreases student dropout rates. (Think of different interest groups that may take sides on this issue.)
- Carbohydrates promote weight gain. (Can you determine if this is a valid statement?)
- Cell phones cause brain tumors. (What research considers this claim?)
- Immigration is good for the US economy. (What research would help you make an informed decision on this topic?)

Many people become very attached to their opinions, even stating them as facts despite the lack of verifiable evidence. Think about political campaigns, sporting rivalries, musical preferences, and religious or philosophical beliefs. When you are reading, writing, and thinking critically, you must be on the lookout for sophisticated opinions others may present as factual information. While it's possible to be polite when questioning another person's opinions when engaging in intellectual debate, thinking critically requires that you do conduct this questioning.

2.2 Problem-Solving

Questions to consider:

- How can determining the best approach to solve a problem help you generate solutions?
- Why do thinkers create multiple solutions to problems?

When we are solving a problem, whether at work, school, or home, we are being asked to perform multiple, often complex, tasks. The most effective problem-solving approach includes some variation of the following steps:

Problem-Solving Steps

Determine	• Determine the issue
Recognize	• Recognize multiple perspectives
Think	• Think of multiple possible results
Research and evaluate	• Research and evaluate the possibilities
Select	• Select the best results
Communicate	• Communicate your findings
Establish	• Establish logical action based on your analysis

Figure 2.3 Problem solving steps

Determining the best approach to any given problem and generating more than one possible solution to the problem constitutes the complicated process of problem-solving. People who are good at these skills are highly marketable because many jobs consist of a series of problems that need to be solved for production, services, goods, and sales to continue smoothly. Think about what happens when a worker at your favorite coffee shop slips on a wet spot behind the counter, dropping several drinks she just prepared. One problem is the employee may be hurt, in need of attention, and probably embarrassed; another problem is that several customers do not have the drinks they were waiting for; and another problem is that stopping production of drinks (to care for the hurt worker, to clean up her spilled drinks, to make new drinks) causes the line at the cash register to back up. A good manager has to juggle all of these elements to resolve the situation as quickly and efficiently as possible. That resolution and return to standard operations doesn't happen without a great deal of thinking: prioritizing needs, shifting other workers off one station onto another temporarily, and dealing with all the people involved, from the injured worker to the impatient patrons.

Determining and Recognizing the Best Approach

Faced with a problem-solving opportunity, you must assess the skills you will need to create solutions. Problem-solving can involve many different types of thinking. You may have to call on your creative, analytical, or critical thinking skills—or more frequently, a combination of several different types of thinking—to solve a problem satisfactorily. When you approach a situation, how can you decide what is the best type of thinking to employ? Sometimes the answer is obvious; if you are working a scientific challenge, you likely will use analytical thinking; if you are a design student considering the atmosphere of a home, you may need to tap into creative thinking skills; and if you are an early childhood education major outlining the logistics involved in establishing a summer day camp for children, you may need a combination of critical, analytical, and creative thinking to solve this challenge.

Generating Multiple Solutions

Why do you think it is important to provide multiple solutions when you are going through the steps to solve problems? Typically, you'll end up only using one solution at a time, so why expend the extra energy to create alternatives? If you planned to explore downtown with a friend who is visiting, you may have created a list of the sites you plan to see and the restaurant where you will eat. You may think that this is enough, but upon arriving downtown you realize multiple streets are blocked off, public transportation is backed up and most restaurants have minimum staff, as downtown tourism is experiencing an employee strike. Now what? A back-up plan would have helped you contemplate alternatives you could substitute for the original plans. You certainly cannot predict every possible contingency—sick children, weather delays, a flat tire, or economic downfalls—but you can be prepared for unexpected issues to come up and adapt more easily if you plan for multiple solutions.

Activity 2.2

Write out at least two possible solutions to these dilemmas:

- You have a test today but your car won't start.
- You have three exams scheduled on a day when you also have work.
- Your car needs new tires, an oil change, and gas—you have no cash. (Is there a trend here?)
- You have to pass a running test for your kinesiology class, but have not worked out in years.

Providing more than one solution to a problem gives people options. You may not need several options, but having more than one solution will allow you to feel more in control and part of the problem-solving process.

2.3 Information Literacy

Questions to consider:

- How do you go about verifying source validity, and why is this important?
- How do you use resources to improve your thinking?
- What is information literacy?

What is Information Literacy?

Human beings are passionate, curious, and always seeking to connect with each other and make sense of things. Learning is more effective when new information is meaningful and linked to some personal experience or prior knowledge. Learning is about both context and content. It is necessary to learn how to assess, evaluate, and connect in order to make information become knowledge. Information literacy skills are the hallmark of the ability to do research. What is important is for you to learn how to find information that "matters" and then figure out why it might matter.

Information literacy is a link between the life experiences of you as a student, the academic world of scholarship, and the post college real world application of learning. An information-literate person has the ability to ask questions and knows the difference between ignorance and understanding. (When do I need information?) Information literacy builds a lifelong ability to determine where information is kept (Where is the best place to find this?) and in what forms knowledge is stored (Which knowledge products will likely have what I need?).

Information literacy relies on the use of a critical mind to discern credible from not credible, valid from not valid. It is actually the core of the first-year experience. It lasts, while the specifics of particular courses fade over time. After all, the nature of research, the core of higher education, is a learning process: "How do I learn about something?" Communication skills are essential to your ability to both learn and share what you've learned.

When conducting any type of thinking, you need to have a firm grasp on **information literacy**, or knowing how to access the sources you may need. Practicing good information literacy skills involves more than simply using a search engine such as Google, although that could be a starting point. You also engage in creative thinking (i.e., generating topics to research), analytical thinking (i.e., reading and examining the parts of sources), and critical thinking (i.e., evaluating sources for accuracy, authority, etc.). Then there is synthesis that is used when incorporating multiple sources into a research project. Information literacy utilizes all of the necessary thinking skills. If you saw the name of a person on the cover of a magazine, for instance, you might assume the person did something important to merit the attention. If you were to google the person's name, you would instantly need to use context clues to determine if the information your search produced is actually about your person and not someone else with the same or a similar name, whether the information is accurate, and if it is current. If it is not, you would need to continue your research with other sources.

Verifying Valid Sources

The American Library Association defines information literacy as a set of skills that allow you to "recognize when information is needed and have the ability to locate, evaluate, and use effectively the needed information."[1] We need information almost all the time, and with practice, you'll become more and more efficient at knowing where to look for answers on certain topics. As information is increasingly available in multiple formats, not only in print and online versions but also through audio and visual means, users of this information must employ critical thinking skills to sift through it all.

Starting your Research

Getting a good grade in college often relies on finding and using the best and most authoritative information on a topic. To do this, you have to think critically, work through the resources you find, and construct your own ideas. In this course we focus on developing research skills, which include finding information appropriate to your needs, evaluating that information, and using it ethically. These skills take time, effort, and reflection to acquire.

What is Research?

When you read the word **research**, you might think of the quick web searches we all do every day when we need basic information: a good recipe for Vietnamese bánh mì sandwiches, what are the top 100 movies of all time, what is Tourette syndrome, and so on. You might also think of writing a lengthy paper and the resources you'll need to find and use within it.

Both of these processes are examples of seeking out information, but as you tackle more projects in college, your instructors will frequently use the word research to mean the process of finding and using authoritative resources. Thinking through the research process can help you be more efficient and effective, not only as it relates to coursework, but also when researching for your personal needs. Research is an ongoing cycle of questions and answers, which can quickly become very complex. Here are some important areas to think about when starting your research:

- Determining the scope of your research

1 "Information Literacy." American Library Association. Accessed February 1, 2020. https://literacy.ala.org/information-literacy/

- Developing your topic and research question
- Identifying key concepts for your topic

Popular and Scholarly Information

Table 2.1 Chart illustrates the differences between popular and scholarly information

Popular	Scholarly
written for the general public; language is clear, simple, and direct	written for specialists in the field; language is scholarly and often complex
articles may be short and unsigned; when signed, author credentials are usually missing	articles are longer and in-depth; author credentials and contact information are clearly listed
most articles are illustrated with photographs; online versions often have videos	most illustrations are charts, graphs, or other ways to present data
often no citations, footnotes, references, or bibliographies	thorough citations, footnotes and references are required
articles are proofread and copy edited	articles are peer reviewed by several subject experts as well as proofread and copyedited
include advertisements for commercial products of all kinds	if present, advertising focuses on publishing, professional societies, and conferences tied to the journal topic

Popular Information

Popular information is found within publications written for the general public rather than for scholarly audiences. They have not gone through a rigorous review process and are less technical than scholarly materials. Articles found within popular sources may not include citations; instead often offer a less-detailed, more surface-level summary of their topic. They might not even list an author. *People* magazine, *Vogue*, and *Rolling Stone* are examples of popular publications. Trending social media applications and sites like Google are also popular. All of these sources can be helpful if your topic has to do with recent events, popular culture, or hobbies.

Scholarly Information

Scholarly information gives you a more in-depth understanding of a topic. This type of information is often found within scholarly books and journal articles. Scholarly books and articles undergo peer review, a rigorous review process by subject experts before publication. They usually contain subject-specific, technical language, and refer to the resources the authors used by including citations. Scholarly materials are often the product of a specific research project and contain information about the methods the authors used to reach their conclusions. These are helpful for projects where it is important to build a strong research-based foundation for your ideas or interpretation.

Peer Review Process

Many instructors will expect you to use scholarly information. Therefore, it's important to have an understanding of how it's made. Here is the typical publication process for a peer reviewed article:

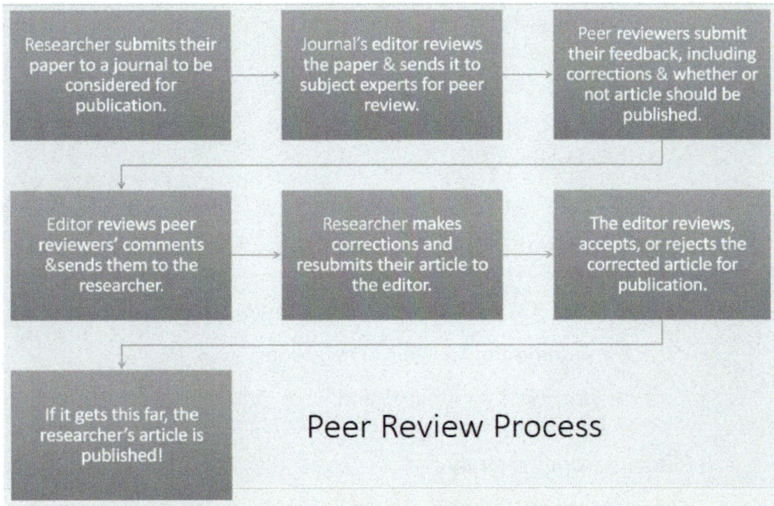

Figure 2.4 The peer-review process by experts that articles go through before being published

2.4 Conducting Research

Questions to consider:

- What are the steps to a good research study?
- What are the parts of a research study in a peer reviewed journal article?
- How should you read a peer reviewed article?

Turning Information Into Knowledge Using Peer Reviewed Journal Articles

Peer reviewed journal articles (PRJA's) are some of the most reliable resources you can use for your academic research. However, you can also use these strategies when evaluating other types of scholarly sources, such as books. Although the sections of books and articles are labeled differently, they generally serve the same purpose. These sections can provide information and structure to help you quickly evaluate the source. For example, the summary section at the beginning of an article or book chapter is called the **abstract**, but in a book, this is called the **introduction**. However they are labeled, you can use the information found within each section to evaluate the source.

The following table illustrates what to expect in each section of a peer reviewed journal article.

Table 2.2

Abstract	• Summary of the entire article • Key findings
Introduction	• Hypothesis of the study • Why the research is being conducted • Reviews past research on the topic
Method	• Procedures of the study and participant information • Participant demographics (ex: age, gender, etc.) • How the study was conducted and what did the participants did (Ex: took a survey)
Results	• Findings from the study • Answer to the hypothesis • Statistical information used to analyze data • Graphs, charts, and tables from data gathered during the study
Discussion	• Answers the hypothesis by accepting or rejecting research questions • Conclusions and review of the findings • Possible applications and value of the findings • Connections to past research (Ex: similar findings) • Implications and future research suggestions

How to Read a Peer Reviewed Journal Article

Start by reading the abstract and the discussion sections. If an article has an abstract, read that first. The abstract is a summary of the entire article. This summary gives you a general idea of what the authors were trying to accomplish, as well as a brief description of their experiment, observations, or analysis. If the abstract is too complex or technical, that is an indication for what the rest of the article will be like. If you can understand most of the language used in the abstract, highlight terms that you don't recognize to look up later. This can be a useful learning experience. However, if you can't understand the article at all, then it may not be the right resource for you, even if it's written by the foremost expert in the field.

Once you have read the abstract, you can skip down to the conclusion, or discussion section. With scholarly articles, you don't always have to read straight through from start to finish. Strategically skipping around and skimming specific sections can help you understand the big takeaways from the research. The **conclusion** usually includes information about major findings and why the author thinks they are important. By reading the conclusion, you can verify that the impression you got from the abstract is correct and check that the article is actually relevant for your research question. This can also inform how you read and interpret the rest of the article.

Explore the Rest of the Article

If you found the abstract and conclusion relevant for your research topic, continue on to read the rest of the article. This will give the details that you will want to use and cite in your work.

Dig into the **Methods** section to understand how the author(s) conducted their research, including how they gathered their data (e.g. surveys, interviews, experiments, or observations) and why they chose that method. Be on alert for approaches that are too general or don't give any detail, such as only stating "We ran a qualitative analysis." If you don't understand a term or phrase, take note of it to look it up later. Reviewing an article's Methods can give you a deeper understanding of how the authors got their results and will put their findings into a better context.

The **Results** and **Discussion** sections provide more specific details about what the authors found. This includes descriptions of overall results and their corresponding data. Important or notable findings may be pulled out in tables, figures, and graphics, to help you understand the data more quickly or completely. Reading the results section will give you the full breadth of the research findings, not just the highlights you saw in the conclusion.

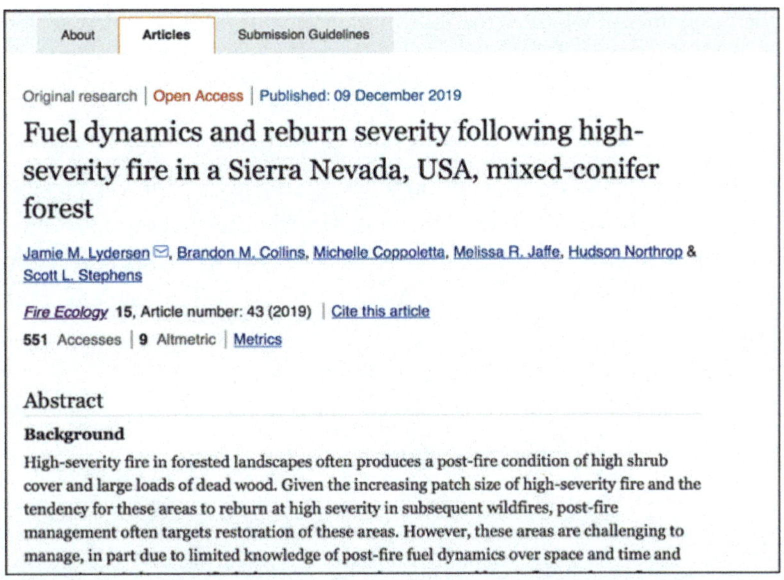
About | Articles | Submission Guidelines

Original research | Open Access | Published: 09 December 2019

Fuel dynamics and reburn severity following high-severity fire in a Sierra Nevada, USA, mixed-conifer forest

Jamie M. Lydersen, Brandon M. Collins, Michelle Coppoletta, Melissa R. Jaffe, Hudson Northrop & Scott L. Stephens

Fire Ecology 15, Article number: 43 (2019) | Cite this article

551 Accesses | 9 Altmetric | Metrics

Abstract

Background

High-severity fire in forested landscapes often produces a post-fire condition of high shrub cover and large loads of dead wood. Given the increasing patch size of high-severity fire and the tendency for these areas to reburn at high severity in subsequent wildfires, post-fire management often targets restoration of these areas. However, these areas are challenging to manage, in part due to limited knowledge of post-fire fuel dynamics over space and time and

Figure 2.5 The most reliable sources of online information may be journals or related research-oriented websites, which include the author names, their credentials, and other data. However, unless they are "peer reviewed," meaning independent experts have read and verified the quality of the information, even credible-looking sites may be more opinion than fact-oriented. (Credit: Springer Open. https://fireecology.springeropen.com)

Validity and Credibility

Before you move on to interpreting your data and addressing the significance of what you found, you need to understand the concepts of validity and credibility. **Validity and credibility** refer to the quality of information. In research, **Validity** asks if the information is logical, sound, or well-grounded. **Credibility** refers to the information being trustworthy. This could involve a certain conclusion, an entire concept, or even how something was measured in a research study. Is the information logical, or justifiable when considering the real world? Does this conclusion make sense? Does the information sound true? Can the information be trusted? When considering research studies, the question is often, did the researchers effectively measure what was trying to be measured? For college students, this is where critical thinking can be practiced.

There are many ways you can check the validity of a piece of information. Can you find contradictory or confirmatory data? Can you find evidence that disputes what you are reading? If so, use this information. It is always useful to mention opposing ideas. Ultimately, doing so might strengthen your own ideas. Is the topic within the expertise of the person offering the information? Was the method chosen to convey this information the best method to use? The credibility of the author is another important aspect of checking your sources. In other words, evaluate the authors. Are they experts on the topic? Do they have credentials to write on this particular topic? Has this author written anything else on this topic?

Finally, consider when your source was published. This date can affect how useful (or not) that source will be for you now. Depending on your topic or assignment, you may need something published within the last five or ten years. This can be the case when researching recent events or technological innovations. For other topics, it may be necessary to consult an older source, such as for research on a historical event or a long-standing theory in your discipline. Keep in mind, if a theory has been around for a long time, it has had more opportunity to be criticized, overturned, built upon, or reinforced. You may need to seek out newer sources about the same topic to figure out whether the information in your original source is outdated today.

The Internet presents its own challenges when it comes to discovering valid and credible information. When looking at a website, you should be able to answer the following questions: Who is responsible for the site (i.e., who is the author)? What can you find out about the responsible party? Where does the site's information come from (e.g., opinions, facts, documents, quotes, excerpts)? For certain topics and types of information, you may need to dig deeper. Take into account the funding behind a website. Look up the author, and see if they have written anything else and if there are any obvious biases present in that writing. What are the key concepts, issues, and "facts" on the site? And finally, can the key elements of the site be verified by another site or source? In other words, if you want to find some information online, you shouldn't just Google the topic and then depend on the first website that pops up.

Strengths and Weaknesses of Web Search Engines

Strengths

- Simple to search and mobile-friendly
- Available to anyone with Internet access, regardless of university affiliation
- Media content, such as videos and images, is much easier to find than with other finding tools

Weaknesses

- Difficult to focus or refine your search and the number of results may be overwhelming
- Has more difficulty finding scholarly materials, such as journal articles
- Search engine algorithms may interpret your meaning incorrectly, based on past searches

Activity 2.3

Reflect on what bias the following sites may have. Without consulting the Internet, write one to two sentences on what ideas the following organizations may present. After you consider these on your own, conduct a search and see if you were accurate in your assumptions about the entities.

a. National Dairy Council
b. Yoga Society
c. People for the Ethical Treatment of Animals (PETA)
d. The American Medical Association

Whatever you write or declare based on sources should be correct and truthful. Reliable sources present current and honest information backed up with evidence you can check. Any source that essentially says you should believe this "because I said so" isn't a valid source for critically thinking, information-literate individuals.

Finding Sources for Your Research Needs

Every search has a different context. Sometimes you just need basic facts and news. In that case, Google would be a good option. However, if you need scholarly information, Google is probably not your best choice. For most academic work, google is not enough.

The San Antonio College Library provides students 24/7 access to these sources in the form of academic research databases. Personalized research help via online chat, email, text messaging, phone, online meeting, and in-person is also available through the San Antonio College Library.

Evaluating Information

Vast amounts of new information are created every minute and it can be overwhelming to make sense of it all. How do you know you've found the best information for your needs? You evaluate it! In this section, we'll discuss how you can more effectively evaluate and fact-check all kinds of information, from news stories to academic articles.

Evaluating information is something you do every day, whether you know it or not. You evaluate information when you determine what to write down in your notes, debate issues with friends, and look up new movie reviews. All this is done before you even start gathering information for a research project.

Evaluating with SIFT

SIFT is an acronym developed by Mike Caulfield (2019) that describes four steps you can use to evaluate sources. The four steps included in SIFT are:

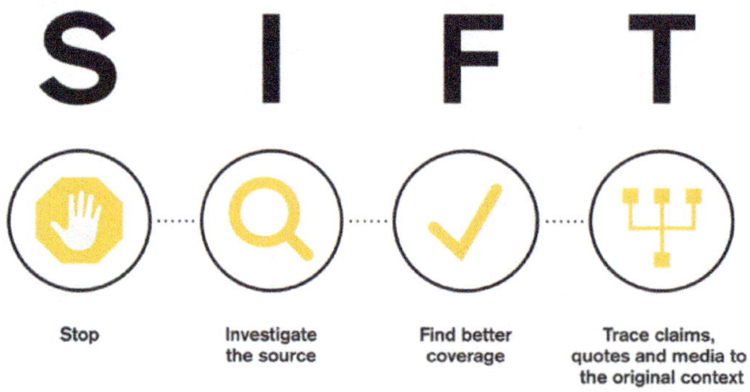

Figure 2.6 SIFT stands for Stop, Investigate, Find better coverage, and Trace claims.

We'll now be exploring each of these steps and how you can integrate them into your everyday habits for evaluating content.

Stop

The first step in SIFT is also the most simple: stop reading and consider why you are engaging with this source instead of another. What drew you to this source, and how is it applicable for your needs? Specifically, you'll want to stop and check these two things:

Check Yourself

Everyone brings their own expectations to their research. These expectations can affect every step of your research process, from the search terms you use to the sources you choose to cite. For example, you may have a preconceived notion of what you think the research should show, but this may not be what the research actually shows.

If a source confirms or denies what you believe to be true, you may have an emotional reaction (e.g. anger, sadness, vindication, excitement). Use your reaction as a reminder to **check yourself** and make sure your emotions are not affecting the sources you use and how you use them.

Make it a habit to check your emotions and ensure that they aren't affecting the choices you make in your research or life. Verifying the truth of a source you agree with or finding additional sources that present a different perspective (even if it may upset you or contradict your beliefs) can strengthen your case.[2]

Checking yourself is particularly important in your everyday life as well. You've likely had friends or family share an article on social media and had the comments explode. How many of the commenters do you think actually read the article? It's possible that even the person who shared it didn't read the whole article before reacting to the headline. When you know the person sharing something, it is natural to rely on their judgment. This can lead to embarrassment if you share or react to something that isn't saying what you thought it was.

---

2 Caulfield, M. (2020, January 1). *The S in SIFT (1): Introduction and the S in SIFT.* YouTube. https://www.youtube.com/watch?v=3VEPbuicH1A

STOP is also a reminder to stay on task. It is easy to get lost exploring interesting tangents while researching. As soon as you find yourself getting distracted, stop and remember your original goal. For a paper or project, this means focusing on your research question and sources that are directly related to it.

Investigate the Source

Once you are sure that you are on task with your research, you can move on to critically evaluate your sources. Even if the sources you've found seem to fit your project's topic well, you will still need to evaluate their quality and context in other ways. Here are some points to consider:

Figure 2.7 When investigating sources consider the author's reputation and purpose, and any conflicts of interest or biases.

You'll need to understand your sources and decide whether each is worth using. If a source you encounter is low quality or if you can't verify that it's reliable, your best strategy is to not use it and move on to other sources.

You should do the same investigation with websites. Don't rely on first impressions to tell you whether a source is good. There are many great academic websites that appear outdated or poorly designed because the creators' expertise lies in content rather than web design. You might have noticed that not all of your professors are great at using Canvas, for example. Your course pages may not be the most attractive, but because your professors are experts in their course topics, you can feel confident in using their content. In contrast, some intentionally misleading websites look sleek and well-supported because their creators have heavily invested in making their work look "reputable."

Find Better Coverage

Most of the time, you will not be able to determine the reliability of a claim or statement based on how it is covered in a single source. **Reliability** refers to the consistency of something, usually the quality of information, being repeatedly trustworthy over time. To get a better understanding of your topic and ensure that the information you are using is reliable, try to find better coverage. Is it possible to find the same information from another source? If yes, that is a good indication that the information or source is reliable. This can take many forms: you might find better coverage through sources that are more detailed, varied, authoritative, or recent. Even if you think your original source is good, verifying what you've found with additional sources will strengthen your research.

Trace it Back

Before trusting or reusing information you've found, make sure you understand its original context by tracing the claims, quotes, and media back to their sources. This is useful whether you are exploring a news source, article, or social media post. T may be the "last" move in SIFT, but it isn't the last thing you need to do. Once you find the original source for a piece of information, you may need to circle back to steps I and F to evaluate any new information you've found.

Evaluating scholarly information takes more than just verifying that it has been peer reviewed. You also need to determine if your source is accurate, reliable, and relevant. In addition to using SIFT, there are some other strategies and considerations that can be useful for quickly assessing a scholarly source.

For example, for a website you should determine who owns this site. Is it a professional organization such as the American Medical Association? You can usually find this info in the About section of the site or in a copyright designation near the end of the landing page. Domain names can help you determine the purpose of the site, but don't make assumptions based on the domain.

Table 2.3

Domain	User
.edu	Used by educational institutions (i.e., colleges, universities, school districts); usually reliable sources of information, but individual members of these institutions may be able to create web pages on the site under the official domain that do not reflect the values of the school
.com/.biz	Used by commercial or business groups; may be valid, but also may be used to sell products, services, or ideas
.gov	Used by government agencies; typically valid
.org	Used by organizations, such as nonprofit groups or religious entities; may present information slanted toward a specific denomination or cause. You'll need to conduct additional research to verify validity.
.net	Originally created for networks or groups of people working on the same problem, .net is still a viable option for noncommercial sites such as personal blogs or family websites. You'll need to conduct additional research to verify validity.
Many other domains exist	Research the validity of domain names outside these most common ones

Citation Search Techniques

A **citation** contains elements (e.g. author, date, title) that uniquely identify a resource. You will primarily find citations in the works cited or reference section of a paper or book. They may also appear on websites, your course syllabus, or other materials provided by your instructor. Your instructors expect you to include citations in all of your work to tell them where your ideas came from. Scholars out in the wider world include citations in their work for the same purpose. You can use their citations to trace back where their ideas originated, the same way your instructors check your work.

Note that different citation styles (MLA, APA, Chicago, etc.) will have different rules or ways of representing common elements of citations, such as author name, title of article or book, and so on. What's important is to focus on recognizing these citation elements rather than the specific rules for a given style.

2.5 Academic Integrity

Questions to consider:

- What are the six values of Academic Integrity?
- What is plagiarism?

Why Academic Integrity Matters

A degree, diploma or certificate achieved without compromising your own integrity and simultaneously upholding campus academic integrity standards, is a true representation of all the hard work and dedication you put into your studies. You will also be well prepared for success in your career as you have put the necessary time and effort into your work, gained much knowledge and developed many valuable skills, such as research, critical thinking and writing skills, and much more.

What Does Academic Integrity Mean?

The International Center for Academic Integrity (2013), defines **Academic Integrity** as a commitment to uphold six fundamental values in the academic community, even when faced with adversity:

- honesty
- trust
- fairness
- respect
- responsibility
- courage

Each of these values is defined below.

Honesty: honest students respect university policies, follow the instructions of their professors and do their work on their own, without any unauthorized help. Dishonest behavior, such as lying, cheating, fraud, theft, impersonating another person, falsification of data and the like, are morally and ethically not acceptable to a person of integrity.

Trust: if you are always honest, you will be able to build a relationship of trust both with your peers and with your instructors. Trust is established over time and is based mostly on your actions.

Fairness: a person of integrity is fair. You are fair to your peers when you do your own work, to authors when you acknowledge their work you use by citing it, to the university when you respect and follow academic integrity standards, and to alumni when your behavior helps to support the value of their degree.

Respect: you show respect when you adhere to your assignment instructions, when you actively participate in learning and show interest in gaining new knowledge, when you contribute your thoughts to the academic discourse while accepting that others may disagree with you, when you credit others for their ideas, and when you show that you are putting your best efforts forward.

Responsibility: you show responsible behavior when you lead by example, when you resist negative peer pressure, and when you discourage others from violating academic integrity principles. Being responsible means being accountable to yourself and others and to do your work to the best of your abilities.

Courage: to uphold academic integrity standards requires courage to resist temptations for the "easy way out" and to speak up against wrongdoing.

Academic Integrity Policy and Procedures

Alamo Colleges Academic Integrity Policy: College personnel with administrative authority may initiate disciplinary proceedings against a student accused of scholastic dishonesty. "Scholastic dishonesty" includes, but is not limited to, cheating on a test, plagiarism, and collusion.

Academic integrity violations cover conduct involving **scholastic dishonesty**. It is a violation of the Student Code of Conduct to engage in or to assist others to engage in the following conduct:

1. Sale of Academic Product. Preparing, selling, offering or advertising for sale, or delivering to another person an Academic Product, in exchange for anything of value.
2. Academic Enticement or Influence. Influencing or attempting to influence an employee, faculty member or administrator.
3. Academic Misconduct - the intentional violation of college policies, such as tampering with grades, misrepresenting one's identity, or taking part in obtaining or distributing any part of a test or assessment.
4. Cheating - the use or attempted use of unauthorized materials, information, or study aids; or an act of deceit by which a student attempts to misrepresent academic skills or knowledge; or unauthorized copying or collaboration.
5. Fabrication - intentional misrepresentation or invention of any information, such as falsifying research, inventing or exaggerating data, or listing incorrect or fictitious references.
6. Collusion - assisting another to commit an act of academic dishonesty, such as paying or bribing someone to acquire a test or assignment, taking a test or doing an assignment for someone else, or allowing someone to do these things for one's own benefit.
7. Plagiarism - the unauthorized or undocumented use or close imitation of the language and thoughts of another author and the representation of them as one's own original work.

See Student Code of Conduct in the Student Handbook available on the SAC website for more details.

What is the best way to avoid committing a violation?

1. Be **honest** in all areas
2. Do your **own** work
3. Submit **original** work
4. Only work with others if your instructor **permitted** it
5. If permitted to work in groups, **acknowledge** contributions of others
6. Acknowledge all your sources of information by **citing** them properly
7. Learn to quote, paraphrase and summarize **properly**
8. Get help if needed
9. Do **not** help another person commit a violation

Understanding Plagiarism

Plagiarism is one of the most frequent academic integrity violations. It ranges in severity from blatant to inadvertent. Plagiarism is defined as the misrepresentation of something as your own. There are many definitions of the word plagiarism. Using someone's words, ideas or other works without giving credit is plagiarism. A student could submit a whole work that is not their own, for example a paper purchased online. A student may get distracted or overwhelmed and forgets to cite sources. This is still plagiarism.

Plagiarism often starts with the note-taking stage of the research process. Thus, when taking notes, be sure to distinguish between paraphrases and direct quotations. When you are copying an exact quotation, note all the information you will need for the citation. It is a good idea to make a system for yourself, perhaps color coding, when doing your research. Make direct quotations one color and your own paraphrasing of ideas another color. Both quotations and paraphrases need to be cited with sources, both within the paper and at the end in a reference page.

Figure 2.8 Students doing research for a group project

Avoiding Plagiarism

You certainly have heard about plagiarism and how important it is not to let yourself participate in it. It is so easy to read through many other people's work and grab a sentence here and there to put into your work. When struggling to come up with ideas, you may also find yourself borrowing from others. Neither of these is a good idea.

While the process of writing authentically and avoiding plagiarism must be focused from the start, you can avoid a world of trouble by double-checking your near-final work with a source identification site or plagiarism detector. Doing so can help you avoid any unintentional reuse of others' work and may simply identify a source you forgot to cite. You must follow best practices to ensure that you don't plagiarize. At SAC, you can get help in the Library or the Writing Center.

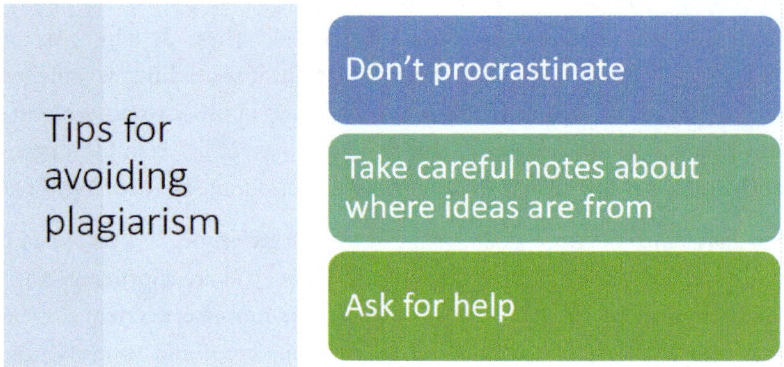

Figure 2.9

Tips for Avoiding Plagiarism

- Don't procrastinate. Good research takes time. Procrastinating makes it likely you'll run out of time to complete your assignment before you need to turn it in. Plan your research well in advance, to make sure you have enough time to get everything done.
- Take careful notes about where the ideas you are using come from. One good practice is to clearly label which ideas are your own and which come from others. For example, in your draft, you could write (ME) after your own ideas, and note citation information (author, date, and especially page numbers) after the information from your sources. You'll need this information for your bibliography anyway, so you'll benefit from having it at the beginning.
- Ask for help when you need it! Your professor or a librarian can help you better understand your assignment or what resources to use. The Writing Center offers tutoring or writing support. If you've got a quick question about how to find or cite a source, use the SAC Library's Live Chat service or stop by the main desk at the library and ask.

Reusing Your Work

Sometimes you might be tempted to reuse old papers or projects you've completed for another class, especially if that work is applicable for your current assignment. Recycling is a form of plagiarism called **self-plagiarism**. This refers to submitting your own previous work, entirely or partially, in another course as new and original. This type of recycled work could be flagged as plagiarism by plagiarism detection software, and is unacceptable in many courses. Different disciplines have differing attitudes toward this kind of recycling, ranging from tolerance in very specific situations to absolutely forbidding it in all cases.

Before you resubmit work or assignments you have completed for a different course or purpose, you should always discuss with your instructor whether it is permitted to recycle your own work like this, whether in part or in its entirety.

Activity 2.4

Consider the following scenarios and provide the best course of action for each.

1. You are a new student and are juggling to keep up with your courses while also working a part-time job. You are a bit stressed about an upcoming exam. A student who is a year ahead of you offers you a copy of an exam and informs you all the exams for this course can be found online. What action would be acceptable?
2. You are having difficulties with one of your courses. You have been stuck on your essay for a whole week already. You are afraid that you may fail the course if you can't turn this situation around. What should you do?

2.6 Citing Your Sources

Questions to consider:

- Why is it important to cite all your sources?
- What is the correct way to cite sources?

Now that you have learned effective strategies for searching for, accessing, and evaluating sources, review the final stage of the research process, using sources in your project. Let's look at the basics about citations, using sources ethically, and copyright.

Why cite sources?

It is important to cite your sources in order to:

- meet the requirements for your assignment
- give the original creators credit for their ideas
- help your readers find and learn from the sources you used
- lend credibility to your argument

You are likely familiar with the first three reasons already, so let's examine the last one in more detail. How does citing sources lend credibility to your argument? Research projects involve reading, analyzing, and synthesizing information from multiple sources and using their ideas to inform your work. There is a common misconception that academic research consists of one person making amazing breakthroughs all alone in their lab or office, but that's not what usually happens in most cases. Instead, research is a process where scholars build on older work while sharing their new ideas. When you cite others' research, you are doing the same thing. By citing a scholar that has done research on your topic area, you are using their authority and experience to support your claims, and adding your own insights.

Cite Purposefully

Citations aren't just there to fill up space. Each citation you include in your work should be relevant and serve a purpose. Maybe you agree with the author and wish to further explore their main points. Or perhaps you disagree with their conclusions and wish to explain your own perspectives. In either case, the ideas you are citing must somehow add to your argument. Keep in mind that no single article or book will be exactly what you need. To strengthen your argument, you need to examine the work of multiple authors.

When to cite?

Whenever you use someone else's ideas, you need to cite them. This is true for any source where there is interpretation involved (opinions, research findings, recent discoveries, statistics, etc). No matter where ideas come from you still need to cite them, whether they are from images, tables, charts, statistics, websites, podcasts, interviews, emails, speeches, songs, movies, or any other source.

There are times when an exact quote is the best option for your work, but most of the time, you'll be paraphrasing the sources you cite. **Paraphrasing** refers to incorporating someone else's ideas into your work and restating them in your own words. This means more than simply swapping out a few words for synonyms. When you paraphrase, you analyze the ideas presented, synthesize that information, and summarize it while citing the original source. By paraphrasing well, you demonstrate that you have understood an author's ideas, and that you can restate them without altering the author's meaning.

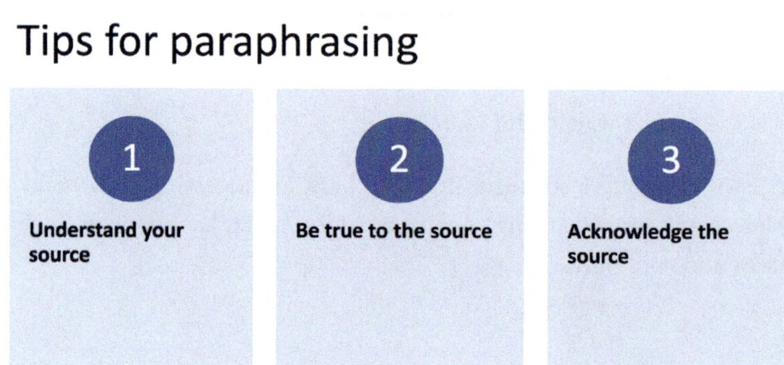

Figure 2.10

Tips for Paraphrasing

- **Understand your source**: when you understand someone else's perspective and how it fits into your argument, only then can you put those ideas in your own words. Most writing guides will recommend that you read and reflect on the main points that may be relevant to your project.
- **Be true to the source**: you must accurately represent the message of the original author in your paraphrasing. This doesn't mean you have to agree with the ideas, just that you explain them accurately.
- **Acknowledge the source**: you must always cite the source whenever you paraphrase. Citing acknowledges that you are using someone else's ideas whether or not you are using the exact words of the original author. Not citing paraphrased material is plagiarism. Your work is strengthened when you show that you have done your research; citing other writers' works is your evidence!

Common knowledge is factual information that can *easily be verified in multiple authoritative sources* (e.g., encyclopedias, dictionaries, reputable websites, and books). You always need to cite things like opinions, ideas, or new research findings, but well-established facts don't need citations. Even if it's something new to you, if it's a long-held fact, it is considered common knowledge and doesn't need to be cited.

Here are some types of common knowledge, with examples of each:

- Widely-known facts: that water boils at 100° Celsius.
- Uncontested historical dates: 1776 was the year the Declaration of Independence was signed in the United States of America.
- Well-known cultural references, such as important facts, people, or historical events within that culture: Suleiman the Magnificent was the longest ruling sultan of the Ottoman Empire.

How to cite?

Once you have done your research and found sources, the next step is working on the assignment. As you complete your work, you will need to communicate your ideas to your audience. You will also need to demonstrate that you know how to integrate others' ideas in your writing in an ethical, clear, and consistent way. This means incorporating citations when paraphrasing or using direct quotes.

Citation Style manuals are guides that help you write particular types of papers (research reports, technical reports, and theses). They also have rules for how to cite sources properly and consistently. Your professor will usually tell you which style manual you should follow for assignments in their class. If not, you should ask.

In addition to helping you configure citations, style manuals also help you structure your writing in a way that is understood by an audience of subject experts. The most common styles used for college writing are APA, MLA and Chicago.

Figure 2.11

- **APA** is mostly used in the Sciences and Social Sciences
- **MLA** is used in many of the Humanities
- **Chicago style** is the preferred style for History and Music

Citation Examples

A book citation includes the author, title, publisher and year of publication. Below is a citation for a book in Chicago style:

Frank, Frederick S. *The First Gothics: A Critical Guide to the English Gothic Novel.* Garland Publishing, 1987.

A book chapter citation contains all the elements of a book citation, plus some extra pieces that indicate the citation is for part of a book, rather than the whole book. These commonly include an editor's name, the chapter title in addition to the book title, and page numbers for the chapter. Generally, a book chapter citation includes two sets of names. The first is the author(s) of the book chapter being cited. The second set represents the editor(s) for the entire book. Below is a citation for a book chapter in MLA style:

> Neves, Marcos Fava, and Luciano Thomé e Castro, "Inserting small holders into sustainable value chains." In *Handbook of Business Practices and Growth in Emerging Markets*, ed. Satyendra Singh. (Singapore: World Scientific, 2010), 235–253.

Journal article citation elements include author and title of the article, journal name, journal volume and issue numbers. Below is an example of an article citation in APA style:

> Upadhyay, R. and Rao, J.M. (2012). Microwave-assisted extraction of chlorogenic acids from green coffee beans. *Food Chemistry, 130*(1), 184–188. doi: 10.1016/ j.foodchem.2011.06.057

Some styles have quick guides available online. The SAC library also has copies of many different style manuals. To find style manuals in your area of study, talk with your professors or a subject specialist librarian, or visit the Writing Center.

Where to cite?

Prepare to cite in TWO places:

- In the body of writing where you
    - Quote
    - Paraphrase
    - Summarize
    - Use or refer to specific audiovisual representations (data, images, tables, figures, video clips, podcasts, performances, etc.)
- In a list of sources at the end of your work or paper, called
    - References **(APA)**
    - Works Cited **(MLA)**
    - Bibliography

At the end of your project, you'll need to compile the sources you used into a bibliography. A **bibliography**, also called "**references**" or "**works cited**," is a comprehensive list of citations at the end of a project. The rules for organizing and formatting a bibliography differ depending on which style you are using. The style manual should provide guidance for how to do this consistently.

The example below shows how the three citations the student used within the body of the text would appear in the corresponding list of sources for the APA and MLA citation styles. The first entry is for a **book**, the second for an **online article** and the third for a **book chapter.**

Although Canada's multicultural policy is liberal and democratic in its goals, there are reasons to be sceptical about its value. Detractors argue that the state should not enshrine differences into policy, but should rather aim to treat everyone the same, or more accurately, provide the conditions such that all members of society can have access to equal opportunities (Barry, 2001). One could even argue that a multicultural policy magnifies cultural differences instead of promoting a homogeneous diversity. The policy has also been attacked for promoting the interests of the English-Canadian majority (Day & Sadick, 2002). Mitchell (1996) goes even further with this, arguing that it is a policy designed to further the capitalist interests of the "elites". At the core of the argument, however, is the question of whether or not the policy is any good . . .	**References** Barry, B. (2001). *Culture and equality: An egalitarian critique of multiculturalism.* Harvard University Press. Day, R. F., & Sadick, T. (2002). The BC land question, liberal multiculturalism, and the spectre of aboriginal nationhood. *BC Studies*, 134, 5–34. https://doi.org/10.14288/bcs/v0i134.162 Mitchell, K. (1996). In whose interest? *Transnational capital and the production of multiculturalism in Canada.* In R. Wilson, & W. Dissanayake (Eds.), Global/Local: Cultural production and the transnational imaginary (pp. 219–254). Duke University Press.

Figure 2.12 APA Style: In-text citations (author/date) and corresponding *Reference List* entry

Although Canada's multicultural policy is liberal and democratic in its goals, there are reasons to be sceptical about its value. Detractors argue that the state should not enshrine differences into policy, but should rather aim to treat everyone the same, or more accurately, provide the conditions such that all members of society can have access to equal opportunities (Barry 118). One could even argue that a multicultural policy magnifies cultural differences instead of promoting a homogeneous diversity. The policy has also been attacked for promoting the interests of the English-Canadian majority (Day and Sadick 30). Mitchell goes even further with this, arguing that it is a policy designed to further the capitalist interests of the "elites". (225) At the core of the argument, however, is the question of whether or not the policy is any good . . .	**Works Cited** Barry, Brian. *Culture and Equality: An Egalitarian Critique of Multiculturalism.* Harvard UP, 2001. Day, Richard F., & Tonio Sadick. "The BC Land Question, Liberal Multiculturalism, and the Spectre of Aboriginal Nationhood. *BC Studies*, vol. 134, Summer 2002, pp. 5–34. doi.org/10.14288/bcs/v0i134.162 Mitchell, Katharyne. "In Whose Interest? Transnational Capital and the Production of Multiculturalism in Canada." *Global/Local: Cultural Production and the Transnational Imaginary*, edited by Rob Wilson, & Wimal Dissanayake Duke UP, 1996, pp. 219–254.

Figure 2.13 MLA Style: In-text citations (author/page) and corresponding *Work Cited* list entry

Figures 2.13 and 2.14 Source: Massachusetts Institute of Technology. (n.d.). What is common knowledge? *Academic integrity at MIT: A handbook for students.* -common-knowledge

In this course you will practice how to find, read, summarize, and cite peer reviewed journal articles. The Peer-reviewed Journal Article Summary Worksheet found in Appendix 3 will guide you through the article summary process.

Chapter Summary

This chapter explored what thinking means and how thinking may impact you as a college student. College students in particular must be prepared to think critically. This includes weighing options, consulting data, gathering opinions, making choices, and then evaluating those decisions. Throughout many of your courses, it will be important to recognize that you must make efforts to ask questions, conduct research, limit assumptions, recognize biases, and gather multiple options. That is why determining the best approach to any given problem and generating more than one possible solution will leave you with options. More than one solution will allow you to feel more in control whether it is for an assignment or your everyday life.

This is why information literacy and knowing how to access reliable information is a critical life skill. As a college student, your job is to continuously seek out information through research. Popular and scholarly peer reviewed information can help you conduct research effectively. It is important to know when to use various resources and how to find them. Do not forget that help is available to you through the campus Library. By utilizing tools such as SIFT, you will be able to evaluate information by stopping, investigating the source, finding coverage, and tracing it back. The SIFT process enables you to determine that your source information is accurate, reliable, and relevant.

When researching, college students must be diligent in upholding academic integrity by citing all sources of information. In all of your academic work, unless information is common knowledge, paraphrasing and quoting requires careful, relevant, and purposeful citation to avoid plagiarism. The type of citation style to use is often determined by the instructor or subject. Remember, the San Antonio College Library is equipped to help you conduct research, evaluate information and maintain academic integrity effectively.

Chapter Citations

Baldwin, A. (2022). *College Success*. Independently published. OpenStax

Iowa State University Library Instruction Services. (2021). Library 160: Introduction to college-level research. Ames, IA: Iowa State University Digital Press.DOI:https://dx.doi.org/10.31274/isudp.2021.72

Kestler, U. and Kwantlen Polytechnic University Library. (2020). Academic Integrity [Online]. Press Books. https://www.oercommons.org/courses/academic-integrity/view#

Chapter 3 Career Exploration, Degree Planning, and Leadership

Figure 3.1 There are many considerations when choosing a career

Chapter Outline*

3.1 Why worry about a career while I'm in college?

3.2 Your Map to Success: The Career Planning Cycle

3.3 Planning Your Degree Path

3.4 Making a Plan

3.5 Developing Your Leadership Skills

Student Survey

How ready are you to plan your career? Take this quick survey to figure it out, ranking questions on a scale of 1–4, 1 meaning "least like me" and 4 meaning "most like me."

1. ____I am feeling certain about my major (or my ability to choose a major soon).

* Endnote references in this chapter retain the numbering from the original article.

2. _____I know what kinds of jobs I can get with my major.
3. _____I am familiar with the requirements I must complete and options I must select to obtain a college degree.
4. _____I have a good idea of what I need to do in each year of college to graduate and achieve career success.
5. _____I am aware of what resources are on campus to help me create a career plan.
6. _____I am exploring ways to develop my leadership skills while in college.

Chapter Outcomes

In this chapter you will learn more about setting the foundation for college and career success by gaining a deeper understanding of how to begin your academic and career planning. It will also help identify the nature of leadership characteristics needed in the workplace.

By the time you complete this chapter, you should be able to do the following:

- Learn what a career is and how it applies to you.
- Identify resources on campus that can help you explore careers and develop a plan.
- Increase self-awareness relative to career aspirations and create a plan to reach career goals.
- List the types of college certificates, degrees, special programs, and majors you can pursue.
- Describe the nature of leadership.
- List the behavioral and situational perspectives on leadership.
- Give examples of transactional and transformation leadership characteristics.

3.1 Why Worry about a Career While I Am in College?

Questions to consider:

- What is the difference between a Job and a Career?
- How do I separate career myths from reality?

A universal definition of a job is "work that you do in exchange for money." It can also be a particular role or title. A career is something for which we train, something that we intend to do permanently—which in actuality means long-term and over time, not necessarily for the rest of our lives. It is a field or area in which we have achieved some success. It occurs progressively and usually consecutively. Here is how some current college students have defined "career":

- "A career is long-term; you do it until you can't anymore."
- "Something you love . . . a dream job."
- "What you plan and strive for while you work."
- "When you are more invested in the activities of the job than just getting a paycheck."[1]

1 Canisius College Student Interviews, Buffalo, NY, September 2019

Shira's Story

When Shira was in college, she had a job at a local ice-cream stand. She made very good money in the summertime, so she could work less during the school year. She also learned a lot about customer service and working with her coworkers as a team. Shira eventually took on more responsibility as a supervisor, creating work schedules and interviewing prospective new employees. She really enjoyed this part of her job because she liked tasks involving helping people do well at work. Her boss, customers, and coworkers told her she was good at it. Unbeknownst to her at the time, this was the beginning of Shira's career in human resources.

How did this happen? As she took classes in psychology and business, Shira saw her courses in organizational psychology and management as applicable to her work. She enjoyed learning about how people interact in the workplace. She learned about human resources, which is typically defined as the department of a business or organization that deals with the hiring, administration, and training of people. She wanted to learn even more, so she got an internship in the human resources department of a bank before she graduated and loved it.

After getting her Bachelor of Science degree in psychology, Shira got her first career-oriented job, as a recruiting specialist at a health insurance company. After about two years of working diligently, Shira got promoted to a job as a human resource generalist, with responsibility for recruiting strategy and process; recruiting specialists now report to her. In addition to working full-time, Shira also is active in her local chapter of the Society for Human Resource Management and will begin studying to take the national certification exams offered through this organization, giving her a highly sought-after professional credential. Within 5 to 10 years, Shira hopes to become a human resources director.

Shira's career path is a straightforward one. She learned a lot about herself early in her college career. She received some experience and studied academic subjects she was interested in. Shira was nervous and uncertain at times, but she remained positive and adjusted her course as needed. She worked hard and made plans to be sure she could get a "good job."

Career Myths and Realities

Because you are a student, many people will want to give you advice as you make your way through college. Your parents might have very definite ideas about what you should major in and the best way to get a job. Your friends, particularly those already in college, might tell you what their experience is, but maybe yours will be very different. Then there are all kinds of things you hear about in the news as to whether there are jobs out there. Government statistics tell us that the unemployment rate is lower than ever before, but many people say it is still very difficult to get a job. So what is the reality for college students looking to begin their careers?

MYTH #1: "Because I am getting a college degree, I will have no problem getting hired and making a lot of money."

REALITY: Your chances of making more money over the course of your lifetime are greater when you have a college degree. However, employers expect more than just a diploma. They also expect that you did well in your studies and engaged in activities and experiences that demonstrate you can put learning into context in a work setting. Internships, practicums, service learning, community-based research, part-time or summer jobs, and more prove to employers that you are capable and eager to begin your career.

MYTH #2: "There is one perfect job for me" or "I will be happy if I find the right career."

REALITY: Finding the right career is not like waving a magic wand or a ticket to living your best Instagram life all of the time. There are jobs and careers for which you might be well-suited based on a combination of features and attributes. The better you know yourself, the better you can make a good match. Additionally, those features and attributes change over time, and by learning good career planning skills, you can adapt easily.

MYTH #3: “I can’t get a good job with (fill in the name of a major).”

REALITY: There are some majors that traditionally result in jobs that earn more than others do. These are usually because the education for these occupations is often rigorous, and both training for and working in the occupation require a high level of skill and knowledge, even over time (engineering, computer science, accounting). However, anybody can get a “good” job with their major. The key is to understand what knowledge, skills, and abilities are required for the jobs you would like and to take action to make sure you have them. People who have a problem getting employment in their field after college may not have fully understood the requirements for being hired, they may have been unable to make the sacrifices necessary for that to happen, or they may have had unrealistic expectations.

MYTH #4: “It is too late to change my career.”

REALITY: It is almost never “too late” to make a career change. There are millions of people who have made career changes, some by going to college in their 30s, 40s, 50s, or even older. In many cases, the best time to make a change is when you are older, because you have more to offer employers, have gained different experiences, and have become more settled in your personal life. Many college students find they are well-positioned to make the most of their college studies when they are more mature.

MYTH #5: “No one will hire me because I am ‘just a student’; I won’t be able to compete with people with more experience.”

REALITY: Employers often like to hire recent graduates or people who are early in their careers because their learning is fresh, and they know how to learn new material and adapt quickly. Additionally, many employers believe that hiring new graduates allows them to train people the way that they would like. New graduates of all ages show persistence and flexibility by having earned a college degree and shown willingness to start something new.

MYTH #6: “I should be passionate about my work. If not, I am doing something wrong. “

REALITY: “Do what you love and you’ll never work a day in your life” and “Do what you love and the money will follow” are terrible advice. No one loves their work every minute of every day, and passion is a very high standard to meet. There are many things about which we might be passionate that would make for jobs that are completely unsuitable for us. What most people who are happy with their work have in common are that they can do it well; it has some impact on people, organizations, information, or things; and they find satisfaction in it. It is often through discovering this that passion for one’s work follows.

Activity 3.1

Consider the various events or conversations you’ve experienced in the past few years that have led you toward a career goal. Have any of the myths or their counterparts listed above impacted your choices? Are you called to reconsider any previous decisions? Why or why not? Are there additional preconceptions you might have that could potentially block you from moving forward with your ideal plans?

What Should I Be?

Have you ever heard statements like these?

- "You are so good at math . . . you should be an accountant."
- "Your best grades have always been in art, but it isn't really practical to become an artist."
- "You like kids so much! You should be a teacher!"

Many people tend to first think of careers based on images they see in society or the media. Prestigious and high-visibility occupations are what many young people aspire to when they are young. How many of you first wanted to be a doctor, firefighter, entertainer, professional athlete, or teacher? As we grow up and get to know the world better, we are exposed to a greater universe of jobs. However, young people in middle and high school also tend to look at careers based on the subjects they are good at (or not good at) in school. These self-perceptions and interests can last long into adulthood. But education and the work world can be extremely different environments with different purposes and expectations. The realities of jobs and careers we choose are vastly more complex than the courses we like or don't and whether we perform well in them in high school. Though we may have some images for "what we are" and "who we should be," there are also many different options, and the choices can be overwhelming. How do we ensure that we make career decisions that are productive for us?

3.2 Your Map to Success: The Career Planning Cycle

Questions to consider:

- What steps should I take to learn about my best opportunities?
- What can I do to prepare for my career while in college?
- What experiences and resources can help me in my search?

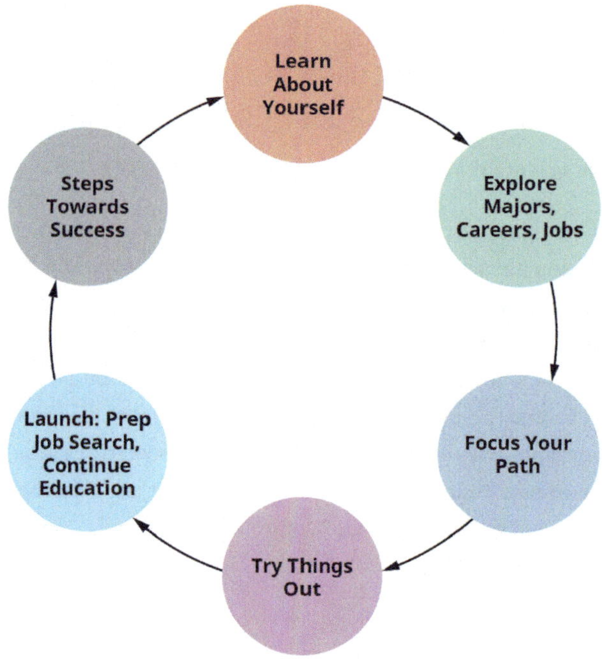

Figure 3.2 You can use the Career Planning Cycle to consider and reconsider your approach and progress in choosing and moving toward a career (Credit: Based on work by Lisa August.)

The Career Planning Cycle helps us apply some concrete steps to figuring out where we might fit into the work world. If you follow the steps, you will learn about who you truly are who you can be as a working professional. Let's look at each of the steps in the Career Planning Cycle in more detail.

Step 1 - Learn About Yourself

To understand what type of work suits us and to be able to convey that to others to get hired, we must become experts in knowing who we are. Gaining self-knowledge is a lifelong process, and college is the perfect time to gain and adapt to this fundamental information. Following are some of the types of information that we should have about ourselves:

- Interests: Things that we like and want to know more about. These often take the form of ideas, information, knowledge, and topics.
- Skills/Aptitudes: Things that we either do well or can do well. These can be natural or learned and are usually skills—things we can demonstrate in some way. Some of our skills are "hard" skills, which are specific to jobs and/or tasks. Others are "soft" skills, which are personality traits and/or interpersonal skills that accompany us from position to position.
- Values: Things that we believe in. Frequently, these are conditions and principles.
- Personality: Things that combine to make each of us distinctive. Often, this shows in the way we present ourselves to the world. Aspects of personality are customarily described as qualities, features, thoughts, and behaviors.

In addition to knowing the things we can and like to do, we must also know how well we do them. What are our strengths? When employers hire us, they hire us to do something, to contribute to their organization in some way. We get paid for what we know, what we can do, and how well or deeply we can demonstrate these things. Think of these as your Knowledge, Skills, and Abilities (KSAs). As working people, we can each think of ourselves as carrying a "tool kit." In our tool kit are the KSAs that we bring to each job.

Awareness of the need to develop your career identity and your vocational worth is the first step. Next, undertaking a process that is mindful and systematic can help guide you through. Often, career assessment is of great assistance in increasing your self-knowledge. It is most often designed to help you gain insight more objectively. You may want to think of assessment as pulling information out of you and helping you put it together in a way that applies to your career. There are two main types of assessments: formal assessments and informal assessments.

Formal Assessments

Formal assessments are typically referred to as "career inventories." It is important to use assessments that are developed to be reliable and valid. Look to your career center for their recommendations; their staff have often spent a good deal of time selecting instruments that they believe work best for students.

Here are some commonly used and useful assessments that you may run across:

- Interest Assessments: Strong Interest Inventory, Self-Directed Search, Campbell Interest and Skill Survey, Harrington-O'Shea Career Decision-Making System
- Personality Measures: Myers-Briggs Type Indicator, CliftonStrengths (formerly Strengths-Quest), Big Five Inventory, Keirsey Temperament Sorter, TypeFocus, DiSC
- Career Planning Software: SIGI 3, FOCUS 2

Informal Assessments

Often, asking questions and seeking answers can help get us information that we need. When we start working consciously on learning more about any subject, things that we never considered may become apparent. Happily, this applies to self-knowledge as well. Some things that you can do outside of career testing to learn more about yourself can include:

Self-Reflection:

- Notice when you do something that you enjoy or that you did particularly well. What did that feel like? What about it made you feel positive? Is it something that you would like to do again? What impact did you make through your actions?
- Most people are the "go to" person for something. What do you find that people come to you for? Are you good with advice? Do you tend to be a good listener, observing first and then speaking your mind? Do people appreciate your repair skills? Are you good with numbers? What role do you play in a group?

Enlist Others:

- Ask people who know you to tell you what they think your strengths are. What kinds of things have they observed you doing well? What personal qualities do you have that they value?

- Find a mentor—such as a professor, an alum, an advisor, or a community leader—from whom you think you could learn new things. Many of your college faculty likely have (or had) other roles and positions.
- Get involved with one or more activities on campus that will let you use skills outside of the classroom. You will be able to learn more about how you work with a group and try new things that will add to your skill set.

No one assessment can tell you exactly what career is right for you; the answers to your career questions are not in a test. The reality of career planning is that it is a discovery process that uses many methods over time to strengthen our career knowledge and belief in ourselves.

Step 2 - Explore Jobs and Careers

Many students seem to believe that the most important decision they will make in college is to choose their major. While this is an important decision, even more important is to determine the type of knowledge you would like to have, understand what you value, and learn how you can apply this in the workplace after you graduate. For example, if you know you like to help people, this is a value. If you also know that you are interested in math and/or finances, you might study to be an accountant. To combine both, you would gain as much knowledge as you can about financial systems and personal financial habits so that you can provide greater support and better help to your clients.

The four factors of self-knowledge (interests, skills/aptitudes, values, and personality), which manifest in your Knowledge, Skills, Abilities (KSAs), are also the factors on which employers evaluate your suitability for their positions. They consider what you can bring to their organization that is in line with their organization's standards and needs.

Along with this, each job has KSAs that define it. You may think about finding a job/career as you look at the figure below.

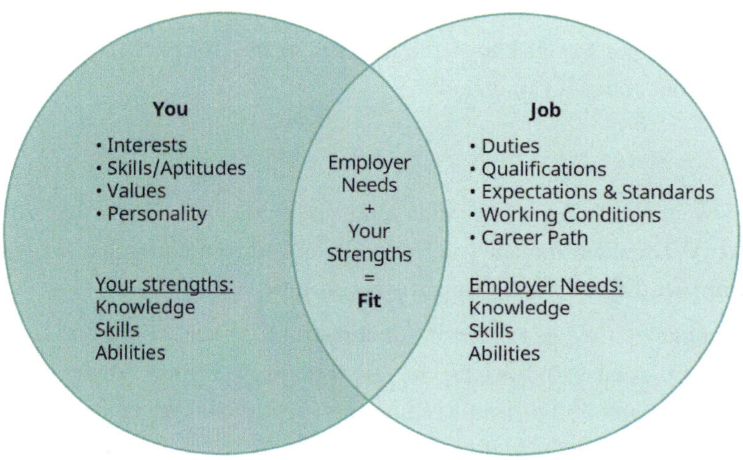

Figure 3.3 Your fit for a job lies at the intersection of your attributes and the elements of the position. When your strengths align with the employer's needs, both can mutually benefit.

The importance of finding the right fit cannot be overstated. Many people do not realize that the KSAs of the person and the requirements of the job have to match in order to get hired in a given field. What is even more important, though, is that when a particular job fits your four factors of self-knowledge and maximizes your KSAs, you are most likely to be satisfied with your work! The "fit" works to help you not only get the job, but also enjoy the job.

So, if you work to learn about yourself, what do you need to know about jobs, and how do you learn it? In our diagram, if you need to have self-knowledge to determine the YOU factors, then to determine the JOB factors, you need to have workplace knowledge. This involves understanding what employers in the workplace and specific jobs require. Aspects of workplace knowledge include:

- Labor Market Information: Economic conditions, including supply and demand of jobs; types of industries in a geographic area or market; regional sociopolitical conditions and/or geographic attributes.
- Industry Details: Industry characteristics; trends and opportunities for both industry and employers; standards and expectations.
- Work Roles: Characteristics and duties of specific jobs and work roles; knowledge, skills, and abilities necessary to perform the work; training and education required; certifications or licenses; compensation; promotion and career path; hiring process.

This "research" may sound a little dry and uninteresting at first but consider it as a look into your future. If you are excited about what you are learning and your career prospects, learning about the places where you may put all your hard work into practice should also be exciting! Most professionals spend many hours not only performing their work but also physically being located at work. For something that is such a large part of your life, it will help you to know what you are getting into as you get closer to realizing your goals.

Holland's Theory of Career Choice

Careers are categorized using interest areas. If a career utilizes your highest interests, you are more likely to feel that the career is a good fit for you. Listed below are the six Holland Occupational Interest Types. The descriptions of "pure types" will rarely be an exact fit for any one person. Your interest profile will more likely combine several types to varying degrees.

1. **Realistic (R).** These people describe themselves as honest, loyal, and practical. They are doers more than thinkers. They have strong mechanical, motor, and athletic abilities; like the outdoors; and prefer working with machines, tools, plants, and animals.
2. **Investigative (I).** These people love problem solving and analytical skills. They are intellectually stimulated and often mathematically or scientifically inclined; like to observe, learn, and evaluate; prefer working alone; and are reserved.
3. **Artistic (A).** These people are the "free spirits." They are creative, emotional, intuitive, and idealistic; have a flair for communicating ideas; dislike structure and prefer working independently; and like to sing, write, act, paint, and think creatively. They are similar to the investigative type but are interested in the artistic and aesthetic aspects of things more than the scientific.
4. **Social (S).** These are "people" people. They are friendly and outgoing; love to help others, make a difference, or both; have strong verbal and personal skills and teaching abilities; and are less likely to engage in intellectual or physical activity.
5. **Enterprising (E).** These people are confident, assertive risk takers. They are sociable; enjoy speaking and leadership; like to persuade rather than guide; like to use their influence; have strong interpersonal skills; and are status conscious.

6. **Conventional (C).** These people are dependable, detail oriented, disciplined, precise, persistent, and practical; value order; and are good at clerical and numerical tasks. They work well with people and data, so they are good organizers, schedulers, and project managers.

Figure 3.4 Hollands Hexagon

Since many career guidance tests are based on Holland's work, let's take a closer look at what careers are matched with the different types. Just as many individuals are more than one personality type, many jobs show a strong correlation to more than one occupational type.

Research careers using resources provided by the Department of Labor. Two excellent Career Exploration Websites are the U.S. Bureau of Labor and Statistics and O*NET Online.

Read online information that is relevant to the professions you are interested in. Good sources for this include professional associations. Just "Googling" information is risky. Look for professional and credible information. The *Occupational Outlook Handbook* has links to many of these sources. Your academic advisor, the Student Enrichment Center, and your academic department can also guide you.

Something to keep in mind as you make choices about your major and career is that the training is not the job. What you learn in your college courses is often foundational information; it provides basic knowledge that you need for more complex concepts and tasks. For example, a second-year student who is a premedical student has the interests and qualities that may make her a good physician, but she is struggling to pass basic chemistry. She starts to think that medical school is no longer an appropriate goal because she does not enjoy chemistry. Does it make sense to abandon a suitable career path because of one 15-week course? In some ways, yes. In medical school, the education is so long and intensive that if the student cannot persevere through one introductory course, she may not be determined to complete the training. On the other hand, if you are truly dedicated to your path, do not let one difficult course deter you.

Table 3.1 Occupational Options by Type

Realistic	• Structured • Clear lines of authority • Work with **things** and **tools** • Casual dress • Focus on tangible results or well-thought- out goals	• Contractor • Emergency medical technician (EMT) • Mechanic • Military career • Packaging engineer
Investigative	• Nonstructured • Research oriented • Intellectual • Work with **ideas** and **data**	• Pharmacist • Lab technician • Nanotechnologist • Geologist • College professor
Artistic	• Nonstructured • Creative • Rewards unconventional and aesthetic approaches • Creation of products and **ideas**	• Advertising career • Architect • Animator • Musician • Journalist
Social	• Collaborative • Collegial • Work with **people** and on people-related problems/ issues • Work as a team or community	• Teacher • Geriatric counselor • Correctional officer • Coach • Nurse
Enterprising	• Typical business environment • Results oriented • Driven • Work with **people** and **data** • Entrepreneurial • Power focused	• Sales manager • Banker • Lawyer • Business owner • Restaurant manager
Conventional	• Orderly • Clear rules and policies • Consistent **processes** • Work with systems to manipulate and organize **data** • Control and handling of money	• Auditor • Insurance underwriter • Bank teller • Office manager • Database manager

Shantelle

The example above describes Shantelle. They were not quite sure which major to choose, and they were feeling pressure because the window for making their decision was closing. They considered their values and strengths—they love helping people and have always wanted to pursue work in medical training. As described above, Shantelle struggled in general chemistry this semester and found that they actually didn't enjoy it at all. They have heard nightmare stories about organic chemistry being even harder. Simultaneously, Shantelle is taking Intro to Psychology, something they thought would be an easier course but that they enjoy even though it is challenging. Much to their surprise, they found the scientific applications of theory in the various types of mental illness utterly fascinating. But given that their life dream was to be a physician, Shantelle was reluctant to give up on medicine because of one measly chemistry course. With the help of an advisor, Shantelle decided to postpone choosing a major for one more semester and take a course in clinical psychology. Since there are so many science courses required for premed studies, Shantelle also agreed to take another science course. Their advisor helped Shantelle realize that it was probably not a wise choice to make such an important decision based on one course experience.

Step 3 - Focus Your Path

When you know yourself and know what to expect from a workplace and a job, you have information to begin to make decisions. As we have discussed throughout this book, you are not attending college solely to get a job. But this is likely one of your goals, and your time in school offers a tremendous opportunity to both prepare for your career (or careers) and make yourself more attractive to organizations where you want to work. Successfully learning the content of your classes and earning good grades are among the most important. Beyond these priorities, you will learn the most about yourself and your potential career path if you engage in activities that will help you make decisions. Simply sitting back and thinking about the decision doesn't always help you take action.

Take advantage of every resource you can while in college. Your college has a wealth of departments, programs, and people dedicated to your success. The more you work to discover and engage with these groups, the more successfully you'll establish networks of support and build skills and knowledge for your career. Make plans to drop by SAC's Student Enrichment Center which offers career services. There, you will learn about events you can attend, and you will get to know some of the people there who can help you.

Step 4 - Try Things Out

In the first two steps of the Career Planning Cycle, you gather information. You may have some ideas about jobs and careers that you may like, but you also may wonder if you will really like them. How will you know? How can you be more certain? It is a great idea to try out a new skill or career field before you commit to it fully. Experiences help you become more qualified for positions. One exciting aspect of college is that there is a huge variety of learning experiences and activities in which to get involved. The following are some ways that you can try things out and get experience.

Figure 3.5 Career fairs are important before (and sometimes after) you graduate, both to explore opportunities and to make actual connections that can lead to a position. (Credit: COD Newsroom / Flickr / Attribution 2.0 Generic (CC-BY 2.0))

Community Involvement, Volunteering, and Clubs

You are in college to develop yourself as an individual. You will gain personally satisfying and enriching experience by becoming more involved with your college or general community. Organizations, clubs, and charities often rely on college students because of their motivation, knowledge, and increasing maturity. The work can increase your skills and abilities, providing valuable experience that will lead to positive results. Volunteering can be an important way to access a profession and get a sense for if you will enjoy it.

Once you join a club or related organization, take the time to learn about their leadership opportunities. Most campus clubs have some type of management structure—treasurer, vice president, president, and so on. You may "move up the ranks" naturally, or you may need to apply or even run for election. Some organizations, such as a campus newspaper, radio station, or dance team, have skill-based semi-professional roles such as advertising manager, sound engineer, or choreographer. These opportunities may not always be available to you as freshmen, but you can take on shorter-term roles to build your skills and make a bigger impact. Managing a fundraiser, planning an event, or temporarily taking on a role while someone else is busy are all ways to engage further.

Internships and Related Experiences

Many employers value experience as much as they do education. Internships and similar fieldwork allow you to use what you have learned and, sometimes more importantly, see how things work "in the real world." These experiences drive you to communicate with others in your field and help you understand the day-to-day challenges and opportunities of people working in similar areas. Even if the internship is not at a company or organization directly in your field of study, you will focus on gaining transferable skills that you can apply later.

When you intern, you are usually treated like you work there full-time. It is not just learning about the job; it is doing the job, much like an entry-level employee. The level of commitment may vary by the type of internship and may be negotiable based on your schedule. Be clear about what is required and what you can handle given your other commitments, because you want to leave a very good impression. (Internship managers are your top resource for employment references and letters of recommendation.)

Table 3.2 Internship and Experiential Learning Terminology

Internship	A period of work experience in a professional organization, in which participants (interns) are exposed to and perform some of the tasks of actual employees. Internships are usually a high commitment and may be paid and/or result in college credit.
Externship/Job Shadowing	Usually a briefer and lower-commitment experience than internships, in which participants are observing work activities and undertaking small projects. Unpaid and not credit-bearing.
Fieldwork	A period or trip to conduct research or participate in the "natural environment" of a discipline or profession. Fieldwork may involve visiting a work site, such as a hospital or nursing home, or being a part of a team gathering data or information.
Apprenticeship	A defined period of on-the-job training in which the student is formally doing the job and learning specific skills. Unlike most internships, apprenticeships are usually formal requirements to attain a license or gain employment in skilled trades, and they are growing in use in health care, IT, transportation, and logistics.
Undergraduate Research	Even as an undergraduate, you may find opportunities to partake in actual research in your field of study. Colleges often have strict guidelines on types and levels of participation, and you will likely need to apply. The benefits include firsthand knowledge of a core academic activity and exposure to more people in your field.
Related Employment	It may be possible to get a regular, low-level paying job directly in your field of study or in a related place of work. While it is not essential, simply being around the profession will better inform and prepare you.
Clinicals, Student Teaching, and Related Experiences	Health care, education, and other fields often have specific requirements for clinicals (learning experience in health care facilities) or student teaching. These are often components of the major and required for both graduation and licensure.
Service Learning	Students learn educational standards through tackling real-life problems in their community. Involvement could be hands-on, such as working in a homeless shelter. Students could also tackle broad issues indirectly, such as by solving a local environmental problem.

Transferable (Marketable) Skills

Through your coursework, campus involvement, job, networking, and internships you should focus as much as possible on building and improving transferable skills. These are abilities and knowledge useful across many industries, job types, and roles. They can be transferred—hence the name—from where you learned them to another career or area of study.

Some examples of transferable skills include communication, leadership, teamwork, computation/quantitative literacy, information technology, research/analysis, and foreign language. Employers believe that transferable skills are critical to the success of their recent college graduate new hires. The top four career competencies that employers want are critical thinking/problem solving, teamwork/collaboration, professionalism/work ethic, and oral/written communication.[2]

These are considered skills because they are not simply traits or personality elements; they are abilities and intelligences you can develop and improve. Even if you are a great writer before starting an internship, you may need to learn how to write in a more professional manner—becoming more succinct, learning the executive summary, conforming to templates, and so on. Once you establish that skill, you can not only mention it on a resume or an interview, but also discuss the process by which you improved, demonstrating your adaptability and eagerness to learn.

Not everyone can land an internship or perform fieldwork. Perhaps you need to work full-time while in school. If so, focus on developing transferable skills in that environment. Take on new challenges in areas where you do not have experience. For example, if you work in retail, ask your manager if you can help with inventory or bookkeeping (building quantitative literacy skills). If you are a waiter, help the catering manager plan a party or order food (building organizational skills). Remember, extending yourself in this way is not simply a means to enhance your resume. By taking on these new challenges, you will see a side of the business you did not have before and learn things that you can apply in other situations.

Now that you have explored career options for yourself, we will now look at other ways you can prepare yourself for moving into your career.

Step 5 - What to Do to Get Ready

Being prepared to find a job means putting evidence of your Knowledge-Skills-Abilities (KSAs) together in a way that employers will understand. It is one thing to say you can do something; it is another to show that you can. The following are things that you will want to compile as a part of your college career.

Resumes and Profiles: The College Version

You may already have a resume or a similar profile (such as LinkedIn), or you may be thinking about developing one. Usually, these resources are not required for early college studies, but you may need them for internships, work-study, or other opportunities. When it comes to an online profile, be very careful and intentional when developing it.

Resume

A resume is a summary of your education, experience, and other accomplishments. It is not simply a list of what you have done; it is a showcase that presents the best you have to offer for a specific role.

A resume is a one-page summary (two, if you are a more experienced person) that generally includes the following information:

- Name and contact information
- Objective and/or summary
- Education—all degrees and relevant certifications or licenses

2 National Association of Colleges and Emplyers. "The Four Career Competencies Employers Value Most." 2019. https://www.naceweb.org/career-readiness/competencies/the-four-career-competencies-employers-value-most/

- While in college, you may list coursework closely related to the job to which you are applying.
- Work or work-related experience—usually in reverse chronological order, starting with the most recent and working backward. (Some resumes are organized by subject/skills rather than chronologically.)[3]
- Career-related/academic awards or similar accomplishments
- Specific work-related skills

While you are in college, especially if you went into college directly after high school, you may not have formal degrees or significant work experience to share. That is okay. Tailor the résumé to the position for which you are applying, and include high school academic, extracurricular, and community-based experience. These show your ability to make a positive contribution and are a good indicator of your work ethic.

Henry Townsend
htownse@stlu.mi.edu

2438 McNair Avenue, Apartment 3
St. Louis, Missouri

Summary
Highly organized audiology major with excellent communication skills and extensive customer service background. Currently focused on gaining clinical experience and leadership skills.

Education
St. Louis University, St. Louis, Missouri
Major: Communication Disorders, Focus on Audiology; Expected Graduation 2024
Activities: Pep Band, Concert Band, Comms Club

Spring Lakes High School, Crimson, Virginia, 2020
Cumulative G.P.A: 3.6
Rotary Public Service Award
Founder and President, Hip Hop Health -- hospital patient music program

Experience
Student Relations Coordinator
St. Louis Children's Hospital — 2021-Present

Circulation Clerk
St. Louis University Library — 2020-Present

Service Desk Representative
Forte Equipment Rental, Virginia Beach — 2019-2021

Skills
American Sign Language, Near Fluent
Google Sheets and Slides, Highly Proficient
Zendesk and Salesforce, Highly Proficient

Figure 3.6 Resumes summarize your accomplishments, education, skills, and experience

Digital Profiles

An online profile is becoming a standard component of professional job seeking and networking. LinkedIn is a networking website used by people from nearly every profession. It combines elements of résumés and portfolios with social media. Users can view, connect, communicate, post events and articles, comment, and

3 Writing@CSU. "Organizing Your Resume." https://writing.colostate.edu/guides/page.cfm?pageid=1517&guideid=77

recommend others. Some professions or industries have specific LinkedIn groups or subnetworks. Other professions or industries may have their own networking sites, to be used instead of or in addition to LinkedIn.

As a college student, it might be a great idea to have a LinkedIn or related profile. It can help you make connections in a prospective field and provide access to publications and posts on topics that interest you. Before you join and develop a public professional profile, however, keep the following in mind:

- Be professional.
- Add relevant experience and information as you attain it.
- Professional networking is different from social media. While LinkedIn has a strong social media component, users are often annoyed by too much nonprofessional sharing.
- LinkedIn is not a replacement for a real resume.

Social Media and Online Activity Never Go Away

It is important to remember that future employers, educational institutions, internship coordinators, and other can see most of what you have posted or done online. Companies are well within their rights to dig through your social media pages, and those of your friends or groups you are a part of, to learn about you. Tasteless posts, inappropriate memes, harassment, pictures or videos of high-risk behavior, and even aggressive and mean comments are all problematic. They may convince a potential employer that you are not right for their organization. Be careful of who and what you retweet, like, and share. It is all traceable, and it can all have consequences.

Building Your ePortfolio

Future employers or educational institutions may want to see the work you have done during school. Also, you may need to recall projects or papers you wrote to remember details about your studies. Your ePortfolio can be one of your most important resources.

Items to include an ePortfolio:

- Evidence of any workshops or special classes you attended. Include a certificate, registration letter, or something else indicating you attended/completed it.
- Evidence of volunteer work, including a write-up of your experience and how it impacted you.
- Related experience and work products from your time prior to college.
- Materials associated with career-related talks, performances, debates, or competitions that you delivered or took part in.
- Products, projects, or experiences developed in internships, fieldwork, clinicals, or other experiences (see below).
- Evidence of "universal" workplace skills such as computer abilities or communication, or specialized abilities such as computation/number crunching.
- Projects, simulations, and case studies.

Preparing an Informational Interview

Throughout this section, we have discussed how important relationships are to your career development. Meeting with someone in your specific career field can be a great way to gain insight into the pros and cons for that position. Conducting this type of information interview can sometimes be a little intimidating but with preparation and understanding, these encounters can be not only helpful, but also rewarding. Here are some ideas to consider when meeting new people who can be helpful to your career:

- Be yourself. You are your own best asset. If you are comfortable with who you are and where you come from, others will be, too.
- Be polite, not too casual. If your goal is to become a professional, look and sound the part.
- Listen.
- Think of some questions ahead of time.
- Say thank you. No need to go on and on, but thank them for any advice they give or simply for taking the time to talk with you.

Letters of Recommendation

Letters of recommendation are often a standard component of convincing people you are the right person to join their organization. Some positions or institutions require a certain quantity of letters and may have specific guidance on who should write them.

Whom should I ask for a letter? They are usually written by instructors, department chairs, club advisors, managers, coaches, and others with whom you've had a good relationship. Maybe it is someone who taught two or three of your courses, or someone you helped in a volunteer or work-study capacity.

How to ask? Be straightforward and direct. They may ask you to provide more information about yourself so that they can write an original letter. If they do so, be thorough but prompt—you do not want to keep them waiting. And if you have a deadline, tell them.

Thank-you notes. They wrote you a letter, so you should write them one in return.

Figure 3.7 When you ask someone to write you a letter of recommendation, be prepared to share information about your goals, your accomplishments, and why you are asking the person in particular. (Credit: US Embassy Jerusalem/Flickr/Attribution 2.0 Generic (CC-BY 2.0))

Step 6 – Steps to Success

A key to success is the ability to manage change, adapt to the unexpected, and handle setbacks. This is also true as you work through the Career Planning Cycle. While this ability may be difficult during the process, it will build a better—and more employable—you. While you cannot prepare for every obstacle or surprise, you can be certain that you will encounter them.

You may go through all of college, and even high school, with one job in mind. You may apply early to a specific program, successfully complete all the requirements, and set yourself on a certain career path. And then something may change.

As described above, changes in your interests or goals are a natural part of developing your career; they are nothing to be ashamed of. Most college students change majors several times. Even once they graduate, many people find themselves enjoying careers they did not envision. Ask the people around you, and many will share stories about how they took a meandering or circuitous path to their profession. Some people end up in jobs or companies that they did not know existed when they started school. Be open to returning to any of the steps in the cycle as circumstances change.

3.3 Planning Your Degree Path

Questions to consider:

- What types of college degrees or certifications can I pursue?
- What is the difference between majors and minors?
- How do preprofessional programs differ from other majors?
- Do some majors have special requirements beyond regular coursework?

Now that you have explored possible careers that would be a good fit for you, it is time to map out the education that is needed to research your career goals.

To set goals for your academic and career path, you must first understand the options available for you to pursue and the requirements you will need to meet. The next section provides an overview of academic programs and college degrees that are common among many colleges and universities in the United States. Please note that each institution will have its own specific options and requirements, so the intention of this section is both to help you understand your opportunities and to familiarize you with language that colleges typically use to describe these opportunities.

Types of Degrees

Whereas in most states high school attendance through the 12th grade is mandatory, or compulsory, a college degree may be pursued voluntarily. There are fields that do not require a degree. Bookkeeping, computer repair, massage therapy, and childcare are all fields where certification programs—tracks to study a specific subject or career without need of a complete degree—may be enough.

However, many individuals will find that an associate's or bachelor's degree is a requirement to enter their desired career field. According to United States Census data published in 2017, more than one-third of the adult population in the country has completed at least a bachelor's degree.

Not every job requires a bachelor's degree, and some require even higher degrees or additional specialized certifications. As you develop your academic plan, it is important to research your field of interest to see what requirements might be necessary or most desirable.

Associate's Degrees and Certificates

To enter an associate degree program, students must have a high school diploma or its equivalent. Associate of Applied Science (AAS) degree programs are intended to help students enter a technical career field, such as automotive technology, graphic design, or entry-level nursing in some states.

Other associate degree programs are intended to prepare a student with the necessary coursework to transfer into a bachelor's degree program upon graduation. These transfer-focused programs usually require similar general education and foundational courses that a student would need in the first half of a bachelor's degree program. Transfer-focused associate degrees may be called Associate of Arts (AA), Associate of Arts in Teaching (AAT)or Associate of Science (AS), or other titles, depending on the focus of study. Transfer Advising Guides (TAGs) inform students what classes to take while enrolled at the Alamo Colleges, so that their classes not only transfer but also count toward their intended four-year degree program at their desired university.

An associate degree is typically awarded when a student has completed at least 60 credits, about 20 courses, meeting the requirements of a specific degree. Some technical associate degrees, such as nursing, may require additional credits in order to meet requirements for special certifications. You may find that your college or university does not offer associate degrees. Most associate degrees are offered by community or junior colleges, or by career and technical colleges.

In addition to associate degrees the Alamo Colleges District also offers certificates that are part of the career and technical offerings at the colleges in the Alamo Colleges District. The certificate programs require fewer semester hours than an AAS and most can be applied toward an AAS degree. The types of certificates available are:

- Marketable Skills Achievement Award: 9 to 14 semester hours. Courses that may lead to immediate employment or add to the student's marketability
- Level I Certificate: 15 to 42 semester hours
- Level II Certificate: 30 to 51 semester hours

Source: San Antonio College Schedule Catalog 2022–2023

General Education

General education, also called core curriculum, is a group of courses that are often set as requirements by your state or by your individual college. These courses provide you with a foundation of knowledge across a breadth of fields and are also intended to help you further develop college-level critical-thinking and problem-solving abilities. For many of the subject areas, you will have a selection of courses to choose from. At San Antonio College, the Core Curriculum consists of 42 credit hours. By taking all the courses in the Core Curriculum, you are considered "core complete" and this block of courses will transfer to any state college or university in Texas. Below is a listing of the Core Curriculum.

Table 3.3 San Antonio College Core Curriculum

While your college may use different labels, general education courses often include a selection of courses from these categories.

Credit Hours Required	Subject Area
6	English composition
6	American History
6	Government/Political Science
3	Social and Behavioral Science
6	Life Sciences
3	Mathematics
3	Creative Arts
6	Language, Philosophy and Culture
3	Speech

Bachelor's Degrees

A bachelor's degree is usually completed with at least 120 credits, or about 40 courses. When someone mentions "a college degree," they are often referring to the bachelor's degree, or baccalaureate degree. Because it takes four years of full-time attendance to complete a bachelor's degree, this degree is also referred to as a "four-year degree." Both associate's degrees and bachelor's degrees are considered undergraduate degrees, thus students working toward these degrees are often called undergraduates. A student with an associate degree may transfer that degree to meet some (usually half) of the requirements of a bachelor's degree; however, completion of an associate degree is not necessary for entry into a bachelor's degree program.

Major Courses

Major courses are courses in your field of interest and provide you with the foundational knowledge required for further study in that field or with the skills necessary to enter your career. Major courses often have a series of prerequisites, or courses that must be taken in sequence prior to other courses, starting with an introductory course and progressing into more depth. Colleges and universities usually require students to select a major by the time they have completed 30 total credits.

Electives

Electives are free-choice courses. Though you may have a choice to select from a menu of options to meet general education and major requirements, electives are even less restricted. Some students may be able to take more electives than others due to their choice of major.

Graduate Degrees

Whereas associate's and bachelor's degrees are considered undergraduate degrees and require high school graduation for entry, advanced degrees called graduate degrees require prior completion of a bachelor's degree. Some professions require graduate degrees as a minimum job qualification, such as pharmacists, lawyers, physical therapists, psychologists, and college professors. In other cases, students may be motivated to pursue a graduate degree to obtain a higher-level job or higher salary, or to be more competitive in their field. Some students are also interested in learning about a subject in greater depth than they did at the undergraduate level. Because graduate degrees do not include general education or free elective courses, they are very focused on career-specific knowledge and skills. Graduate degrees include master's, doctoral, and professional degrees. Master's degrees often require 30–60 credits and take one to two years of full-time attendance to complete. Some master's degrees, like those for counselors, require supervised job experience as a component of the degree and therefore require more credits.

Doctorate and professional degrees are the highest level of advanced degrees. Very few careers require this level of education for entry, so fewer individuals pursue these degrees. Doctorates are offered in many subjects and primarily prepare students to become researchers in their field of study. This in-depth level of education often requires an additional 90–120 credits beyond the bachelor's degree and may or may not require a master's degree prior to entry.

Professional degrees are a specific type of doctorate-level degree that focus on skills to be applied in a practical, or hands-on, career rather than as a researcher. The most common professional degrees are Doctor of Medicine (MD) for aspiring medical doctors, Juris Doctor (JD) for aspiring lawyers, Doctor of Pharmacy (PharmD) for aspiring pharmacists, and Doctor of Education (EdD) for aspiring school and college or university administrators. If the career you are pursuing requires a graduate degree, you should keep this end goal in mind as you plan for the timeline and finances required to meet your goals.

3.4 Making an Academic Plan

Question to consider:

- How can you use the services of the Academic Advisors to ensure that you are following the right degree plan to reach your degree or transfer goals?

SAC has academic advisors who can help you navigate your academic plan and fit your courses and requirements together with your other life obligations to help you meet your goals.

An advisor is an expert on college and major requirements and policies, while you are the expert on your life circumstances and your ability to manage your study time and workload. It is also an advisor's responsibility to understand the details of your degree requirements. This person can teach you how to best utilize college resources to make decisions about your academic and career path. An advisor can help you connect with other college staff and faculty who might be integral to supporting your success. Together with your advisor, you can create a semester-by-semester plan for the courses you will take and the specific requirements you will meet. It is wise to meet with your advisor every semester to both check your progress and learn about new opportunities that might lend you a competitive advantage in entering your career or transferring to the university of your choice.

It is important to follow your degree plan or transfer advising guide. The plans and guides available at SAC can be found in the SAC catalog. Following your plan will ensure that you do not take the classes you do not need and complete your degree as quickly as possible. By taking classes on your plan, you are ensuring they can be covered by financial aid or VA benefits. SAC uses Alamo GPS, found in ACES, to help students keep on track to their degree.

Alamo GPS - Track Your Progress

Goal + Plan = Success

3.5 Developing Your Leadership Skills

Questions to consider:

- What is the nature of leadership?
- What are core traits of successful leaders?
- What leadership skills will be needed in the future?

The many definitions of leadership each have a different emphasis. Some definitions consider leadership an act or behavior, such as initiating structure so group members know how to complete a task. Others consider a leader to be the center or nucleus of group activity, an instrument of goal achievement who has a certain personality, a form of persuasion and power, and the art of inducing compliance. Some look at leadership in terms of the management of group processes. In this view, a good leader develops a vision for the group, communicates that vision, orchestrates the group's energy and activity toward goal attainment, "[turns] a group of individuals into a team," and "[transforms] good intentions into positive actions."

As you just read earlier, Leadership is one of the needed transferable skills.

Leadership is frequently defined as a social (interpersonal) influence relationship between two or more persons who depend on each other to attain certain mutual goals in a group situation. Effective leadership helps individuals and groups achieve their goals by focusing on the group's maintenance needs and task needs. Maintenance needs are the needs for individuals to fit in and work together by having, for example, shared norms. Task needs refer to the need for the group to make progress toward attaining the goal that brought them together.

Finally, it is important to note that while managers may be successful in directing and supervising their subordinates, they often succeed or fail because of their ability or inability to lead. As noted above, effective leadership often calls for the ability to manage, and effective management often requires leadership.

The Leader

Leaders are people who take charge of or guide the activities of others. They are often seen as the focus or orchestrater of group activity, the people who set the tone of the group so that it can move forward to attain its goals. Leaders provide the group with what is required to fulfill its maintenance and task-related needs.

Leader Emergence

Organizations have two kinds of leaders: formal and informal. A formal leader is that individual who is recognized by those outside the group as the official leader of the group. Often, the formal leader is appointed by the organization to serve in a formal capacity as an agent of the organization. Jack Welch was the formal leader of General Electric, and Leonard Bernstein was the formal leader of the New York Philharmonic symphony. Practically all managers act as formal leaders as part of their assigned role. Organizations that use self-managed work teams allow members of the team to select the individual who will serve as their team leader. When this person's role is sanctioned by the formal organization, these team leaders become formal leaders. Increasingly, leaders in organizations will be those who "best sell" their ideas on how to complete a project—persuasiveness and inspiration are important ingredients in the leadership equation, especially in high-involvement organizations.[22]

Informal leaders, by contrast, are not assigned by the organization. The informal leader is that individual whom members of the group acknowledge as their leader. Athletic teams often have informal leaders, individuals who exert considerable influence on team members even though they hold no official, formal leadership position. In fact, most work groups contain at least one informal leader. Just like formal leaders, informal leaders can benefit or harm an organization depending on whether their influence encourages group members to behave consistently with organizational goals.

Leadership Traits

The last three decades of the 20th century witnessed continued exploration of the relationship between traits and both leader emergence and leader effectiveness. Edwin Locke from the University of Maryland and several his research associates, in their recent review of the trait research, observed that successful leaders possess a set of core characteristics that are different from those of other people.[45] Although these core traits do not solely determine whether a person will be a leader—or a successful leader—they are seen as preconditions that endow people with leadership potential. Among the core traits identified are:

- *Drive*—a high level of effort, including a strong desire for achievement as well as high levels of ambition, energy, tenacity, and initiative
- *Leadership motivation*—an intense desire to lead others
- *Honesty and integrity*—a commitment to the truth, where word and deed correspond
- *Self-confidence*—an assurance in oneself, one's ideas, and one's ability
- *Cognitive ability*—conceptually skilled, capable of exercising good judgment, having strong analytical abilities, possessing the capacity to think strategically and multidimensionally
- *Knowledge of the business*—a high degree of understanding of the company, industry, and technical matters
- *Other traits*—charisma, creativity/originality, and flexibility/adaptiveness

While leaders may be "people with the right stuff," effective leadership requires more than simply possessing the correct set of motives and traits. Knowledge, skills, ability, vision, strategy, and effective vision implementation are all necessary for the person who has the "right stuff" to realize their leadership potential.[47] According to Locke, people endowed with these traits engage in behaviors that are associated with leadership. As followers, people are attracted to and inclined to follow individuals who display, for example, honesty and integrity, self-confidence, and the motivation to lead.

Thus, a person is not born with self-confidence. Self-confidence is developed, honesty and integrity are a matter of personal choice, motivation to lead comes from within the individual and is within his control, and knowledge of the business can be acquired. While cognitive ability does in part find its origin in the genes, it still needs to be developed. Finally, drive, as a dispositional trait, may also have a genetic component, but it too can be self- and other-encouraged. It goes without saying that none of these ingredients are acquired overnight.

Leadership Behaviors

It is now common to think of effective leadership in terms of what leaders do. CEOs and management consultants agree that effective leaders display trust in their employees, develop a vision, keep their cool, encourage risk, bring expertise into the work setting, invite dissent, and focus everyone's attention on that which is important.

A group of Ohio State University researchers, under the direction of Ralph Stogdill, began an extensive and systematic series of studies to identify leader behaviors associated with effective group performance. Their results identified two major sets of leader behaviors: consideration and initiating structure.

Consideration is the "relationship-oriented" behavior of a leader. It is instrumental in creating and maintaining good relationships (that is, addressing the group's maintenance needs) with organizational members. Consideration behaviors include being supportive and friendly, representing people's interests, communicating openly with group members, recognizing them, respecting their ideas, and sharing concern for their feelings.

Initiating structure involves "task-oriented" leader behaviors. It is instrumental in the efficient use of resources to attain organizational goals, thereby addressing the group's task needs. Initiating structure behaviors include scheduling work, deciding what is to be done (and how and when to do it), providing direction to organizational members, planning, coordinating, problem-solving, maintaining standards of performance, and encouraging the use of uniform procedures.

After consideration and initiating structure behaviors were first identified, many leaders believed that they had to behave one way or the other. If they initiated structure, they could not be considerate, and vice versa. It did not take long, however, to recognize that leaders can simultaneously display any combination of both behaviors.

Researchers at the University of Michigan also began to investigate leader behaviors. They attempted to identify behavioral elements that differentiated effective from ineffective leaders.

The two types of leadership behavior that stand out in these studies are job centered and organizational member centered. Job-centered behaviors are devoted to supervisory functions, such as planning, scheduling, coordinating work activities, and providing the resources needed for task performance. Employee-member-centered behaviors include consideration and support for organizational members.

Subsequent research at Michigan and elsewhere has found additional behaviors associated with effective leadership: support, work facilitation, goal emphasis, and interaction facilitation.

The Leadership Grid®

Much of the credit for disseminating knowledge about important leader behaviors must go to Robert R. Blake and Jane S. Mouton, who developed a method for classifying styles of leadership compatible with many of the ideas from the Ohio State and Michigan studies.[66] In their classification scheme, *concern for results* (production) emphasizes output, cost effectiveness, and (in for-profit organizations) a concern for profits. *Concern for people* involves promoting working relationships and paying attention to issues of importance to group members. As shown in **Exhibit 12.9**, the Leadership Grid® demonstrates that any combination of these two leader concerns is possible, and five styles of leadership are highlighted here.

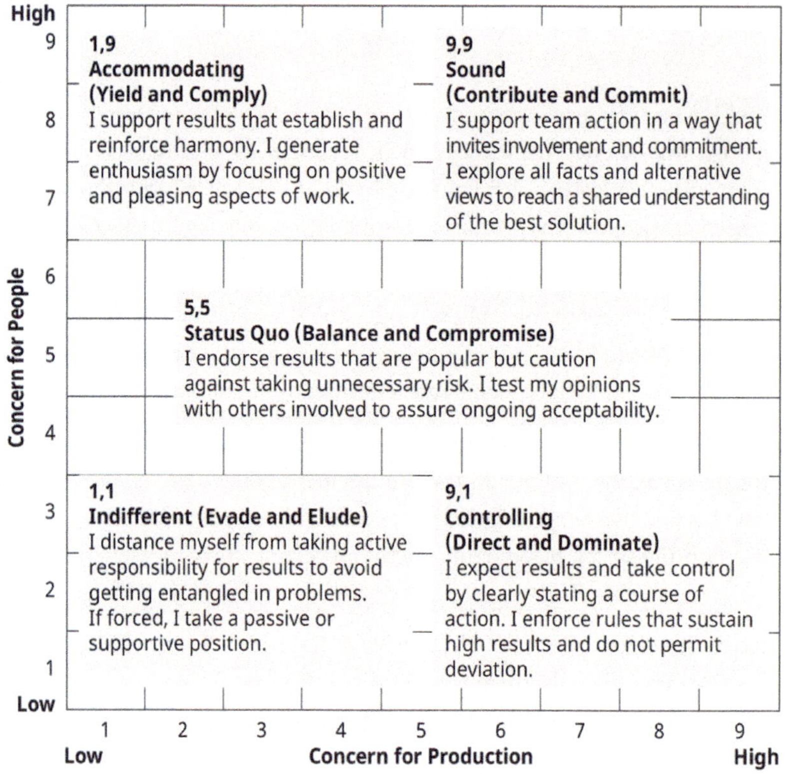

Figure 3.8 Blake and Mouton's Managerial Grid® (Source: Adapted from R. McKee and B. Carlson. 1999. The Power to Change, p. 16.)

Blake and Mouton contend that the sound (contribute and commit) leader (a high concern for results and people, or 9,9) style is universally the most effective.[67] While the Leadership Grid® is appealing and well structured, research to date suggests that there is no universally effective style of leadership (9,9 or otherwise).[68] There are, however, well-identified situations in which a 9,9 style is unlikely to be effective. Organizational members of high-involvement organizations who have mastered their job duties require little production-oriented leader behavior. Likewise, there is little time for people-oriented behavior during an emergency. Finally, evidence suggests that the "high-high" style may be effective when the situation calls for high levels of initiating structure. Under these conditions, the initiation of structure is more acceptable, favorably affecting follower satisfaction and performance, when the leader is also experienced as warm, supportive, and considerate.

Styles of Leaders

Leaders who subscribe to the notion that "if it ain't broke, don't fix it" are often described as ***transactional leaders***. They are extremely task oriented and instrumental in their approach, frequently looking for incentives that will induce their followers into a desired course of action.[92] These reciprocal exchanges take place in the context of a mutually interdependent relationship between the leader and the follower, frequently resulting in interpersonal bonding.[93]. The transactional leader moves a group toward task accomplishment by initiating structure and by offering an incentive in exchange for desired behaviors.

The ***transformational leader***, on the other hand, moves and changes (fixes) things "in a big way"! Unlike transactional leaders, they do not cause change by offering inducements. Instead, they inspire others to take action through their personal values, vision, passion, and belief in and commitment to the mission.[94] Through charisma (idealized influence), individualized consideration (a focus on the development of the follower), intellectual stimulation (questioning assumptions and challenging the status quo), and/or inspirational motivation (articulating an appealing vision), transformational leaders move others to follow.

The **transformational leader**, also referred to as a visionary leaders, are those who influence others through an emotional and/or intellectual attraction to the leader's dreams of what "can be." Vision links a present and future state, energizes, and generates commitment, provides meaning for action, and serves as a standard against which to assess performance.[95] Evidence indicates that vision is positively related to follower attitudes and performance. As pointed out by Warren Bennis, a vision is effective only to the extent that the leader can communicate it in such a way that others come to internalize it as their own.[97]

As people, transformational leaders are engaging. They are characterized by extroversion, agreeableness, and openness to experience.[98] They energize others. They increase followers' awareness of the importance of the designated outcome. They motivate individuals to transcend their own self-interest for the benefit of the team and inspire organizational members to self-manage (become self-leaders).[100] Transformational leaders move people to focus on higher-order needs (self-esteem and self-actualization). When organizations face a turbulent environment, intense competition, products that may die early, and the need to move fast, managers cannot rely solely on organizational structure to guide organizational activity. In these situations, transformational leadership can motivate followers to be fully engaged and inspired, to internalize the goals and values of the organization, and to move forward with dogged determination!

Transformational leadership is positively related to follower satisfaction, performance, and acts of citizenship. These effects result from the fact that transformational leader behaviors elicit trust and perceptions of procedural justice, which in turn favorably impact follower satisfaction and performance.[101] As R. Pillai, C. Schriesheim, and E. Williams note, "when followers perceive that they can influence the outcomes of decisions that are important to them and that they are participants in an equitable relationship with their leader, their perceptions of procedural justice [and trust] are likely to be enhanced." Trust and experiences of organizational justice promote leader effectiveness, follower satisfaction, motivation, performance, and citizenship behaviors.

Leadership Needs in the 21st Century

What will the leaders of tomorrow be like? Professor Conger suggests that the effective leaders of the 21st century will have to be many things.[110]

They will have to be *strategic opportunists*; only organizational visionaries will find strategic opportunities before competitors. They will have to be *globally aware*; with 80 percent of today's organizations facing significant foreign competition, knowledge of foreign markets, global economics, and geopolitics is crucial. They must be able to manage a highly decentralized organization; movement toward the high-involvement organization will accelerate as environmental demands for organizational speed, flexibility, learning, and leanness increase. They will have been *sensitive to diversity*; during the first few years of the 21st century, fewer than 10 percent of those entering the workforce in North America will be White, Anglo-Saxon males, and the incoming women, minorities, and immigrants will bring with them a vastly separate set of needs and concerns. They will have to be *interpersonally competent*; a highly diverse workforce will necessitate a leader who is extremely aware of and sensitive to multicultural expectations and needs. They will have to be *builders of an organizational community*; work and organizations will serve as a major source of need fulfillment, and in the process, leaders will be called on to help build this community in such a way that organizational members develop a sense of ownership for the organization and its mission.

Leaders of the 21st-century organization have a monumental challenge awaiting them and a wealth of self-enriching and fulfilling opportunities. The challenge and rewards awaiting effective leaders are awesome!

There are many opportunities for you to start developing your leadership skills while in college through formal and informal roles. As a student, you can take a leadership role in group projects, become an officer in a student organization, or sign up for the Student Leadership Institute. You can also hone your leadership skills at any jobs or internships you hold while in college. Taking advantage of these types of opportunities will give you a boost above your competitors when you start applying for your first position in the career you are working towards.

Chapter Summary

This chapter began by helping you explore the many career options available and which careers would be the best fit for you. You learned how to create a plan to reach your career goals through activities such as networking, creating a resume, informational interviewing, and having an online presence. The various types of degrees were explored to help you create an academic plan.

You learned about the importance of leadership in the 21st century and the nature and types of leaders. Developing your leadership skills will be a key component of your success in your dream career.

References

22. J.A. Conger. 1993. The brave new world of leadership training. *Organizational Dynamics* 21(3):46–59.

45. S.A. Kirkpatrick & E.A. Locke. 1991. Leadership: Do traits matter? The Executive 5(2):48–60. E.A. Locke, S. Kirkpatrick, J.K. Wheeler, J. Schneider, K. Niles, H. Goldstein, K. Welsh, & D.-O. Chad. 1991. *The essence of leadership: The four keys to leading successfully*. New York: Lexington.

47. Locke et al., 1991; T.A. Stewart. 1999 (Oct. 11). Have you got what it takes? *Fortune* 140(7):318–322.

66. R.R. Blake & J.S. Mouton. 1964. *The managerial grid*. Houston: Gulf; R.R. Blake & J.S. Mouton. 1981. *The versatile manager: A grid profile*, Homewood, IL: Dow Jones-Irwin; R.R. Blake & J.S. Mouton. 1984. *The new managerial grid III*. Houston: Gulf.

67. R.R. Blake & J.S. Mouton. 1981. Management by grid® principles or situationalism: Which? *Group and Organization Studies* 6:439–455.

68. L. L. Larson, J. G. Hunt, & R. N. Osborn. 1976. The great hi-hi leader behavior myth: A lesson from Occam's razor. *Academy of Management Journal* 19:628–641.

92. G.A. Yukl. 1981. *Leadership in organizations*. Englewood Cliffs, NJ: Prentice-Hall.

93. B. Kellerman. 1984. *Leadership: Multidisciplinary perspectives*. Englewood Cliffs, NJ: Prentice-Hall; F. L. Landy. 1985. Psychology of work behavior. Homewood, IL: Dorsey Press.

94. J.M. Burns. 1978. Leadership. New York: Harper & Row; B. M. Bass. 1985. *Leadership and performance beyond expectations*. New York: Free Press.

95. R.L. Daft. 2018. *The Leadership Experience* 7th edition. Mason, OH: Cengage Learning.

97. Bennis, 1989.

98. T. A. Judge & J.E. Bono. 2000. Five-factor model of personality and transformational leadership. *Journal of Applied Psychology* 85:751–765.

100. C.C. Manz & H.P. Sims, Jr. 1987. Leading workers to lead themselves: The external leadership of self-managed work teams. *Administrative Science Quarterly* 32:106–129.

101. Pillai, Schriesheim, & Williams, 1999.

110. Conger, 1993.

Chapter 4 Time Management and Goal Setting

Figure 4.1 We hold time in our hands

Chapter Outline

4.1 Procrastination

4.2 Managing Time

4.3 Prioritizing and Task Completion

4.4 Goal Setting

4.5 Creating your Work Schedule

Student Survey

How do you feel about your time management and goal setting abilities? Take this quick survey to figure it out, ranking questions on a scale of 1–4, 1 meaning "least like me" and 4 meaning "most like me." These questions will help you determine how the chapter concepts relate to you right now. As you are introduced to new concepts and practices, it can be informative to reflect on how your understanding changes over time. We will revisit these questions at the end of the chapter to see whether your feelings have changed.

1. _____ I regularly procrastinate completing tasks that do not interest me or seem challenging.
2. _____ I use specific time management strategies to complete tasks.
3. _____ I find it difficult to prioritize tasks because I am not sure what is important.

4. _____ I am pleased with my ability to manage my time.
5. _____ I use my goals to prioritize my activities.
6. _____ I am aware of how to formulate a specific goal.
7. _____ I keep a study schedule.
8. _____ I know how to break down large tasks into small doable pieces.

Chapter Outcomes

In this chapter you will learn about two of the most valuable tools used for academic success: prioritizing and time management. By the time you complete this chapter, you should be able to do the following:

- Articulate how time management differs from high school to college.
- Outline the reasons and effects of procrastination and provide strategies to overcome it.
- Describe ways to evaluate your time management skills.
- Discuss the importance and the process of prioritization.
- Articulate the importance of goal setting and motivation.
- Identify strategies and specific tactics for managing your time.
- Articulate the characteristics of a SMART Goal.
- Formulate specific steps of an action plan.
- Apply the concept of breaking down a large assignment into small parts and setting deadlines.

4.1 Procrastination

Questions to consider:

- Why do we procrastinate?
- What are the effects of procrastination?
- How can we avoid procrastination?

A very unfortunate but all-too-common situation in higher education is the danger students face from poor time management. Many college administrators who work directly with students are aware that a single mishap or a case of poor time management can set into motion a series of events that can seriously jeopardize a student's success. In some of the more extreme instances, the student may even fail to graduate because of it.

To better understand how one instance of poor time management can trigger a cascading situation with disastrous results, imagine that a student has an assignment due in a business class. She knows that she should be working on it, but she is not in the mood. Instead, she convinces herself that she should think a little more about what she needs to complete the assignment and decides to do so while looking at social media or playing a couple more rounds of a game on her phone. In a little while, she suddenly realizes that she has become distracted, and the evening has slipped away. She has little time left to work on her assignment. She stays up later than usual trying to complete the assignment but cannot finish it. Exhausted, she decides that she will work on it in the morning during the hour she had planned to study for her math quiz. She knows there will not be enough time in the morning to do a decent job on the assignment, so she decides she will put together what she has and hopes she will at least receive a passing grade.

At this point in our story, an evening of procrastination has not only resulted in a poorly done business class assignment, but now she is going to take a math quiz that she has not studied for. She will take the quiz tired from staying up too late the night before. Her lack of time management has now raised potential issues in two courses. She will now have to work harder on both courses to improve her grades. Any other problems she has with future assignments in either course could cause a domino effect of circumstances that begin to overwhelm her.

In our imagined situation, you can see how events set into motion by a little procrastination can quickly spiral out of control. You can think of similar experiences in your own life, when one small bit of poor time management set off a chain of events that threatened to cause big problems.

The High Cost of Poor Time Management

It is not just your academic performance that can be affected by cascading events that have a domino effect on your college path. Dropping out of school is not your only danger. There are other consequences that affect the financial cost to you as a student if your lack of time management skills causes you to delay finishing college.

Based on independent research, a *Washington Post* article details the monetary impact delaying graduation by two semesters can have on a student.[1]

According to the article, there is a significant cost associated with delaying graduation from college by only one year (by dropping and retaking courses, taking less than a full credit load, etc.). Not only will you pay for additional tuition, textbooks, and other fees. If you are using student loans, you will also accumulate interest on those loans. On average this would come to an extra $12,557 in actual costs and $6,040 in interest at a public university, or $18,992 in tuition and fees and $7,823 in interest (over 10 years) at a private school. That is a lot of extra cost to you!

While a loss of $26,815 may seem like a lot of money, it pales in comparison to the other financial areas impacted by a single extra year in school. The *Washington Post* article estimates that one year's delay of graduation would cost you an additional $46,355 based on average lost earnings. To make matters worse, like the story of the student that procrastinates finishing her business assignment, there is a spiraling effect that takes place with loss of income when it comes to retirement investments. The figure cited by the *Washington Post* as lost retirement earnings for taking five years instead of four years to graduate is $82,074. That brings the average total cost for only two extra semesters to over $150,000. Measured by the financial cost to you, even a slight delay in graduation can have a serious impact.

Table 4.1 Average Cost of an Additional Year of a 4 Year College

Tuition, textbooks, and fees (SAC-$2618 does not include 3Peat class)	$15,774
Interest on student loans ($1,442.98 5-year loan)	$6,932
Lost wages	$6,932
Lost retirement earnings	$82,074
Average total loss:	**$151,115**

Credit: *Washington Post*. Note the numbers in the table above have been averaged between the two scenarios described.

Any situation that brings about a graduation delay can increase the cost of college. This also includes attending school part-time. While in some instances responsibilities may make it impossible to go to school full-time, from a financial perspective you should do all you can to graduate as soon as you can.

While it may not be possible to prevent life challenges while you are in college, you can do a great deal to prevent the chaos and the chain reaction of unfortunate events that they can cause. This can be accomplished through thoughtful prioritization and time management efforts.

What follows in the rest of this chapter is a close look at the nature of time management and prioritization in ways that can help keep you on track to graduate college on time.

The Reasons behind Procrastination

There are several reasons we procrastinate, and a few of them may be surprising. On the surface we often tell ourselves it is because the task is something we do not want to do, or we make excuses that there are other things more important to do first. In some cases, this may be true, but there can be other contributors to procrastination that have their roots in our physical well-being or our own psychological motivations.

Lack of Energy

Sometimes we just do not feel up to a certain task. It might be due to discomfort, an illness, or just a lack of energy. If this is the case, it is important to identify the cause and remedy the situation. It could be something as simple as a lack of sleep or improper diet. Regardless, if a lack of energy is continually causing you to procrastinate to the point where you are starting to feel stress over not getting things done, you should assess the situation and address it.

Lack of Focus

Much like having low physical energy, a lack of mental focus can be a cause of procrastination. This can be due to mental fatigue, being disorganized, or allowing yourself to be distracted by other things. Again, like low physical energy, this is something that may have further-reaching effects in your life that go beyond the act of simply avoiding a task. If it is something that is recurring, you should accurately assess the situation.

Fear of Failure

This cause of procrastination is not one that many people are aware of, especially if they are the person avoiding tasks because of it. To put it in simple words, it is a bit of trickery we play on ourselves by avoiding a situation that makes us psychologically uncomfortable. Even though they may not be consciously aware of it, the person facing the task is afraid that they cannot do it or will not be able to do it well. If they fail at the task, it will make them appear incompetent to others or even to themselves. Where the self-trickery comes in is by avoiding the task. In the person's mind, they can rationalize that the reason they failed at the task was because they ran out of time to complete it, not that they were incapable of doing it in the first place.

It is important to note that a fear of failure may not have anything to do with the actual ability of the person suffering from it. They could be quite capable of doing the task and performing well, but it is the fear that holds them back.

Social-Cultural Challenges

Many college students are pulled in a variety of directions because of family demands and money challenges. First generation college students often have various obstacles as they navigate college without help or support of family. Having to learn how and where to access help can be an obstacle to successfully battling procrastination.

Analysis Question

Consider something right now that you may be procrastinating about. Are you able to identify the cause?

The Effects of Procrastination

In addition to the causes of procrastination, you must also consider what effects it can have. Again, many of these effects are obvious and commonly understood, but some may not be so obvious and may cause other issues.

Loss of Time

The loss of time as an effect of procrastination is the easiest to identify since the act of avoiding a task comes down to not using time wisely. Procrastination can be thought of as using the time you have to complete a task in ways that do not accomplish what needs to be done.

Loss of Goals

Another of the more obvious potentially adverse effects of procrastination is the loss of goals. Completing a task leads to achieving a goal. These can be large or small (e.g., from doing well on an assignment to being hired for an excellent job). Without goals you might do more than delay work on a task—you may not complete it at all. The risk of the loss of goals is very impactful.

Loss of Self-Esteem

Often, when we procrastinate, we become frustrated and disappointed in ourselves for not getting important tasks completed. If this continues to happen, we can begin to develop a low opinion of ourselves and our own abilities. We begin to suffer from low self-esteem and might even begin to feel like there is something wrong with us. This can lead to other increasingly negative mental factors such as anger and depression. As you can see, it is important for our own well-being to avoid this kind of procrastination effect.

Stress

Procrastination causes stress and anxiety, which may seem odd since the act of procrastination is often about avoiding a task. Anyone who has noticed that nagging feeling when they know there is something they should be doing is familiar with this.

On the other hand, some students see that kind of stress as a boost of mental urgency. They put off a task until they feel that surge of motivation. While this may have worked in the past, they quickly learn that procrastinating when it comes to college work includes an underestimation of the tasks to be completed—sometimes with disastrous results.

Managing Procrastination

Questions to consider:

- What strategy helps me prioritize my top tasks?
- How do I make the best use of my time when prioritizing?
- How do I make sure I tackle unpleasant tasks instead of putting them off?
- What is the best way to plan for long-term tasks?
- How do I find time in a busy schedule?

Now that you understand a few of the major problems procrastination can produce, let us look at methods to manage procrastination and get you on to completing the tasks, no matter how unpleasant you think they might be.

Get Organized

Much of this chapter is dedicated to defining and explaining the nature of time management. The most effective way to combat procrastination is to use time and project management strategies such as schedules, goal setting, and other techniques to get tasks accomplished on time.

Put Aside Distractions

Several of the methods discussed in this chapter deal specifically with distractions. Distractions are time-killers and are the primary way people procrastinate. It is easy to just play a video game a little while longer, check out social media, or finish watching a movie when we are avoiding a task. Putting aside distractions is one of the primary functions of setting priorities.

Reward Yourself

Rewarding yourself for the completion of tasks or meeting goals is an effective way to avoid procrastination. An example of this would be rewarding yourself with the time to watch a movie you would enjoy *after* you have finished the things you need to do, rather than using the movie to keep yourself from getting things done.

Be Accountable—Tell Someone Else

A strong motivational tool is to hold ourselves accountable by telling someone else we are going to do something and when we are going to do it. This may not seem like it would be highly effective, but on a psychological level we feel more compelled to do something if we tell someone else. It may be related to our need for approval from others, or it might just serve to set a level of commitment. Either way, it can help us stay on task and avoid procrastination—especially if we take our accountability to another person seriously enough to warrant contacting that person and apologizing for not doing what we said we were going to do.

Breaking Down the Steps and Spreading Them over Shorter Work Periods

The concept behind this strategy is to break tasks into smaller, more manageable units that do not require as much time to complete. As an illustration of how this might work, imagine you are assigned a two-page paper to include references. You estimate that to complete the paper—start to finish—would take you between four and a half and five hours. You look at your calendar over the next week and see that there simply are no open five-hour blocks (unless you decided to only get three hours of sleep one night). Rightly so, you decide that going without sleep is not a good option. While looking at your calendar, you do see that you can squeeze in an hour or so every night.

Table 4.2 More Strategies that Work

<table>
<tr>
<td></td>
<td>Daily Top Three
The idea behind the daily top three approach is that you determine which three things are the most important to finish that day, and these become the tasks that you complete. It is an amazingly simple technique that is effective because each day you are finishing tasks and removing them from your list. Even if you took one day off a week and completed no tasks on that day, a daily top three strategy would have you finishing 18 tasks in a single week. That is a sizable number of things crossed off your list.</td>
</tr>
<tr>
<td></td>
<td>Pomodoro Technique
The Pomodoro Technique is named after a type of kitchen timer, but you can use any clock or countdown timer. This technique was developed by Francesco Cirillo. The basic concept is to use a timer to set work intervals followed by a short break. The intervals are usually about 25 minutes long and are called pomodoros, which comes from the Italian word for tomato because Cirillo used a tomato-shaped kitchen timer to keep track of the intervals.

In the original technique there are six steps:
1. Identify a task.
2. Set the timer for 25 minutes.
3. Work on the task with no distractions.
4. When the alarm sounds, take a 5 minute break.
5. Repeat process three more times.
6. Take a longer break (15–30 minutes) and start again.

There are several reasons this technique is deemed effective for many people. One is the benefit that is derived from quick cycles of work and short breaks. This helps reduce mental fatigue and the lack of productivity caused by it. Another is that it tends to encourage practitioners to break tasks down to things that can be completed in about 25 minutes, which is something that is usually manageable from the perspective of time available. It is much easier to squeeze in three 25-minute sessions of work during the day than it is to set aside a 75-minute block of time.

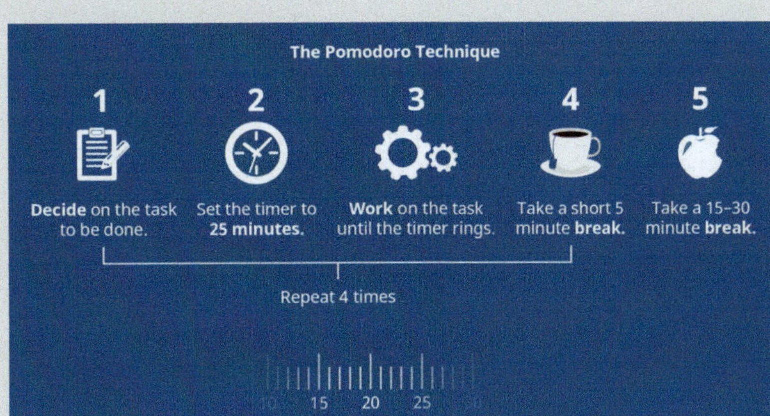</td>
</tr>
</table>

Eat the Frog

Of our three quick strategies, eat the frog has the strangest name and may not sound the most inviting. The name comes from a famous quote, attributed to Mark Twain: "Eat a live frog first thing in the morning and nothing worse will happen to you the rest of the day." Eat the Frog is also the title of a best-selling book by Brian Tracy that deals with time management and avoiding procrastination.

How this applies to time and task management is based on the concept that if a person takes care of the biggest or most unpleasant task first, everything else will be easier after that.

Although stated in a humorous way, there is a good deal of truth in this. First, we underestimate how much worry can impact our performance. If you are continually distracted by anxiety over a task you are dreading, it can affect the task you are working on at the time. Second, not only will you have a sense of accomplishment and relief when the task you are concerned with is finished and out of the way, but other tasks will seem lighter and not as difficult.

Activity 4.1 Try Three Time Management Strategies

Over the next two weeks, try each of the three methods described above to see which ones might work for you. Is there one you favor over the others? Might each of these three approaches serve you better in different situations or with different tasks? Do you have a creative alternative or a way to use some combination of these techniques? The key is to find which system works best for you.

4.2 Managing Time

Questions to consider:

- Is time management different in college from what I am used to?
- How different is college schoolwork from high school work?

How to Manage Time

The simplest way to manage your time is to accurately plan for how much time it will take to do each task and then set aside that amount of time. How you divide the time is up to you. If it is going to take you five hours to study for a final exam, you can plan to spread it over five days, with an hour each night, or you can plan on two hours one night and three hours the next. You would not want to plan to study only a few hours the night before the exam and find that you fell noticeably short of the time you estimated you would need. If that were to happen, you would have run out of time before finishing, with no way to go back and change your decision. In this kind of situation, you might even be tempted to "pull an all-nighter," which is a phrase that has been used among college students for decades. It means going without sleep for the entire night and using that time to finish an assignment. While this method of trying to make up for poor planning is common enough to have a name, rarely does it produce the best work.

Of all the parts of time management, accurately predicting how long a task will take is usually the most difficult—and the most elusive. Part of the problem comes from the fact that most of us are not perfectly accurate timekeepers, especially when we are busy applying ourselves to a task. The other issue that makes it so difficult to accurately estimate time on task is that our estimations must also account for things like interruptions or unforeseen problems that cause delays.

When it comes to academic activities, many tasks can be dependent upon the completion of other things first, or the time a task takes can vary from one instance to another, both of which add to the complexity and difficulty of estimating how much time and effort are required.

For example, if an instructor assigned three chapters of reading, you would not really have any idea how long each chapter might take to read until you looked at them. The first chapter might be 30 pages long while the second is 45. The third chapter could be only 20 pages made up mostly of charts and graphs for you to compare. By page count, it might seem the third chapter would take the least amount of time but studying charts and graphs to gather information can take longer than regular reading.

To make matters even more difficult, when it comes to estimating time on a task for something as common as reading, not all reading takes the same amount of time. Fiction, for example, is usually read faster than a technical manual. But something like the novel *Finnegan's Wake* by James Joyce is considered so difficult that most readers never finish it.

Knowing Yourself

While you can find all sorts of estimates online as to how long a certain task may take, it is important to know these are only averages. People read at different speeds, people write at different speeds, and those numbers even change for everyone depending on the environment.

If you are trying to read in surroundings that have distractions (e.g., conversations, phone calls, etc.), reading 10 pages can take you a lot longer than if you are reading in a quiet area. Similarly, you may be reading in a quiet environment (e.g., in bed after everyone in the house has gone to sleep), but if you are tired, your attention and retention may not be what it would be if you were refreshed.

The only way you are going to be able to manage your time accurately is to know yourself and to know how long it takes you to do each task. But where to begin?

Activity 4.2

Many people are not aware of how they spend their time. They make assumptions about how much time it takes to do certain things, but they never really take an accurate account.

In this activity, write down all the things you do in one day. You will want to cover the main activities of your day—for example, working, eating, driving, shopping, gaming, being engaged in entertainment, etc. Document how long each activity takes. You may want to try this activity for a week. Are you spending time in areas that help you meet your goals? The Week of Your Life Worksheet in Appendix 4 can help you keep track.

4.3 Prioritizing and Task Completion

Questions to consider:

- Why is prioritization important?
- What are the steps involved in prioritization?
- How do I deal with situations where others' priorities are different from my own?
- What do I do when priorities conflict?
- What are the best ways to make sure I complete tasks?

Prioritization: Self-Management of What You Do and When You Do It

Another key component in time management is that of prioritization. Prioritization can be thought of as ordering tasks and allotting time for them based on their identified needs or value. This next section provides insight into helping prioritize tasks and actions based on need and value and how to better understand the factors that contribute to prioritization.

How to Prioritize

The enemy of good prioritization is panic, or at least making decisions based on strictly emotional reactions. Before assigning priority to a task, it is important to take the time to carefully consider its value in an intellectual manner. It is very natural for us to want to remove a stressful situation as soon as we can. We want the adverse emotions out of the way as quickly as possible. But when it comes to juggling multiple problems or tasks to complete, prioritizing them first may mean the difference between completing everything satisfactorily or completing nothing at all.

Make Certain You Understand the Requirements of Each Task

One of the best ways to make good decisions about the prioritization of tasks is to understand the requirements of each. If you have multiple assignments to complete and you assume one of those assignments will only take an hour, you may decide to put it off until the others are finished. Your assumption could be disastrous if you find, once you begin the assignment, that there are several extra components that you did not account for and the time to complete will be four times as long as you estimated. Or, one of the assignments may be dependent on the results of another—like participating in a study and then writing a report on the results. If you are not aware that one assignment depends upon the completion of the other before you begin, you could inadvertently do the assignments out of order and must start over. Because of situations like this, it is critically important to understand exactly what needs to be done to complete a task before you determine its priority.

Make Decisions on Importance, Impact on Other Priorities, and Urgency

After you are aware of the requirements for each task, you can then decide your priorities based on the importance of the task and what things need to be finished in which order.

> ***To summarize:*** *the key components to prioritization are making certain you understand each task and making decisions based on importance, impact, and urgency.*

To better see how things may need to be prioritized, some people make a list of the tasks they need to complete and then arrange them in a quadrant map based on importance and urgency. Traditionally this is called the Eisenhower Decision Matrix. Before becoming the 34th president of the United States, Dwight Eisenhower served as the Allied forces supreme commander during World War II and said he used this technique to better prioritize the things he needed to get done.

Determining Priorities

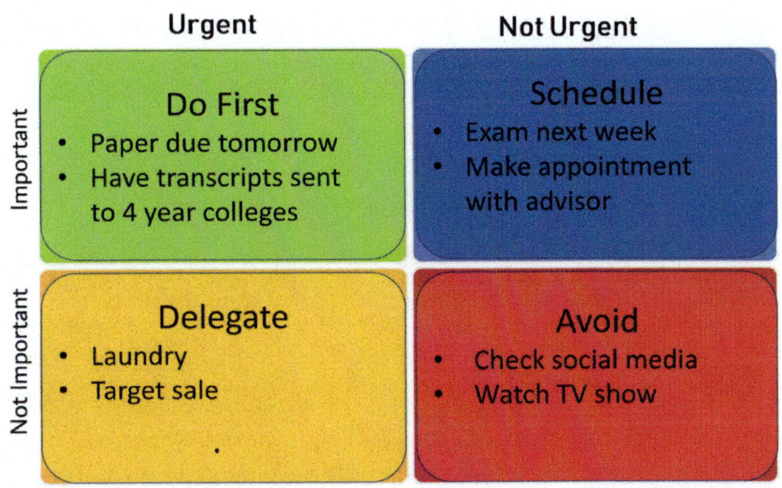

Figure 4.2 The Eisenhower Matrix can help organize priorities and ensure that you focus on the correct tasks.

> *Activity 4.3*
>
> In this activity you will begin by making a list of things you need or want to do today. Then draw the four quadrants shown above. Write each item you listed in one of the four squares; choose the square that best describes it based on its urgency and its importance. When you have completed writing each task in its appropriate square, you will see a prioritization order of your tasks. Obviously, those listed in the Important and Urgent square will be the things you need to finish first. After that will come things that are "important but not urgent," followed by "not important, but urgent," and finally "not urgent and not important."

Who Is Driving Your Tasks?

Another thing to keep in mind when approaching time management is that while you may have greater autonomy in managing your own time, many of your tasks are being driven by different individuals. These individuals are unaware of the other things you need to do and often have goals that conflict with your other tasks. This means that different instructors, your manager at work, or even your friends may be trying to assert their needs into your priorities. An example of this might be a boss that would like you to work a few hours of overtime, but you were planning to apply that time to do research for a paper.

Just like assessing the requirements and needs for each priority, doing the same with how others may be influencing your available time can be an important part of time management. In some cases, keeping others informed about your priorities may help avert conflicts (e.g., letting your boss know you will need time on a certain evening to study, letting your friends know you plan to do a journal project on Saturday but can do something on Sunday, etc.).

It will be important to be aware of how others can drive your priorities and for you to listen to your own good judgment. Time management in college is as much about managing all the elements of your life as it is about managing time for class and completing assignments.

As an illustration, imagine a situation where you think you can only complete one of two assignments that are both important and urgent, and you must make a choice of which one you will finish and which one you will not. It is important to know all the ramifications of whatever decision you make. Consider these things:

- Which assignment is worth the most?
- Is this assignment a foundational assignment for other assignments?
- Do any of your classes allow for "late assignments" with a penalty?
- Is there a way for you to finish both assignments?
- Conference with instructors. Is there another solution to the problem?

Completing the Tasks

Another important part of time management is to develop approaches that will help you complete tasks in a manner that is efficient and works for you. Most of this comes down to a little planning and being as informed about the specifics of each task as you can be.

Knowing What You Need to Do

As discussed in previous parts of this chapter, many learning activities have multiple components, and sometimes they must occur in a specific order. Additionally, some elements may not only be dependent on the order they are completed but can also be dependent on how they are completed. To illustrate this, we will analyze a task usually considered simple: attending a class session. In this analysis we will look at not only what must be accomplished to get the most out of the experience, but also at how each element is dependent upon others and must be done in a specific order. The graphic below shows the interrelationship between the different activities, many of which might not initially seem significant enough to warrant mention, but it becomes obvious that other elements depend upon them when they are listed out this way.

As you can see from the graphic below, even a task as simple as "going to class" can be broken down into a few different elements that have a good deal of dependency on other tasks. One example of this is preparing for the class lecture by reading materials ahead of time to make the lecture and any complex concepts easier to follow. If you did it the other way around, you might miss opportunities to ask questions or receive clarification on the information presented during the lecture.

Understanding what you need to do and when you need to do it can be applied to any task, no matter how simple or how complex. Knowing what you need to do and planning for it can go a long way toward success and preventing unpleasant surprises.

Table 4.3 Many of your learning activities are dependent on others, and some are gateways to other steps

Many Tasks are Dependent on Foundational Tasks

Element or Task Needed for Success	Task it Depends Upon
Pre-class Prep	
• Completing previous homework • Reading appropriate material for lecture • Taking notes on areas that need clarification	• Understanding homework assigned from previous class • Making certain appropriate reading material is identified • Reading appropriate material for lecture
During Class	
• Understanding lecture • Taking notes on lecture • Asking questions for clarification • Taking part in class discussion • Receive assignments for next class	• Reading appropriate material • Understanding lecture
Post Class	
• Understanding assigned homework • Making certain appropriate reading material is identified • Ask questions for clarification • Reviewing and rewriting notes	• Receive assignments for next class

Knowing How You Will Get It Done

After you understand what needs to be done to complete a task (or its component parts), the next step is to create a plan for completing everything.

This may not be as easy or as simple as declaring that you will finish part one, then move on to part two, and so on. Each component may need different resources or skills to complete, and it is in your best interest to identify those ahead of time and include them as part of your plan.

A good analogy for this sort of planning is to think about it in much the same way you would prepare for a lengthy trip. With a long journey you would not walk out the front door and then decide how you were going to get where you were going. There are too many other decisions to be made and tasks to be completed around each choice. If you decided you were going by plane, you would need to purchase tickets, and you would have to schedule your trip around flight times. If you decided to go by car, you would need gas money and a map or GPS device. What about clothes? The clothes you need will depend on how long you will be gone and what the climate will be like. If it is far enough away that you will need to speak another language, you may need to either acquire that skill or at least plan for something or someone to help you translate.

What Resources Will You Need?

The first part of this list may appear to be so obvious that it should go without mention, but it is by far one of the most critical and one of the most overlooked. Have you ever planned a trip but forgotten your most comfortable pair of shoes or neglected to book a hotel room? If a missing resource is important, the entire project can come to a complete halt. Even if the missing resource is a minor component, it may dramatically alter the result.

Learning activities are much the same in this way, and it is also important to keep in mind that resources may not be limited to physical objects such as paper or ink. Information can be a critical resource as well. One of the most often overlooked aspects in planning by new college students is just how much research, reading, and information they will need to complete assignments.

For example, if you had an assignment in which you were supposed to compare a novel with a film adapted from that novel, it would be important to have access to the movie and book as resources. Your plans for completing the work could quickly fall apart if you learned that on the evening you planned to watch the film, it was no longer available.

What Skills Will You Need?

Poor planning or a bad assumption in this area can be disastrous, especially if some part of the task has a steep learning curve. No matter how well you planned the other parts of the project, if there is some skill needed that you do not have and you have no idea how long it will take to learn, it can be an unpleasant situation.

Imagine a scenario where one of your class projects is to create a poster. You intend to use imaging software to produce professional graphics and charts for the poster, but you have never used the software that way before. It seems easy enough, but once you begin, you find the charts keep printing out in the wrong resolution. You search online for a solution, but the only thing you can find requires you to recreate them all over again in a different setting. Unfortunately, that part of the project will now take twice as long.

It can be extremely difficult to recover from a situation like that, and it could have been prevented by taking the time to learn how to do it correctly before you began or by at least including in your schedule some time to learn and practice.

Set Deadlines

Of course, the best way to approach time management is to set realistic deadlines that consider which elements depend on which others and the order in which they should be completed. Giving yourself two days to write a 20-page work of fiction is not very realistic when even many professional authors average only 6 pages per day. Your intentions may be well founded, but your use of unrealistic deadlines will not be successful.

Setting appropriate deadlines and sticking to them is particularly important—so much so that several sections in the rest of this chapter touch on effective deadline practices.

Be Flexible

It is ironic that the item on this list that comes just after a strong encouragement to make deadlines and stick to them is the suggestion to be flexible. The reason that *being flexible* has made this list is because even the best-laid plans and most accurate time management efforts can take an unexpected turn. The idea behind being flexible is to readjust your plans and deadlines when something does happen to throw things off. The worst thing you could do in such a situation is panic or just stop working because the next step in your careful planning has suddenly become a roadblock. The moment when you see that something in your plan may become an issue is when to begin readjusting your plan.

Adjusting a plan along the way is incredibly common. Many professional project managers have learned that something *always* happens or there is always some delay, and they have developed an approach to deal with the inevitable need for some flexibility. You could say that they are even planning for problems, mistakes, or delays from the very beginning, and they will often add a little extra time for each task to help ensure an issue does not derail the entire project or that the completion of the project does not miss the final due date.

The Importance of Where You Do Your Work

Figure 4.3 Where you do work can be as important as when. (Credit: Mads Bodker/Flickr/Attribution 2.0 Generic (CC BY 2.0)

A large part of ensuring that you can complete tasks on time comes to setting up conditions that will allow you to do the work well. Much of this is about the environment where you will do your work. This not only includes physical space such as a work area, but other conditions like being free from distractions and your physical well-being and mental attitude.

The Right Space

Simple things, like where you are set up to do your work, can not only aid in your efficiency but also affect how well you can work or even if you can get the work completed at all. One example of this might be typing on a laptop. While it might seem more comfortable to lie back on a couch and type a long paper, sitting up at a desk or table increases your typing speed and reduces the number of mistakes. Even the kind of mouse you use can impact how you work. Using a mouse that is comfortable for you can make a significant difference.

There are many other factors that can come into play too. Do you have enough space? Is the space cluttered, or do you have the room to keep reference materials and other things you might need within arm's reach? Are there other ways you could work that might be even more efficient? For example, buying an inexpensive second monitor—even secondhand—might be the key to decreasing the amount of time you spend when you can have more than one document displayed at a time.

The key is to find what works for you and to treat your workspace as another valuable resource needed to get the task finished.

Distraction Free

Few things are more frustrating than trying to do work while distractions are going on around you. If other people are continually interrupting you or there are things that keep pulling your attention from the task at hand, everything takes longer, and you are more prone to mistakes.[4]

Many people say they work better with distractions, but the truth is that an environment with too many interruptions is rarely helpful when focus is required. Before deciding that the television or talkative roommates do not bother you when you work, take an honest accounting of the work you produce with interruptions compared to the work you do without distractions.

If you find that your work is better without distractions, it is helpful to create an environment that reduces interruptions. This may mean you have to go to a private room, use headphones, or go somewhere like a library to work. Regardless, the importance of a distraction-free environment cannot be emphasized enough.

Research has clearly demonstrated that multitasking, task switching and dual tasking result in more mistakes and a lower retention of information. Our brains are not efficient in shifting from one activity to another. Single tasking produces the best quality work and better retention of information. Single-tasking is also the most effective use of time.

Working at the Right Time

Most people are subject to their own rhythms, cycles, and preferences throughout their day. Some are alert and energetic in the mornings, while others are considered "night owls" and prefer to work after everyone else has gone to sleep. It can be important to be aware of your own cycles and to use them to your advantage. Rarely does anyone do their best work when they are exhausted, either physically or mentally. Just as it can be difficult to work when you are physically ill, it can also be a hindrance to try to learn or do mental work when you are tired or emotionally upset.

Your working environment includes your own state of mind and physical well-being. Both have a major influence on your learning and production ability. Because of this, it is not only important to be aware of your own condition and work preferences, but to try to create conditions that help you in these areas. One approach is to set aside a specific time to do certain kinds of work. You might find that you concentrate better after you have eaten a meal. If that is the case, make it a habit of doing homework every night after dinner. Or you might enjoy reading more after you are ready for bed, so you do your reading assignments just before you go to sleep at night. Some people find that they are more creative during a certain time of the day or that they are more comfortable writing with subtle lighting. It is worth taking the time to find the conditions that work best for you so that you can take advantage of them.

4.4 Goal Setting

Questions to consider:

- How do I set motivational goals?
- What are SMART goals?
- What is the importance of an action plan?
- How do I keep to my plan?

Set Goals That Motivate You

The first thing to know about goal setting is that a goal is a specific result you desire. If the goal is not something you are really interested in, there is little motivational drive to achieve it. Think back to when you were much younger, and some well-meaning adults set a goal for you—something that did not really appeal to you at all. How motivated were you to achieve the goal? More than likely, if you were successful at all in meeting the goal, it was because you were motivated by earning the approval of someone or receiving a reward, or you were concerned with avoiding something adverse that might happen if you did not do what you were told. From an honest perspective in that situation, your real goal was based on something else, not the meeting of the goal set for you. To get the most from the goals you set, make sure they are things that you are interested in achieving. That is not to say you should not set goals that are supported by other motivations (e.g., If I finish studying by Friday, I can go out on Saturday), but the idea is to be intellectually honest with your goals.

Set SMART Goals

Goals should also be SMART. In this case, the word *smart* is not only a clever description of the type of goal, but it is also an acronym that stands for Specific, Measurable, Attainable, Relevant, and Time-bound. The reason these are all desirable traits for your goals is because they not only help you plan how to meet the goal, but they can also contribute to your decision-making processes during the planning stage.

What does it mean to create SMART goals?

- Specific—For a goal to be specific, it must be defined enough to determine the goal. The goal of *getting a respectable job when I graduate* is too general. It does not define what a respectable job is. In fact, it does not even necessarily include a job in your chosen profession. A more specific goal would be something like *being hired as a nurse in a place of employment where it is enjoyable to work and that has room for promotion.*
- Measurable—The concept of *measurable* is one that is often overlooked when setting goals. What this means is that the goal should have clearly defined outcomes that are detailed enough to measure and can be used for planning of how you will achieve the goal. For example, setting a goal of *doing well in school* is a bit undefined, but making a goal of *graduating with a GPA (Grade Point Average) above 3.0* is measurable and something you can work with. If your goal is measurable, you can know ahead of time how many points you will have to earn on a specific assignment to stay in that range or how many points you will need to make up in the next assignment if you do not do as well as you planned.
- Attainable—*Attainable* or *achievable* goals means they are reasonable and within your ability to accomplish. While a goal of *making an extra one million dollars by the end of the week* is something that would be nice to achieve, the odds that you could make that happen in a single week are not very realistic.
- Relevant—For goal setting, *relevant* means it applies to the situation. In relation to college, the goal of *getting a horse to ride* is not relevant, but *getting dependable transportation* is something that would contribute to your success in school.
- Time-bound—Time-bound means you set a specific time limit to achieve the goal. *I will get my paper written by Wednesday* is time-bound. You know when you must meet the goal. *I will get my paper written sometime soon* does not help you plan how and when you will accomplish the goal.

Another useful approach to goal setting is to create SMART goals and then write them down. For most people there is a higher level of commitment when we write something down. If you have your goals written out, you can refer to each component of the SMART acronym and make certain you are on track to achieve it.

In the following table you can see some examples of goals that do and do not follow the SMART system. As you read each one, think about what elements make them SMART or how you might change those that are not.

Table 4.4 Chart gives an understanding of well written SMART goals

Writing SMART Goals

Goal	Is it SMART?	
I am going to be rich someday.	No	Nothing specific, measurable, or time-bound in this goal.
I will graduate with my AA degree within 2 years.	Yes	The statement calls out specific, measurable, and time-bound details. The other attributes of attainable and relevant are implied.
I am going to save $________ to buy a newer car by June.	Yes	All SMART attributes are covered in this goal.
I would like to do well in all my courses next semester.	No	While this is clearly time-bound and meets most of the SMART goal attributes, it is not specific or measurable without defining what "do well" means.
I am going to start being a nicer person.	No	While most SMART attributes are implied, there is nothing measurable in this goal.
I will earn at least a 3.0 GPA in all my courses next semester.	Yes	All the SMART attributes are in this goal.
I am going to start being more organized.	No	While most SMART attributes are implied, there is nothing measurable in this goal.

Activity 4.4

Try writing two SMART goals—something with a one-week time limit and something that you will accomplish over the next year. Make certain that you include all the appropriate elements—Specific, Measurable, Attainable, Relevant, and Time-bound. List three actions you can take to help reach each of the goals.

Make an Action Plan

Like anything else, making a step-by-step action plan of how you will attain your goals is the best way to make certain you achieve them. It does not matter if it is a smaller goal with immediate results (e.g., finishing all your homework due by Friday) or something bigger that takes several years to accomplish (graduating with my degree in the proper amount of time). The planning techniques you use for time management and achieving goals can be similar. In fact, accurate goal setting is very much a part of time management if you treat the completion of each task as a goal. What follows is an example of a simple action plan that lists the steps for writing a short paper. You can use something like this or modify it in a way that would better suit your own preferences.

Table 4.5 Table is an example of how to create an action plan

WRITING AN ACTION PLAN		
Task	**Objective**	**When**
Choose topic.	Select something interesting.	It needs to be done by Monday!
Write an outline, look for references.	Create the structure of paper and outline each part.	Monday, 6:00 p.m.
Research references to support outline, look for good quotes.	Strengthen paper and resources.	Tuesday, 6:00 p.m.
Draft paper introduction and first page draft.	Get main ideas and thesis statement down.	Wednesday, 7:00 p.m.
Write the second page and closing draft.	Finish main content and tie it all together.	Thursday, 6:00 p.m.
Rewrite and polish final draft.	Clean-up for grammar, writing style, and effective communication.	Friday, 5:00 p.m. (free weekend)

Stick with It!

As with anything else, the key to reaching goals is to keep at it, keep yourself motivated, and overcome any obstacles along the way. In the following graphic you will find seven methods that successful people use to accomplish this.

Figure 4.4 Success Strategies

4.5 Creating Your Work Schedule

Questions to consider:

- How can I use small periods of time that are usually wasted?
- How can setting time limits on activities help me capture bits of time?

Analyzing Your Schedule and Creating Time to Work

Of all the strategies covered in this chapter, this one may require the most discipline, but it can also be the most beneficial in time management. The fact is most of us waste time throughout the day. Some of it is due to a lack of awareness, but it can also be caused by the constraints of our current schedules. An example of this is when we have 15 to 20 minutes before we must leave to go somewhere. We do not utilize that time because we are focused on leaving or where we are going, and we might not be organized enough to accomplish something in that short of a time. A good deal of our 24- hour days are spent a few minutes at a time waiting for the next thing scheduled to occur. These small units of time add up to a fair amount each day.

The intent of this strategy is to take advantage of the many lost minutes throughout our day. This may take careful observation and consideration on your part, but the results of using this as a method of time management are more than worth it.

The first step is to look for those periods of time that are wasted or that can be repurposed. To identify them, you will need to pay attention to what you do throughout the day and how much time you spend doing it. The example of waiting for the next thing in your schedule has already been given, but there are many others. How much time do you spend in activities after you have finished doing them but are still lingering because you have not begun to do something else (e.g., letting the next episode play while binge-watching, reading social media posts or waiting for someone to reply, surfing the Internet, etc.)? You might be surprised to learn how much time you use up each day by just adding a few unproductive minutes here and there.

If you set a limit on how much time you spend on each activity, you might find that you can recapture time to do other things. An example of this would be limiting yourself to reading news for 30 minutes. Instead of reading the main things that interest you and then spending an additional amount of time just looking at things that you are only casually interested in because that is what you are doing now, you could stop after a certain allotted period and use the extra time you have gained on something else.

After you identify periods of lost time, the next step will be to envision how you might restructure your activities to bring those extra minutes together into useful blocks of time.

Figure 4.5 Graduation-college success

Summary

This chapter pointed out the dangers of poor time management, both in cost and even the potential risk to graduation. Sections of the text covered how time management for college can be different from what students may have experienced before. The chapter also contained several suggestions on how to effectively manage time (including predicting time on tasks), how to use technology to your advantage, and how to prioritize tasks. Other topics included goal setting and motivation, some specific strategies for time and task management, and avoiding procrastination.

Notes

1. Spending a Few Extra Years in College May Cost You More Than You Think, Danielle Douglas-Gabriel, June 21, 2016. https://www.washingtonpost.com/news/grade-point/wp/2016/06/21/spending-a-few-extra-years-in-college-may-cost-you-more-than-you-think/?noredirect=on&utm_term=.f06be365e5d6

Chapter 5 Learning, Motivation, GRIT, and Mindset

Figure 5.1 Becoming proficient at American Sign Language requires Grit and a growth mindset.

Chapter Outline

Student Survey

How do you feel about motivation and mindset? These questions will help you determine how the chapter concepts relate to you right now. As we are introduced to new concepts and practices, it can be informative to reflect on how your understanding changes over time. Take this quick survey, ranking questions on a scale of 1–4, 1 meaning "least like me" and 4 meaning "most like me."

1. _____ I am a highly motivated learner.
2. _____ I push through difficult tasks even when I do not feel like it.
3. _____ I have a positive mindset when trying new things.
4. _____ I do not easily give up when I have negative experiences.

Chapter Outcomes

This chapter explores the many ways we are motivated and the theoretical approaches to motivation. You will learn ways to increase your resilience and grit while keeping a positive mindset. Through assessments, you will discover your learning preference and the best way you process academic content.

The goal of this material is to help you do the following:

- Describe the difference between intrinsic and extrinsic motivation.
- Differentiate between the different theories of motivation.
- Identify different strategies to increase grit.
- Explore a variety of strategies to engage in a positive mindset.

5.1 Learning Theory

Metacognition is one of the distinctive characteristics of the human mind that enables us to reflect on our own mental states. It is defined as "thinking about thinking." Metacognition is reflected in many day-to-day activities, such as when you realize that one strategy is better than another for solving a particular type of problem, or when you are able to recognize how your own experiences and perspectives may impact how you understand, react to, or judge certain situations.

Metacognition includes two clusters of activities: knowledge about cognition and regulation of cognition. **Metacognitive knowledge** refers to a person's knowledge or understanding of cognitive processes. In other words, it is the ability to think about what you know and how you know it. This includes knowledge about your own strengths and limitations as well as factors that may interact to help or hinder your learning. **Metacognitive regulation** builds on this knowledge and refers to a person's ability to regulate cognitive processes during problem-solving. You use metacognitive knowledge to make decisions about how to approach new problems or how to effectively learn new information and skills. This involves using various self-regulatory mechanisms like planning ahead, monitoring your progress, and evaluating your own efficiency and effectiveness in learning a task.

To give a concrete example of these metacognitive activities, let's apply them to how you study for an exam. Knowing that your cell phone's notifications tend to distract you from studying is an example of metacognitive knowledge: you are aware of your phone's potential to hinder your learning. Metacognitive regulation requires you to take *action* based on this knowledge and would involve you making the conscious decision to put your cell phone where you cannot see or hear it or to turn it off completely, while you study. In doing so, you regulate your use of your phone to help yourself be more successful in preparing for your exam.

Stages of the Learning Process

We said earlier that metacognitive knowledge involves thinking about the cognitive process, about what you know and how you know it. An important first step in developing metacognitive knowledge about yourself as a learner is to develop an awareness of how we learn new things. Consider the experiences you've had with learning something new, such as learning to tie your shoes or drive a car. You probably began by showing interest in the process, and after some struggling, it became second nature. These experiences were all part of the learning process, which can be described in four stages:

1. **Unconscious incompetence**: This will likely be the easiest learning stage—you don't know what you don't know yet. During this stage, a learner mainly shows interest in something or prepares for learning. For example, if you wanted to learn how to dance, you might watch a video, talk to an instructor, or sign up for a future class. Stage 1 might not take long.
2. **Conscious incompetence**: This stage can be the most difficult for learners because you begin to register how much you need to learn—*you know what you don't know*. This is metacognition at work! Think about the saying "It's easier said than done." In stage 1 the learner only has to discuss or show interest in a new experience, but in stage 2, they begin to apply new skills that contribute to reaching the learning goal. In the dance example above, you would now be learning basic dance steps. Successful completion of this stage relies on practice.
3. **Conscious competence**: You are beginning to master some parts of the learning goal and are feeling some confidence about what you do know. For example, you might now be able to complete basic dance steps with few mistakes and without your instructor reminding you how to do them. Stage 3 requires skill repetition, and metacognition helps you identify where to focus your efforts.
4. **Unconscious competence**: This is the final stage in which learners have successfully practiced and repeated the process they learned so many times that they can do it almost without thinking. At this point in your dancing, you might be able to apply your dance skills to a freestyle dance routine that you create yourself. However, to feel you are a "master" of a particular skill by the time you reach stage 4, you still need to practice constantly and reevaluate which stage you are in so you can keep learning. For example, if you now felt confident in basic dance skills and could perform your own dance routine, perhaps you'd want to explore other kinds of dance, such as tango or swing. That would return you to stage 1 or 2, but you might progress through the stages more quickly this time since you have already acquired some basic dance skills.

Figure 5.2 Stages of the learning process. (Source: https://mindwerx.com/wp-content/uploads/Four-stages-of-learning-competence.jpg)

Bloom's Taxonomy

In 1956, Dr. Benjamin Bloom, an American educational psychologist who was particularly interested how people learn, chaired a committee of educators that developed and classified a set of learning objectives, which came to be known as **Bloom's taxonomy**. This classification system has been updated a little since it was first developed, but it remains important for both students and teachers in helping to understand the skills and structures involved in learning.

Bloom's taxonomy divides the cognitive domain of learning into six main learning-skill levels, or learning-skill stages, which are arranged hierarchically—moving from the simplest of functions like remembering and understanding, to more complex learning skills, like applying and analyzing, to the most complex skills—evaluating and creating. The lower levels are more straightforward and fundamental, and the higher levels are more sophisticated. See Figure 5.3 below.

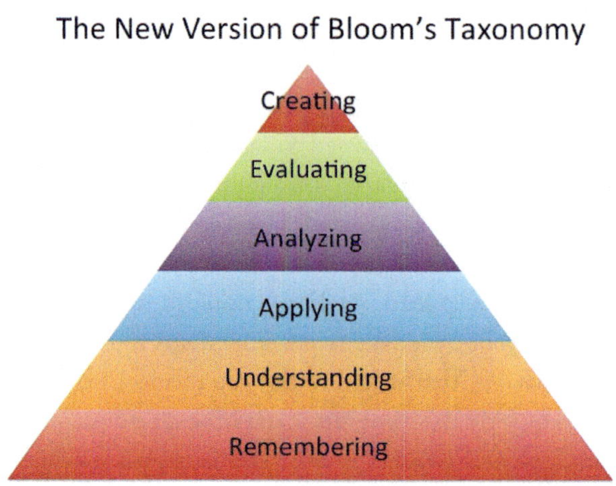

Figure 5.3 Bloom's Cognitive Taxonomy. (Source: https://www.flickr.com/photos/21847073@N05/5857112597)

The following table describes the six main skillsets within the cognitive domain and gives you information on the level of learning expected for each. Read each description closely for details of what college-level work looks like in each domain (note that the table begins with remembering, the lowest level of the taxonomy).

Table 5.1 Levels of Bloom's Taxonomy with Descriptions and Examples

Main Skill Levels Within the Cognitive Domain	Description	Examples of Related Learning Skills (specific actions related to the skillset)
Remembering	When you are skilled in remembering, you can recognize or recall knowledge you've already gained, and you can use it to produce or retrieve definitions, facts, and lists. *Remembering may be how you studied in grade school or high school, but college will require you to do more with the information.*	identify · relate · list · define · recall · memorize · repeat · record · name
Understanding	Understanding is the ability to grasp or construct meaning from oral, written, and graphic messages. *Each college course will introduce you to new concepts, terms, processes, and functions. Once you gain a firm understanding of new information, you'll find it easier to comprehend how or why something works.*	restate · locate · report · recognize · explain · express · identify · discuss · describe · review · infer · illustrate · interpret · draw · represent · differentiate · conclude
Applying	When you apply, you use or implement learned material in new and concrete situations. *In college, you will be tested or assessed on what you've learned in the previous levels. You will be asked to solve problems in new situations by applying knowledge and skills in new ways. You may need to relate abstract ideas to practical situations.*	apply · relate · develop · translate · use · operate · organize · employ · restructure · interpret · demonstrate · illustrate · practice · calculate · show · exhibit · dramatize
Analyzing	When you analyze, you have the ability to break down or distinguish the parts of material into its components, so that its organizational structure may be better understood. *At this level, you will have a clearer sense that you comprehend the content well. You will be able to answer questions such as what if, or why, or how something would work.*	analyze · compare · probe · inquire · examine · contrast · categorize · differentiate · contrast · investigate · detect · survey · classify · deduce · experiment · scrutinize · discover · inspect · dissect · discriminate · separate
Evaluating	With skills in evaluating, you are able to judge, check, and even critique the value of material for a given purpose. *At this level in college, you will be able to think critically, Your understanding of a concept or discipline will be profound. You may need to present and defend opinions.*	judge · assess · compare · evaluate · conclude · measure · deduce · argue · decide · choose · rate · select · estimate · validate · consider · appraise · value · criticize · infer
Creating	With skills in creating, you are able to put parts together to form a coherent or unique new whole. You can reorganize elements into a new pattern or structure through generating, planning, or producing. *Creating requires originality and inventiveness. It brings together all levels of learning to theorize, design, and test new products, concepts, or functions.*	compose · produce · design · assemble · create · prepare · predict · modify · plan · invent · formulate · collect · generalize · document combine · relate · propose · develop · arrange · construct · organize · originate · derive · write

Multiple Intelligences

When you learn, you may be using a variety of intelligences as explained in **Howard Gardner's theory of multiple intelligences**. Gardner proposes that there are eight different forms of intelligence, each of which functions independently of the others. Each person has a mix of all eight abilities—more of some and less of others—that helps to constitute that person's individual cognitive profile. These eight intelligences are summarized in Table 5.2 below.

Since most tasks—including learning in college—require several forms of intelligence and can be completed in more than one way, it is possible for people with various profiles of talents to succeed on a task equally well. In writing an essay, for example, a student with high interpersonal intelligence but rather average verbal intelligence might use her interpersonal strength to get a lot of help and advice from classmates and the teacher. A student with the opposite profile might work well on his own but without the benefit of help from others. Both students might end up with essays that are good, but good for different reasons.

Table 5.2 Descriptions and Examples of Multiple Intelligences

Multiple Intelligences According to Howard Gardner	
Form of intelligence	**Examples of activities using the intelligence**
Linguistic: Verbal skill; ability to use language well	• verbal persuasion • writing a term paper skillfully
Musical: Ability to create and understand music	• singing, playing a musical instrument • composing a tune
Logical-Mathematical: logical skill; ability to reason, often using mathematics	• solving mathematical problems easily and accurately • developing and testing hypotheses
Spatial: Ability to imagine and manipulate the arrangement of objects in the environment	• completing a difficult jigsaw puzzle • assembling a complex appliance (e.g. a bicycle)
Bodily-Kinesthetic: a sense of balance; coordination in use of one's body	• dancing • gymnastics
Interpersonal: Ability to discern others' nonverbal feelings and thoughts	• sensing when to be tactful • sensing a "subtext" or implied message in a person's statements
Intrapersonal: Sensitivity to one's own thoughts and feelings	• noticing complex or ambivalent feelings in oneself • identifying true motives for an action in oneself
Naturalist: Sensitivity to subtle differences and patterns found in the natural environment	• identifying examples of species of plants or animals • noticing relationships among species and natural processes in the environment

This model can be useful as a way for students to think about how you approach your learning. Multiple intelligences suggest that there is (or may be) more than one way to be "smart," and that you can benefit from identifying your personal strengths and preferences.

5.2 Motivation

Questions to consider:

- What is motivation and why is it important?
- How can one increase their motivation levels?
- What are the different types of motivation and how do they differ from one another?

Motivation refers to the driving force or inner desire that compels an individual to act towards achieving a particular goal. It is a key factor in determining the level of effort, persistence, and dedication an individual puts into their tasks or activities. It can come from both external factors such as rewards or recognition, as well as internal factors such as personal values, beliefs, and interests. In general, we discuss motivation as being **intrinsic** (arising from internal factors) or **extrinsic** (arising from external factors). Intrinsically motivated behaviors are performed because of the sense of personal satisfaction they bring, while extrinsically motivated behaviors are performed to receive something from others.

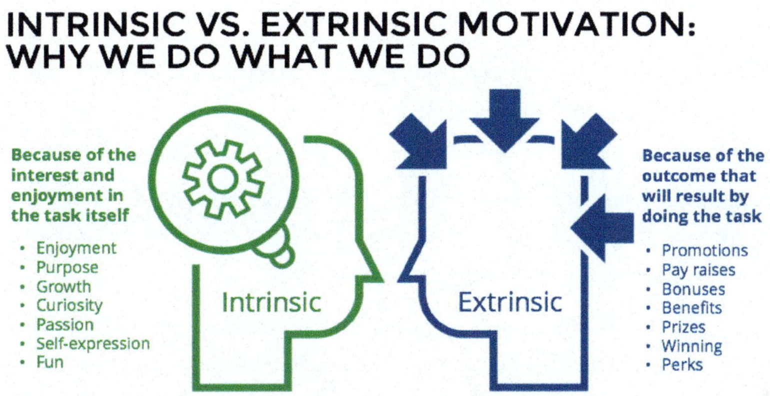

Figure 5.4 Intrinsic motivation comes from within the individual, while extrinsic motivation comes from outside the individual.
(Image from Google Images, author unknown)

Think about why you are currently in college. Are you here because you enjoy learning and want to pursue an education to make yourself a more well-rounded individual? If so, then you are intrinsically motivated. However, if you are here because you want to get a college degree to make yourself more marketable for a high-paying career or to satisfy the demands of your parents, then your motivation is more extrinsic in nature.

Case Scenario

Sophie is a first-year college student majoring in psychology. She has always been interested in understanding human behavior and has chosen this major to pursue her passion. Sophie is a diligent student and strives to do her best in all her classes.

Sophie's psychology professor is known to be a tough grader, and the class assignments require a lot of reading and research. However, Sophie is intrinsically motivated to learn and absorb as much knowledge as she can. She is genuinely interested in the subject matter and finds the coursework challenging yet exciting. Sophie enjoys the mental stimulation that comes with the assignments and the satisfaction of learning something new. Her motivation is not driven by external rewards, such as good grades or praise from her professor.

However, Sophie's motivation also has an extrinsic component. Her parents have high expectations of her academic performance, and she does not want to disappoint them. She also knows that good grades are important for future career prospects, and this external reward serves as a motivator to keep her on track with her studies. Sophie's desire to succeed academically is driven by both intrinsic and extrinsic factors.

Locus of control is a psychological concept that refers to the extent to which people believe that they have control over the events and outcomes in their lives. It is a dimension of personality that describes the extent to which individuals believe that their actions and decisions can influence their environment and outcomes.

People with an **internal locus of control** believe that their actions and decisions have a direct impact on their lives, while people with an **external locus of control** believe that their outcomes are determined by external factors such as luck, chance, or powerful others.

Overall, locus of control is an important concept in understanding how individuals perceive and respond to their environment, and it can have important implications for their behavior and well-being.

Whether you attribute an outcome to something internal or external to you and if you view the outcomes as within your control has a significant impact on your behaviors and motivation.

Like motivation itself, theories of it are full of diversity. For convenience in navigating through the diversity, we have organized theories around different perspectives about motivation. We will now explore four different approaches to motivation: behavioral, humanistic, cognitive, and social.

5.3 Behavioral Theory of Motivation

Questions to consider:

- What role do rewards and incentives play in motivating people?
- How do personal goals impact motivation?
- What are the consequences of a lack of motivation in various aspects of life?

The behavioral theory of motivation states that we are motivated by the consequences of our behaviors. If our actions lead to a positive consequence, then we are likely to continue the behavior so that we can continue to experience the reward. On the other hand, if our behavior leads to a negative outcome, sometimes called a punishment, then we are likely to stop that behavior to avoid any future negative consequences.

As a student, you may choose to study regularly for a difficult class because you want the reward of a good grade and the ability to continue on with your studies to reach your dream career. You may also want to make your family proud. By not studying, you are likely to experience negative consequences such as having to spend time and money retaking the class and disappoint your family. According to B. F. Skinner, rewards work because they reinforce positive behaviors. Also, when we have positive outcomes, we are likely to have positive emotions around the behavior which becomes another motivation to continue the positive behavior.

Case Scenario

Meet John, a 20-year-old community college student who is pursuing an associate degree in computer science. John is a talented student with a passion for technology, but he often struggles to stay motivated and focused on his studies.

Behavioral Motivation: John's behavior is that he spends a lot of time playing video games and hanging out with friends. This has led to him falling behind in his coursework and he is at risk of failing the class.

Since John is experiencing negative consequences to his behaviors, he decides to implement a behavioral motivation strategy and sets some goals for himself. He decides to complete all his coursework for the day before playing video games or hanging out with his friends. He also sets the goal of earning a B in the class.

Video games and spending time with friends have now become rewards for John.

As John starts to see progress towards his goals and experiences the rewards of his hard work, he becomes more motivated and engaged in his studies. He also feels more confident in his abilities and is proud of himself for taking control of his motivation and achieving success.

5.4 Humanistic Theory of Motivation

Question to consider:

- What needs must be met before we can be motivated to reach our full potential?

Maslow's Hierarchy of Needs is a motivational theory developed by psychologist Abraham Maslow in the mid-20th century. It proposes that human needs can be categorized into a hierarchy of five levels, ranging from basic physiological needs to more complex psychological needs.

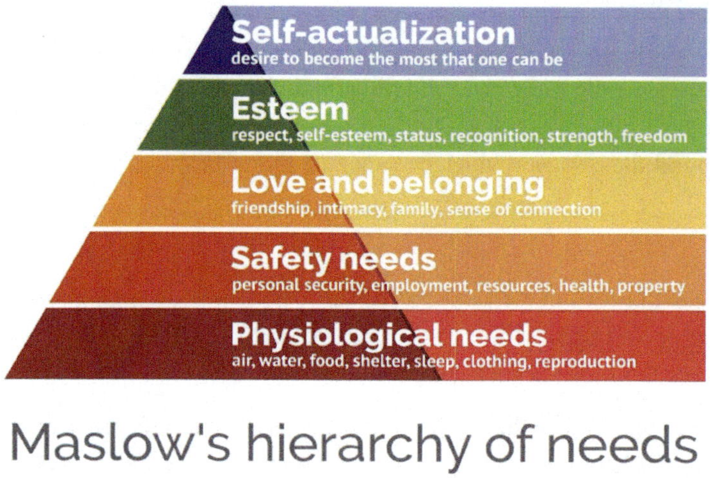

Figure 5.5 Maslow's Hierarchy of Needs Model (adapted from Google images, author unknown)

- **Physiological Needs:** These are the most fundamental needs that humans require for survival, such as food, water, shelter, warmth, and rest.
- **Safety Needs**: Once physiological needs are met, individuals seek safety and security, including protection from physical harm, financial security, and stability.
- **Love and Belonging Needs**: After physiological and safety needs are met, individuals seek social connections and relationships, including love, friendship, and a sense of belonging.
- **Esteem Needs:** Once individuals feel a sense of belonging, they seek esteem, including self-esteem and the esteem of others. This includes respect, recognition, and achievement.
- **Self-Actualization Needs:** At the highest level, individuals strive to achieve their full potential and fulfill their personal goals and aspirations. This includes personal growth, creativity, and self-fulfillment. According to Maslow, self-actualization is a natural human tendency and represents the highest form of psychological development. It involves a deep sense of personal fulfillment and a desire to achieve one's goals and aspirations.

According to Maslow's theory, individuals must satisfy lower-level needs before moving on to higher level needs. The theory suggests that people are motivated by a hierarchy of needs, and that the fulfillment of these needs is necessary for personal growth, self-actualization, and well-being.

Case Scenario

Meet Alex, a 25-year-old community college student who recently enrolled in a two-year program to become a licensed practical nurse. Alex is a single parent with a three-year-old daughter and works part-time to support her family. Alex is excited about the opportunity to advance her career and provide a better life for her daughter. Read how Alex moves through the level of needs towards self-actualization:

Physiological Needs: Alex is often tired and stressed from working and taking care of her daughter. She struggles to find time to prepare healthy meals and often relies on fast food to save time. Alex's lack of sleep and poor diet have started to affect her health, and she has developed digestive issues. Alex knows that she needs to take care of her basic needs to be able to focus on her studies, so she makes an effort to eat healthier and get more rest.

Safety Needs: Alex lives in a low-income area, and she is concerned about her safety and the safety of her daughter. She makes sure to always lock her doors and windows, and she installed a security system to protect her home. Alex also avoids walking alone at night and takes public transportation instead.

Love and Belonging Needs: Alex's family lives far away, and she does not have a lot of friends in her community. She feels isolated and lonely at times, which affects her mood and motivation. Alex joins a student organization on campus for single parents, which helps her connect with other students who share similar experiences. Alex also enrolls her daughter in a daycare program on campus, which allows her to focus on her studies and provides her daughter with socialization opportunities.

Esteem Needs: Alex is proud of herself for pursuing her education and working hard to provide for her family. However, she sometimes feels self-doubt and imposter syndrome, wondering if she is good enough to succeed in her program. Alex seeks out support from her instructors and advisors, who provide her with positive feedback and encouragement. She also sets small achievable goals for herself and celebrates her accomplishments.

Self-Actualization Needs: Alex is passionate about helping others and has always dreamed of becoming a nurse. She is excited about the opportunities that her program will provide her and is determined to succeed. Alex strives to be the best student she can be and actively participates in class discussions and clinical experiences. She also seeks out mentorship opportunities with experienced nurses to learn from their experiences and knowledge.

5.5 Cognitive Theories of Motivation

Questions to consider:

- How do thoughts impact motivation?
- Is it possible to accomplish something you don't believe you can?
- What is helpful when you feel helpless to achieve a task?

Figure 5.6 Relationship Between Goals and Beliefs
(adapted from Google images, author unknown)

Cognitive theories of motivation focus on how an individual's thoughts, beliefs, and expectations influence their motivation to engage in certain behaviors. These theories suggest that people are actively involved in the process of setting goals, evaluating their progress, and making decisions about their behavior based on their internal cognitive processes.

One of the most well-known cognitive theories of motivation is the **Expectancy-Value Theory**, which proposes that individuals are motivated to engage in activities based on their expectations of success and the value they place on the outcomes of those activities. This theory suggests that people are more likely to engage in behaviors that they believe will lead to desirable outcomes, and that they will be more motivated to engage in those behaviors if they believe they have a high chance of success.

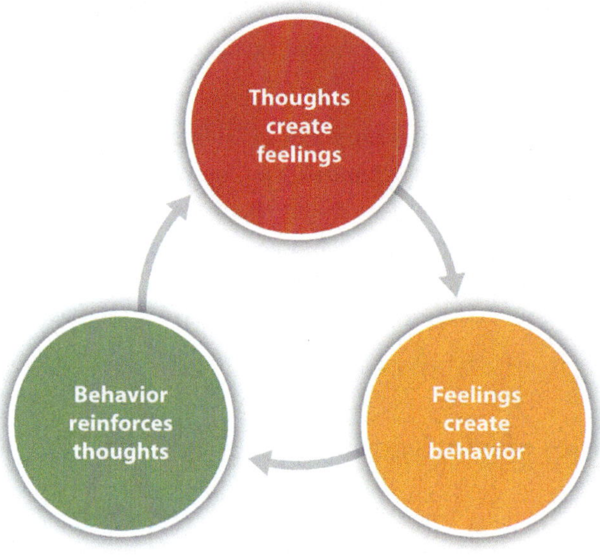

Figure 5.7 Expectancy-Value Model (adapted from Google images, author unknown)

Self-Efficacy Theory is another cognitive theory. Self-efficacy is a person's belief in their ability to successfully perform specific tasks or achieve specific goals. It is a concept introduced by psychologist Albert Bandura, who described it as an individual's belief in their capacity to execute behaviors necessary to produce specific performance attainments. Self-efficacy is not a measure of skills or knowledge but rather a person's confidence in their ability to use those skills or knowledge to achieve a desired outcome. A person with high self-efficacy tends to be more persistent and confident in the face of obstacles, while a person with low self-efficacy may be more likely to give up or avoid challenging tasks. Self-efficacy can be developed through experiences of mastery, modeling, social persuasion, and reducing negative emotional states.

If a person's sense of self-efficacy is exceptionally low, he or she can develop **learned helplessness**, a perception of complete *lack* of control in mastering a task. The attitude is like depression, a pervasive feeling of apathy, and a belief that effort makes no difference and does not lead to success. Learned helplessness was originally studied by the psychologist Martin Seligman (1995).

In people, learned helplessness leads to characteristic ways of dealing with problems. They tend to attribute the source of a problem to themselves, generalize the problem to many aspects of life, and see the problem as lasting or permanent. More optimistic individuals, in contrast, are more likely to attribute a problem to outside sources, to see it as specific to a particular situation or activity, and to see it as temporary or time limited.

As already noted, high self-efficacy is a strong belief in one's capacity to carry out a *specific* task successfully. Therefore, self-efficacy focuses attention on a temporary or time-limited activity (the task), even though the cause of successful completion (oneself) is "internal."

Overall, cognitive theories of motivation emphasize the importance of internal factors, such as beliefs, expectations, and perceptions, in shaping and driving human behavior.

Figure 5.8 Yes you can! Si Se Puede!

Case Scenario

Meet Miguel, a 21-year-old first-generation college student who is pursuing an associate degree in computer science. Miguel is highly motivated to succeed in his studies and is driven by a strong sense of self-efficacy.

Self-Efficacy: Miguel's belief in his ability to succeed is a key factor in his motivation and academic success. He has a strong sense of confidence in his own abilities and feels empowered to take on new challenges and achieve his goals.

To build and maintain his self-efficacy, Miguel engages in several strategies to enhance his learning experience. He sets realistic and achievable goals for himself and creates a plan to achieve them. He breaks down complex tasks into smaller, more manageable steps, which helps him to feel more in control of his academic workload.

Miguel also seeks out support and guidance from his professors and peers, which helps him to feel more connected to his academic community and builds his confidence in his ability to succeed. He participates actively in class discussions and seeks feedback from his professors to help him identify areas where he can improve.

As Miguel continues to learn and grow in his program, his strong sense of self-efficacy continues to fuel his motivation and academic success. He finds satisfaction and fulfillment in his coursework, and his dedication to his studies pays off in his academic performance and long-term career goals. Miguel is proud of himself for pursuing his education and is confident in his ability to achieve his dreams and make a positive impact in the world.

5.6 Social Theory of Motivation

Questions to consider:

- Can external factors like environment and culture influence motivation?
- What types of social support can help you stay motivated?

Social learning theorists view learning as a process of adopting ways of thinking from the culture and community. Therefore, social interaction is a crucial part of the learning process. One of the leading thinkers in the social learning tradition was Lev Vygotsky.

Vygotsky believed that our **culture** provides us with "cognitive tools" that affect the way we think. Our **language**, for example, is a cultural tool. While language serves a similar function in all cultures, the unique features of a language can influence how we think.

An example of this is **linguistic capital.** Linguistic capital in Hispanic culture refers to the social, cultural, and economic value that is attributed to the mastery of Spanish language skills. In many Hispanic communities, the ability to speak Spanish fluently is highly valued and is often seen as a symbol of cultural identity, heritage, and tradition. Being able to communicate effectively in Spanish can also provide individuals with access to various social, cultural, and economic opportunities, such as better jobs, higher education, and greater social mobility.

In addition, in the United States, Spanish is the second most commonly spoken language, and it is becoming increasingly important for individuals to be able to speak Spanish fluently, especially in industries such as healthcare, education, and customer service. Thus, the mastery of Spanish language skills can provide individuals with a competitive advantage in the job market and can enhance their **cultural capital** in the eyes of others.

In the context of college students, the social theory of motivation suggests that students' motivation may be influenced by their peers, professors, and other members of their academic community. For example, students may be motivated by the expectations and approval of their professors or the desire to fit in with their peers.

Moreover, the social theory of motivation highlights the importance of social support and collaboration in promoting motivation. College students who feel supported by their social networks are more likely to feel motivated and persist in their academic pursuits.

Case Scenario

Let's consider the case of Kiara, a first-generation college student. Kiara grew up in a low-income community where few people went to college, and her parents did not pursue higher education. Despite these challenges, Kiara was motivated to attend college and pursue a career in healthcare.

According to social learning theory, Kiara's motivation to pursue higher education may have been influenced by the behavior and attitudes of the people around her. For instance, she may have observed the success and prestige that college graduates in her community had achieved and modeled their behavior. Additionally, her teachers and guidance counselors may have encouraged her to pursue higher education and provided her with the necessary support and resources to succeed.

As Kiara progressed through college, her motivation to continue her studies may have been further reinforced by positive experiences and feedback from her professors and peers. She may have also received validation and recognition from her family and community for her academic achievements, which further reinforced her motivation to succeed.

Overall, social learning theory can help explain the complex interplay of social factors that motivate first-generation college students to pursue higher education and succeed academically. By understanding the role of social learning in academic achievement, educators and policymakers can develop strategies to provide support and resources to first-generation college students to help them succeed in college and beyond.

5.7 Self-Regulation

Question to consider:

- How can one maintain motivation over a long period of time?

Self-regulation refers to the process by which individuals monitor and control their own thoughts, emotions, and behaviors to achieve their goals and adapt to changing circumstances. It involves a range of cognitive, emotional, and behavioral processes that allow individuals to regulate their own thoughts, feelings, and actions. The **self-regulation theory** is a theoretical framework describing the process by which individuals monitor and control their own behavior to achieve their goals. It proposes that self-regulation involves three main stages: the self-monitoring stage, the self-evaluation stage, and the self-reinforcement stage.

The self-monitoring stage involves individuals observing and tracking their own behavior to understand their current performance level. This may involve tracking progress toward a goal or monitoring specific behaviors to identify patterns or areas for improvement.

The self-evaluation stage involves individuals comparing their current performance to their desired level of performance and evaluating whether they are on track to achieve their goals. This may involve setting benchmarks or standards for performance and using these to assess progress.

The self-reinforcement stage involves individuals using rewards or punishments to reinforce their own behavior and increase the likelihood of achieving their goals. This may involve rewarding oneself for making progress toward a goal or punishing oneself for failing to meet a benchmark or standard.

Overall, the self-regulation model proposes that individuals can use a range of strategies to monitor, evaluate, and reinforce their own behavior to achieve their goals. By understanding and applying these strategies, individuals can become more effective at self-regulation and more successful in achieving their desired outcomes. To learn more about your own self-regulation, take the Self-Regulation Questionnaire in Appendix 5.

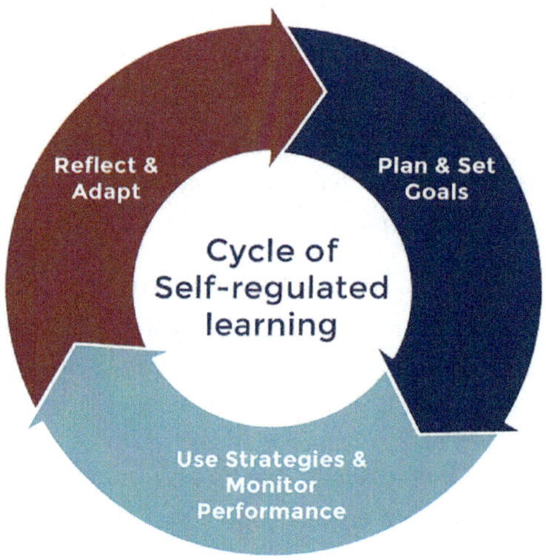

Image by Kristin O'Connell

Figure 5.9 Self-Regulation Model

Emotional intelligence is an important element of self-regulation. It can be defined as the ability of individuals to recognize their own and other people's emotions, discern between different feelings and label them appropriately, use emotional information to guide thinking and behavior, and manage and/or adjust emotions to adapt to environments or achieve one's goal(s). Those with high levels of emotional intelligence are able to recognize and reflect on their own emotions (intrapersonal intelligence) and those of the people around them (interpersonal intelligence); they are also able to respond to those emotions in ways that minimize negative consequences and support the achievement of intended goals.

5.8 Resilience and Grit

Questions to consider:

- What are some examples of times when you have demonstrated resilience in the face of adversity?
- How do you maintain a positive mindset when faced with challenges or setbacks?
- What strategies do you use to stay motivated and focused when pursuing long-term goals?
- How do you bounce back from failure, and what have you learned from your past failures?

Grit can be defined as personal perseverance toward a task or goal. In learning, it can be thought of as a trait that drives a person to keep trying until they succeed. It is not tied to talent or ability but is simply a tendency to not give up until something is finished or accomplished.

Figure 5.10 U.S. Army veteran and captain of the U.S. Invictus team, Will Reynolds, races to the finish line. (Credit: DoD News/Flickr/Attribution 2.0 Generic (CC-BY 2.0))

This personality trait was defined as "grit" by the psychologist Angela Duckworth[1]. In a 2007 study Duckworth and colleagues found that individuals with high grit were able to maintain motivation in learning tasks despite failures. The study examined a cross section of learning environments, such as GPA scores in Ivy League universities, dropout rates at West Point, rankings in the National Spelling Bee, and general educational attainment for adults. What the results showed was that grit and perseverance were better predictors of academic success and achievement than talent or IQ.

In the college setting, Angela Duckworth's definition of grit remains the same: it is the combination of passion and perseverance for long-term goals. However, she explains that grit in the college setting is particularly important because college is a time when students face significant challenges and setbacks.

According to Duckworth, grit in college involves several key components. Firstly, it requires having a clear sense of purpose or direction, which allows students to stay motivated and focused on their goals. Secondly, it involves the ability to persevere in the face of adversity, such as academic difficulties, personal challenges, or social pressures. This means being able to stay committed to one's goals despite setbacks or failures.

Thirdly, grit in college also involves developing effective strategies for learning and problem-solving. This means being able to adapt to new situations, seek out feedback and support, and persist through challenging coursework.

Overall, Duckworth emphasizes that grit is a key factor in college success, as it allows students to stay focused, motivated, and resilient in the face of challenges. By developing grit, students can increase their chances of achieving their long-term academic and career goals.

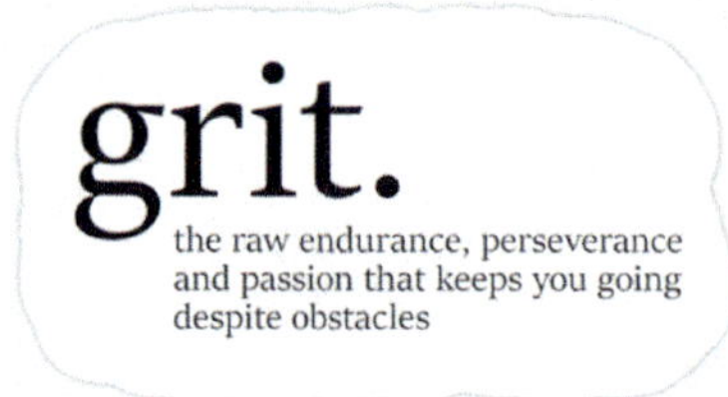

Figure 5.11 Definition of Grit

College students can apply grit in several ways:

1. Set clear goals: College students can apply grit by setting clear and specific goals that align with their values and interests. These goals should be challenging yet achievable and should provide a sense of direction and purpose.
2. Focus on long-term success: Gritty college students understand that success is not immediate and requires consistent effort over time. They focus on the long-term and avoid distractions that may interfere with their goals.
3. Persevere through challenges: College students can apply grit by persisting through challenges and setbacks. This may involve seeking out support and resources, developing effective problem-solving strategies, and maintaining a positive attitude.
4. Practice self-discipline: Gritty college students practice self-discipline by developing habits that support their goals, such as prioritizing their time, staying organized, and avoiding procrastination.
5. Embrace failure as an opportunity to learn: Gritty college students view failure as a natural part of the learning process and use it as an opportunity to reflect on their progress and adjust their approach.
6. Purpose is a major contributor to anything we pursue. If you have a strong purpose in any activity, you have reason to persist at it. Think in terms of end goals and why doing something is worth it. Purpose answers the question of "Why should I accomplish this?"
7. Have hope in what you are doing.

By applying these strategies, college students can cultivate grit and increase their chances of achieving their long-term academic and career goals.

The *New York Times* best-selling author Paul G. Stoltz has taken grit and turned it into an acronym (GRIT) to help people remember and use the attributes of a grit mindset[2]. Each of these elements is explained in the table below.

Table 5.3 The GRIT Acronym as Outlined by Paul G. Stoltz

Growth	Your propensity to seek and consider new ideas, additional alternatives, different approaches, and fresh perspectives
Resilience	Your capacity to respond constructively and ideally make use of all kinds of adversity
Instinct	Your gut-level capacity to pursue the right goals in the best and smartest ways
Tenacity	The degree to which you persist, commit to, stick with, and go after whatever you choose to achieve

Case Scenario

Rodrigo's story is an example of applying grit. He is a first-generation college student who grew up in a low-income family. He had to work part-time jobs throughout high school to support his family, and he faced numerous academic challenges due to a lack of resources and support. Despite these challenges, Rodrigo was determined to attend college and pursue a degree in engineering. During his first semester, Rodrigo struggled to keep up with the rigorous coursework and balance his job and family responsibilities.

However, he refused to give up on his dreams and sought out academic support services, such as tutoring and study groups. He also reached out to professors and advisors for guidance and mentorship. With hard work and perseverance, Rodrigo gradually improved his grades and became more confident in his academic abilities. He also joined several student organizations and began to build a supportive network of peers and mentors.

Over time, Rodrigo's determination and grit paid off, and he earned a high GPA and was even offered a scholarship for his outstanding academic performance. Despite facing numerous challenges, Rodrigo's commitment to his goals and his willingness to seek out help and support allowed him to overcome obstacles and achieve success in college.

Activity 5.1 Get a Grit Partner

Research indicates that having a grit partner is one of the most effective ways to statistically increase your chances of graduation. A grit partner does not have to be a formal relationship. Your partner can simply be a classmate—someone that you can talk with. It can be an instructor you admire or someone else that you establish a connection with. It can even be a family member who will encourage you—someone you do not want to disappoint. What you are looking for is someone who will help motivate you, either by their example or by their willingness to give you a pep talk when you need it. The key is that it is someone you respect and who will encourage you to do well in school. Right now, think about someone who could be your grit partner. Keep in mind that you may not have the same grit partner throughout your entire college experience. You may begin with another classmate but later find that a school staff member steps into the role. Later, as you near graduation, you may find that your favorite instructor motivates you more to do well in school than anyone else. Regardless, the importance of finding the social connection that helps your grit is important.

A psychological tendency that can undermine motivation is **negative bias**. Negative bias can lead individuals to dwell on negative thoughts and feelings, which can undermine their motivation and persistence. This can make it difficult for individuals to maintain their focus on long-term goals, especially when faced with setbacks or challenges.

Grit and negative bias are connected in that individuals with high levels of grit are more likely to resist negative bias. Individuals with high levels of grit tend to be more resilient and better able to cope with adversity. They have a powerful sense of purpose and are committed to achieving their goals. Overall, grit can be a valuable trait in combating negative bias, as it can help individuals stay committed, motivated, and resilient in the face of challenges.

Figure 5.12 Some level of worry and concern is natural, but an overwhelming number of negative thoughts about yourself, including doubt in your abilities and place in school, can impede your learning and stifle your success. (Credit: Inzmam Kahn/Pexels)

What follows are methods for overcoming negative bias and negative self-talk. Each focus on being aware of any negative attitude or emphasizing the positive aspects in a situation.

- **Awareness:** The first step in overcoming negative bias and negative self-talk is to become aware of them.
- **Challenging negative thoughts:** Once you have identified negative bias and negative self-talk, challenge them by asking yourself if they are accurate or if there is evidence to support them. Often, negative biases and self-talk are based on assumptions and beliefs that are not necessarily true.
- **Reframing:** Reframe negative thoughts into more positive and constructive ones. Instead of focusing on the negative, try to find a positive aspect of the situation or challenge. For example, instead of saying "I can't do this," reframe it as "This is a challenge, but I am capable of overcoming it."
- **Positive self-talk:** Practice positive self-talk regularly. This involves intentionally replacing negative thoughts with positive ones. For example, instead of saying "I'm not good enough," say "I am capable and confident."
- **Keep a gratitude and accomplishment journal:** Sometimes we need help remembering positive experiences, and we can prompt our memories by keeping a journal. In your journal you can

write or paste anything that you appreciated or that has positive outcomes. Whenever you are not feeling up to a challenge or when negative bias is starting to wear on you, you can look over your journal to remind yourself of previous accomplishments in the face of adversity.

- **Seeking support:** Surround yourself with people who are positive and supportive. This can help you maintain a positive mindset and provide encouragement when you are struggling with negative bias or self-talk. Seek out a therapist or counselor if you need additional support.

Overall, overcoming negative bias and negative self-talk requires intentional effort and practice. By becoming aware of these patterns of thinking, challenging, and reframing negative thoughts, practicing positive self-talk, and seeking support, you can develop a more positive and constructive mindset.

5.9 It Is All in the Mindset

Questions to consider:

- How does your mindset affect your academic performance?
- How can you cultivate a growth mindset?
- What are some strategies for maintaining a positive and focused mindset?
- How can a growth mindset help you build resilience and cope with the pressures and uncertainties of college life?

In this next section, you will examine the significance of certain mindsets and how they can hinder or promote your own learning efforts.

Figure 5.13 Many fields of study and work create intersections of growth and fixed mindset. (Credit: mentatdgt / Pexels)

Fixed versus Growth Mindset

Fixed mindset and growth mindset are two different ways of thinking about our abilities and potential for learning and growth. These terms were first coined by psychologist Carol Dweck who has extensively researched the effects of these mindsets on individuals' achievement and success[3].

A fixed mindset is the belief that one's abilities and intelligence are fixed and unchangeable. People with a fixed mindset tend to avoid challenges, give up easily, and see effort as fruitless. They may feel threatened by criticism and see the success of others as reflecting their own shortcomings. In a fixed mindset, failure is seen as a sign of lack of ability and can lead to feelings of helplessness and resignation.

On the other hand, a growth mindset is the belief that abilities and intelligence can be developed and improved through dedication, hard work, and learning. People with a growth mindset embrace challenges, persist in the face of setbacks, and see effort as necessary for success. They are open to feedback and see the success of others as a source of inspiration and learning. In a growth mindset, failure is seen as an opportunity to learn and grow, rather than a reflection of ability.

A fixed vs. growth mindset is particularly relevant for college students, as it can influence their academic performance and overall college experience. College students with a fixed mindset may believe that their intelligence and abilities are predetermined, leading them to avoid challenges and view failure as a sign of inability. They may be more likely to give up easily, resist feedback, and avoid seeking help when needed. As a result, they may struggle to achieve their academic goals and feel overwhelmed or discouraged by college life's demands.

In contrast, college students with a growth mindset believe that they can improve their intelligence and abilities through hard work, learning, and dedication. They are more likely to embrace challenges, persist in the face of setbacks, and seek out feedback and help from others. They are also more likely to take risks and try new things, which can help them develop new skills and interests.

Research has shown that college students with a growth mindset tend to perform better academically, have more positive attitudes towards learning, and report higher levels of well-being and satisfaction with their college experience. They are also more likely to develop important skills such as critical thinking, problem-solving, and resilience, which can benefit them in their future careers and personal lives.

In the following graphic, based on Dr. Dweck's research, you can see how many of the components associated with learning are impacted by these two mindsets.

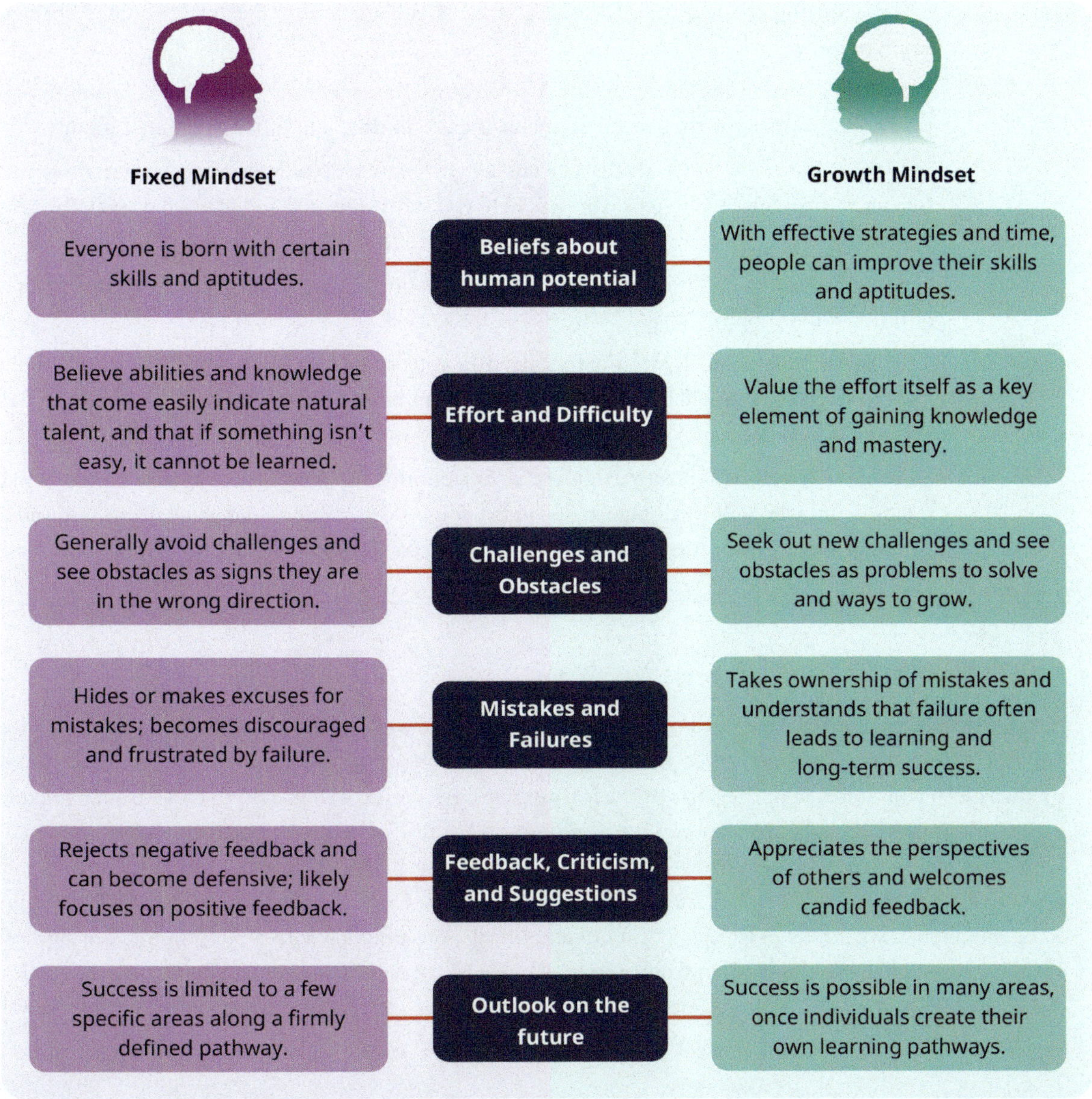

Figure 5.14 The differences between fixed and growth mindset are clear when aligned to key elements of learning and personality. (Credit: Based on work by Dr. Carol Dweck)

Ways to Improving Your Ability to Learn with a Growth Mindset:

1. Embrace challenges: Growth mindset involves seeing challenges as opportunities for growth rather than as threats to your abilities. Therefore, as a college student, you should embrace challenging tasks and assignments, even if they seem difficult at first.
2. Learn from criticism: Instead of taking criticism as a personal attack, try to view it as an opportunity to learn and improve. Ask yourself what you can learn from the feedback and how you can use it to improve your work.

3. Cultivate a love of learning: Focus on the process of learning rather than the end result. This means enjoying the journey of learning, even if you make mistakes or encounter obstacles along the way.
4. Develop a growth mindset vocabulary: Use positive language when discussing your abilities and your potential for growth. Instead of saying "I can't do this," say "I haven't figured it out yet."
5. Set achievable goals: Set goals that are challenging but achievable, and break them down into smaller, more manageable steps. This will help you stay motivated and focused on your progress.
6. Seek out challenges: Seek out opportunities to learn and grow, even if they are outside of your comfort zone. This might mean taking on new responsibilities, joining a club or organization, or trying a new hobby.
7. Practice self-reflection: Take time to reflect on your successes and failures and what you can learn from them. This will help you develop a better understanding of your strengths and weaknesses and how you can continue to grow and improve.
8. Surround yourself with positive influences: Surround yourself with people who have a growth mindset and who will encourage and support your efforts to learn and grow. This might mean joining a study group, attending networking events, or seeking out a mentor or coach.

Activity 5.2

In this exercise, do a self-analysis and think of some areas where you may find yourself hindered by a fixed mindset. Using the outline presented below, in the far-right column, write down how you can change your own behavior for each of the parts of the learning process. What will you do to move from a fixed to a growth mindset? For example, say you were trying to learn to play a musical instrument. In the Challenges row, you might pursue a growth path by trying to play increasingly more difficult songs rather than sticking to the easy ones you have already mastered. In the Criticism row, you might take someone's comment about a weakness in timing as a motivation for you to practice with a metronome. For Success of others, you could take inspiration from a famous musician that is considered a master and study their techniques. Whatever it is that you decide you want to use for your analysis, apply each of the growth characteristics to determine a course of action to improve.

Something I want to get better at: ______________________________

Parts of the learning process	Growth characteristic	What will you do to adopt a growth mindset?
Challenges	Embraces challenges	
Obstacles	Persists despite setbacks	
Effort	Sees effort as a path to success	
Criticism	Learns from criticism	
Success of Others	Finds learning and inspiration in the success of others	

Summary

Metacognition is a thinking process that allows you to reflect on your thinking. This is important in order to learn well. As you learn, you move through four stages from unconscious incompetence to conscious competence. Blooms Taxonomy explains how as people's learning becomes more sophisticated they are better able to apply the learning. It is possible to learn in a variety of ways based on the combination of multiple intelligences that the individual possesses.

Four theories of motivation are explored—behavioral, humanistic, cognitive, and social. Each of these theories looks at how we are motivated from a different perspective. Most of the time, our behaviors are impacted by a combination of these motivators. It is important to be aware of what motivates you so that you can take more control of your choices. Self-regulation allows you to set goals, take action towards reaching the goals, and reflect in order to make any adjustments that are needed.

In addition, this chapter covered grit and mindset. Grit is the ability to persist towards your goals even in the face of adversity. Having a growth mindset means that you believe that through hard work and overcoming challenges you can become more intelligent. Those with a fixed mindset believe that their intelligence is set and cannot change. Those with a growth mindset are more likely to reach their academic goals.

Content from the following OER Resources:

***College Success*, OpenStax**

GRIT and Mindset sections, Applicable citations in this chapter from the book:

1. Duckworth, A.L.; Peterson, C.; Matthews, M.D.; Kelly, D.R. (June 2007). "Grit: Perseverance and passion for long-term goals". *Journal of Personality and Social Psychology*. 92(6): 1087–1101. doi:10.1037/0022-3514.92.6.1087. PMID 17547490.
2. Stoltz, Paul G. (2014). "GRIT The New Science of What It Takes To Persevere, Flourish, Succeed". ClimbStrong Press
3. Dweck, C.S. & Leggett, E.L. (1988). *A Social-Cognitive Approach to Motivation and Personality*

***Educational Psychology* by Nicole Arduini-Van Hoose**

https://www.oercommons.org/courses/edpsych/view

Applicable citations in this chapter from the book:

Social Cognitive Learning Theory. Authored by: Nicole Arduini-Van Hoose. Provided by: Hudson Valley Community College.

Psychology 2e. Authored by: Rose M. Spielman, William J. Jenkins, Marilyn D. Lovett. Provided by: Open Stax. Retrieved from: https://openstax.org/books/psychology-2e. License: CC BY: Attribution

Theories of Motivation. Authored by: Nicole Arduini-Van Hoose. Provided by: Hudson Valley Community College. Retrieved from: . License: CC BY-NC-SA: Attribution-NonCommercial-ShareAlike

Educational Psychology. Authored by: Kelvin Seifert and Rosemary Sutton. Provided by: The Saylor Foundation. Retrieved from: https://courses.lumenlearning.com/educationalpsychology. License: CC BY: Attribution

Behaviorism and Motivation. Authored by: Nicole Arduini-Van Hoose. Provided by: Hudson Valley Community College. Retrieved from: https://courses.lumenlearning.com/edpsy/chapter/behaviorism-and-motivation/. License: CC BY-NC-SA: Attribution-NonCommercial-ShareAlike

Deficiency-Growth Theory: Maslow's Hierarchy of Needs. Authored by: Nicole Arduini-Van Hoose. Provided by: Hudson Valley Community College. Retrieved from: https://courses.lumenlearning.com/edpsy/chapter/deficiency-growth-theory/. License: CC BY-NC-SA: Attribution-NonCommercial-ShareAlike

Educational Psychology. Authored by: Gary D. Borich and Martin L. Tombari. License: CC BY: Attribution

Maslow's Hierarchy of Needs. Authored by: Chiquo. Provided by: Wikimedia Commons. Retrieved from: https://upload.wikimedia.org/wikipedia/commons/8/88/Maslow%27s_Hierarchy_of_Needs.jpg. License: CC BY-SA: Attribution-ShareAlike

Self-Determination Theory. Authored by: Nicole Arduini-Van Hoose. Provided by: Hudson Valley Community College. License: CC BY-NC-SA: Attribution-NonCommercial-ShareAlike

Educational Psychology. Authored by: Bohlin. License: CC BY: Attribution

Self-Efficacy Theory. Authored by: Nicole Arduini-Van Hoose. Provided by: Hudson Valley Community College. Retrieved from: https://courses.lumenlearning.com/edpsy/chapter/self-efficacy-theory/. License: CC BY-NC-SA: Attribution-NonCommercial-ShareAlike

Foundations of Educational Technology by Penny Thompson is licensed under a Creative Commons Attribution-NonCommercial 4.0 International License, except where otherwise noted.

Expectancy-Value Theory. Authored by: Nicole Arduini-Van Hoose. Provided by: Hudson Valley Community College. Retrieved from: https://courses.lumenlearning.com/edpsy/chapter/expectancy-value-theory/%20u200e. License: CC BY-NC-SA: Attribution-NonCommercial-ShareAlike

Attribution Theory. Authored by: Nicole Arduini-Van Hoose. Provided by: Hudson Valley Community College. Retrieved from: https://courses.lumenlearning.com/edpsy/chapter/attribution-theory/. License: CC BY-NC-SA: Attribution-NonCommercial-ShareAlike

Section on Learning Theories:

Source: *Learn to Learn*, https://www.oercommons.org/courseware/lesson/73880/overview?section=5

Personal Learning Preferences. Authored by: Laura Lucas, Heather Syrett, and Edgar Granillo. Provided by: Austin Community College. License: CC BY-NC-SA-4.0

Multiple Intelligences. Located at: https://courses.lumenlearning.com/educationalpsychology/chapter/multiple-intelligences/. License: CC BY: Attribution

Source: https://www.learning-theories.com/metacognition-flavell.html

Section on Emotional Intelligence:

Learning to Learn, https://www.oercommons.org/courseware/lesson/73880/overview?section=5

https://www.learning-theories.com/metacognition-flavell.html

Personal Learning Preferences. Authored by: Laura Lucas, Heather Syrett, and Edgar Granillo. Provided by: Austin Community College. License: CC BY-NC-SA-4.0

Chapter 6 Academic Skills Needed for Success in College

Figure 6.1 Student Taking Notes

Chapter Outline

Student Survey

On a scale of 1 (I need significant improvement) to 4 (I'm doing great), reflect on how you're doing right now on these statements:

1. _____ I am reading at a college level.
2. _____ I take good notes that help me study for exams.
3. _____ I understand how to manage all the reading I need to do for college.
4. _____ I recognize the need for different notetaking strategies for different college subjects.
5. _____ I set aside enough time to prepare for tests.
6. _____ I know what to do to prepare for tests.
7. _____ I know how to manage my test anxiety

Chapter Outcomes

In this chapter we will explore skills you probably think you already understand—reading, notetaking, effective study practices, and test-taking strategies. The goal is to make sure you have honed these skills well enough to lead you to success in college. By the time you finish this chapter, you should be able to do the following:

- Demonstrate the usefulness of strong reading and notetaking for college students.
- Outline the importance of memory when studying and note some opportunities to strengthen memory.
- Discuss specific ways to increase the effectiveness of studying by capitalizing on your strengths.
- Articulate test-taking strategies that minimize anxiety and maximize results.

6.1 Preparing to Read for Specific Disciplines in College

Question to consider:

- How can you best prepare to read for college?

Research supports the idea that reading is good for you. Students who read at or above reading level throughout elementary and secondary school have a higher chance of starting—and more importantly, finishing—college. Educational researchers convincingly claim that reading improves everything from grades to vocabulary.

If you do not particularly enjoy reading, don't despair. We read for a variety of reasons, and you may just have to step back and take a bigger picture of your reading habits to understand why you avoid engaging in this important skill. The myriad distractions we now face as well as the intense information overload we can suffer on a daily basis in all aspects of our lives can combine to make it difficult to slow down to read, an activity that demands at least a modicum of attention in a way that most television and music do not. You may need to adjust your schedule for more reading time, especially in college, because every class you take will expect you to read more pages than you probably have in the past.

Different disciplines in college may have specific expectations, but you can depend on all subjects asking you to read to some degree. In this college reading requirement, you can succeed by learning to read actively, researching the topic and author, and recognizing how your own preconceived notions affect your reading. Reading for college isn't the same as reading for pleasure or even just reading to learn something on your own because you are casually interested.

Allowing Adequate Time for Reading

You should determine the reading requirements and expectations for every class very early in the semester. You also need to understand why you are reading the particular text you are assigned. Do you need to read closely for minute details that determine cause and effect? Or is your instructor asking you to skim several sources so you become more familiar with the topic? Knowing this reasoning will help you decide your timing, what notes to take, and how best to undertake the reading assignment.

Figure 6.2 If you plan to make time for reading while you commute, remember that unexpected events like delays and cancellations could impact your concentration.

6.2 Effective Reading Strategies

Questions to consider:

- What is active reading?
- What are some strategies to use to help with active reading?
- What are the steps in the SQ3R reading strategy?

No universal law exists for how much reading instructors and institutions expect college students to undertake for various disciplines. Suffice it to say, it is a LOT. For most students, it is the volume of reading that catches them most off guard when they begin their college careers. A full course load might require 10–15 hours of reading per week, some of that covering content that will be more difficult than the reading for other courses.

You cannot possibly read word-for-word every single document you need to read for all your classes. That does not mean you give up or decide to only read for your favorite classes or concoct a scheme to read 17 percent for each class and see how that works for you. You need to learn to skim, annotate, and take notes. All of these techniques will help you comprehend more of what you read which is why we read in the first place.

Active Reading Strategies

Active reading differs significantly from skimming or reading for pleasure. You can think of active reading as a sort of conversation between you and the text.

When you sit down to determine what your different classes expect you to read and you create a reading schedule to ensure you complete all the reading, think about when you should read the material strategically, not just how to get it all done. You may also want to consider:

- Reading the textbook chapters and other reading assignments before you go into a lecture about that information. Don't wait to see how the lecture goes before you read the material, or you may not understand the information in the lecture. *Reading before class helps you put ideas together between your reading and the information you hear and discuss in class.*
- When scheduling your reading time, take into account that different disciplines have different types of texts. For example, you may look at a poem for your world literature class and assume that it will not take you long to read because it is relatively short compared to the dense textbook you have for your economics class. But reading and understanding a poem can take a considerable amount of time when you realize you may need to stop numerous times to review the separate word meanings and how the words form images and connections throughout the poem.

The SQ3R Reading Strategy

You may have heard of the SQ3R method for active reading in your early education. This valuable technique is perfect for college reading. The title stands for Survey, Question, Read, Recite, Review, and you can use the steps on virtually any assigned passage. Designed by Francis Pleasant Robinson in his 1961 book *Effective Study*, the active reading strategy gives readers a systematic way to work through any reading material.

Survey is similar to skimming. You look for clues to meaning by reading the titles, headings, introductions, summary, captions for graphics, and keywords. You can survey almost anything connected to the reading selection. In this step, you decide what the general meaning is for the reading selection.

Question is your creation of questions to seek the main ideas, support, examples, and conclusions of the reading selection. Try to create valid questions about what you are about to read that have come into your mind as you engaged in the Survey step. Try turning the headings of the sections in the chapter into questions. Next, how does what you are reading relate to you, your school, your community, and the world?

Read is when you actually read the passage. Try to find the answers to questions you developed in the previous step. When you finish reading the selection, stop to make notes. Answer the questions by writing a note in the margin, or other white space of the text .

You may also carefully underline or highlight text in addition to your notes. Use caution here that you do not try to rush this step by haphazardly circling terms or the other extreme of underlining huge chunks of text. Do not over-mark. You are not likely to remember what these cryptic marks mean later when you come back to use this active reading session to study. The text is the source of information—your marks and notes are just a way to organize and make sense of that information.

Recite means to speak out loud. By reciting, you are engaging other senses to remember the material—you read it (visual) and you said it (auditory). Stop reading momentarily to answer your questions or clarify confusing sentences or paragraphs. You can recite a summary of what the text means to you. If you are not in a place where you can verbalize, such as a library or classroom, you can accomplish this step adequately by saying it in your head. You may even want to try explaining the content to a friend. During this step, you can also write down the answers to your questions.

Review is a recap. Go back over what you read and add more notes, ensuring you have captured the main points of the passage, identified the supporting evidence and examples, and understood the overall meaning. You may need to repeat some or all the SQR3 steps during your review depending on the length and complexity of the material. Before you end your active reading session, write a short (no more than one page is optimal) summary of the text you read.

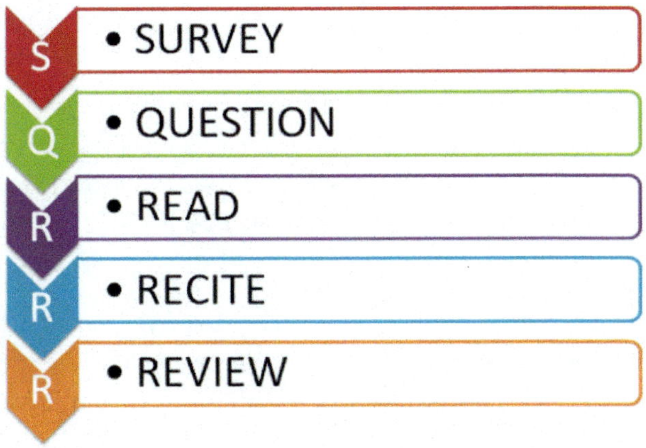

Figure 6.3 Source: https://klumbcomprehensionstrategies.weebly.com/sq3r.html

6.3 Learning Styles

Questions to consider:

- What are learning styles, and do they really work?
- How do I take advantage of learning styles in a way that works for me?
- How can I combine learning styles for better outcomes?
- What opportunities and resources are available for students with disabilities?

Several decades ago, a new way of thinking about learning became very prominent in education. It was based on the concept that each person has a preferred way to learn. It was thought that these preferences had to do with each person's natural tendencies toward one of their senses. The idea was that learning might be easier if a student sought out content that was specifically oriented to their favored sense. For example, it was thought that a student who preferred to learn visually would respond better to pictures and diagrams.

Over the years there were many variations on the basic idea, but one of the most popular theories was known as the VAK model. VAK was an acronym for the three types of learning, each linked to one of the basic senses thought to be used by students: visual, aural, and kinesthetic. What follows is an outline of each of these and the preferred method.

Visual: The student prefers pictures, images, and the graphic display of information to learn. An example would be looking at an illustration that showed how to do something.

Aural: The student prefers sound as a way to learn. Examples would be listening to a lecture or a podcast.

Kinesthetic: The student prefers using their body, hands, and sense of touch. An example would be doing something physical, such as examining an object rather than reading about it or looking at an illustration.

The Truth about Learning Styles

In many ways these ideas about learning styles made some sense. Because of this, educators encouraged students to find out about their own learning styles. They developed tests and other techniques to help students determine which particular sense they preferred to use for learning, and in some cases learning materials were produced in multiple ways that focused on each of the different senses. That way, each individual learner could participate in learning activities that were tailored to their specific preferences.

While it initially seemed that dividing everyone by learning styles provided a leap forward in education, continued research began to show that the fixation on this new model might not have been as effective as it was once thought. In fact, in some cases, the way learning styles were actually being used created roadblocks to learning. This was because the popularization of this new idea brought on a rush to use learning styles in ways that failed to take into account several important aspects that are listed below:

- A person does not always prefer the same learning style all the time or for each situation. For example, some learners might enjoy lectures during the day but prefer reading in the evenings. Or they may prefer looking at diagrams when learning about mechanics but prefer reading for history topics.
- There are more preferences involved in learning than just the three that became popular. These other preferences can become nearly impossible to make use of within certain styles. For example, some prefer to learn in a more social environment that includes interaction with other learners. Reading can be difficult or restrictive as a group effort. Recognized learning styles beyond the original three include: **social** (preferring to learn as a part of group activity), **solitary** (preferring to learn alone or using self-study), or **logical** (preferring to use logic, reasoning, etc.).

Knowing and Taking Advantage of Learning Styles in a Way That Works for You

The problem with relying on learning styles comes from thinking that just one defines your needs. Rather than being constrained by a single learning style or limiting your activities to a certain kind of media, you may choose the media that best fits your needs for what you are trying to learn at a particular time.

Following are a couple of ways you might combine your learning style preference with a given learning situation:

- You are trying to learn how to build something but find the written instructions confusing so you watch a video online that shows someone building the same thing.
- You have a long commute on the bus but reading while riding makes you dizzy. You choose an aural solution by listening to pre-recorded podcasts or a mobile device that reads your texts out loud.

These examples show that by recognizing and understanding what different learning styles have to offer, you can use the techniques that are best suited for you and that work best under the circumstances of the moment. You may also find yourself using two learning styles at the same time—as when you watch a live demonstration or video in which a person shows you how to do something while verbally explaining what you are being shown. This helps to reinforce the learning as it utilizes different aspects of your thinking. Using learning styles in an informed way can improve both the speed and the quality of your learning.

6.4 Studying

Questions to consider:

- How do you prepare yourself and your environment for successful studying?
- What study strategies will be most beneficial to you?
- Does your study space aid or distract you?

Preparing to Study

Studying is hard work, but you can still learn some techniques to help you be a more effective learner. Two major and interrelated techniques involve avoiding distractions to the best of your ability and creating a study environment that works to help you concentrate.

Avoiding Distractions

We have always had distractions—video games, television shows, movies, music, friends—even housecleaning can distract us from doing something else we need to do, like study for an exam. That may seem extreme, but sometimes vacuuming is the preferred activity to buckling down and working through calculus problems! Cell phones, tablets, and portable computers that literally bring a world of possibilities to us anywhere have brought distraction to an entirely new level. When was the last time you were with a large group of people when you didn't see at least a few people on devices?

Figure 6.4 Video games are a common distraction, but we need to be aware that even tedious activities like cleaning can be a distraction from studying.

When you study, your biggest challenge may be to block out all the competing noise. And letting go of that connection to our friends and the larger world, even for a short amount of time, can be difficult. Perhaps the least stressful way to allow yourself a distraction-free environment is to make the study session a definite amount of time: long enough to get a significant amount of studying accomplished but short enough to hold your attention.

When you prepare for your optimal study session, remember to do these things:

- Put your phone out of sight—in another room or at least some place where you will not see or hear it vibrate or ring. Just flipping it over is not enough.
- Turn off the television or music (more on that in the next section).
- Unless you are deliberately working with a study group, study somewhere alone if possible or at least far enough away from others to not hear them talking.

Study Environment

Sometimes you just need to plop down and study whenever and wherever you can manage—in the car waiting for someone, on the bus, at the Little League field as you cheer on your shortstop. And that's OK if this is the exception. For long-term success in studying, though, you need a better study setting that will help you get the most out of your limited study time. Whatever your space limitations, carve out a place that you can dedicate to reading, writing, note taking, and reviewing. What do you have now that you consider your study space? Is it set up for your optimal success?

If it is at all possible, try to make this area exclusive to your study sessions and something you can leave set up all the time and a place out of the way of family or roommate traffic. For example, Martina thought setting up her study station on the dining room table was a good idea at first. The view was calming, and the table was big enough to spread out and could even hold all her materials to study architectural drawings, her favorite subject. But then she needed the table for a small family dinner party, so she had to find a cubbyhole to hide away her supplies with some needing to go into a closet in the next room. Now she was spread out over multiple study spaces. And the family TV was in an adjacent room, not visible from the table but certainly an auditory distraction. Martina ultimately decided to forgo her view and create a smaller station in an unused bedroom so she could leave her supplies out and have a quieter area. You may have to try out numerous places to determine what works best for you.

Activity 6.1

Describe every element in your ideal study environment and explain why it's there as well as how it will make more efficient use of your time, limit distractions, or in some other way strengthen your ability to study.

After you have described your ideal study environment, think about how you can adapt that environment if you cannot be in your favorite place to study. How do you make your own space in the library, a student lounge, or a dedicated space on campus for student studying?

Debunking Study Myths

MYTH #1: You can multitask while studying.

How many times do you eat in the car? Watch TV while you write out a grocery list? Listen to music while you cook dinner? What about type an e-mail while you are on the phone with someone else and jot down notes about the call? The common term for this attempt to do more than one thing at a time is multitasking, and almost everyone does it at some point. The problem is that multitasking does not really work. Of course, it exists, and we do it. For instance, we walk and chew gum or drive and talk but we are not really thinking about two or more distinct things or doing multiple processes simultaneously.

MYTH #2: Highlighting main points of a text is useful.

Another myth of studying that seems to have a firm hold is that the idea of highlighting text—in and of itself—is the best way to review study material. It is one way, and you can get some benefit from it, but do not trick yourself into spending too much time on this surface activity and consider your study session complete. Annotating texts or notes is a first-step type of study practice. If you allow it to take up all your time, you think you are fully prepared for an exam because you put in the time. Actually, you need much more time reviewing and retrieving your lessons and ideas from the text or class lecture as well as quizzing yourself to accomplish your goal of learning so you can perform well on the exam. Highlighting is a task you can do rather easily, and it makes you feel good because you are actively engaging with your text, but true learning needs more steps.

MYTH #3: Studying effectively is effortless.

There is nothing effortless, or even pleasant at times, about studying. This is why so many students do not put in the time necessary to learn complex material: it takes time, effort, and, in some cases, a little drudgery. When done right, learning takes focus, deliberate strategies, and time. Think about a superstar athlete who puts in countless hours of drills and conditioning so that she makes her work on the field look easy.

Analysis Questions

When are you most liable to multitask? How could you be more aware of this practice and try to eliminate it, especially when it comes to studying? How can you make your initial text highlighting more time efficient so you can include other study practices?

6.5 Taking Notes

Questions to consider:

- How can you prepare to take notes to maximize the effectiveness of the experience?
- What are some specific strategies you can employ for better notetaking?
- Why is annotating your notes after the notetaking session a critical step to follow?

Strong notes build on your prior knowledge of a subject, help you discuss trends or patterns present in the information, and direct you toward areas needing further research or reading.

It is not a good habit to transcribe every single word a speaker utters—even if you have an amazing ability to do that. Most of us do not have that court-reporter-esque skill level anyway, and if we try, we will end up missing valuable information. Learn to listen for main ideas and distinguish between these main ideas and details that typically support the ideas. Include examples that explain the main ideas.

The act of taking notes does not necessarily make you a successful learner. It is what you do with the notes later that makes your notes effective. Take your lecture notes and combine them with your textbook notes (yes, you need to take notes on both the lecture and the textbook). Then take time to organize your notes using one of many different styles—use the style that appeals to you or is most effective for your purpose. Typically, students take linear notes during a lecture, line after line of notes. However, linear notes are not effective to use during study time. You need to repackage your notes, using your selected style or a combination of styles, and then use them when you study.

Think of all notes as potential study guides. In fact, if you only take notes without actively working on them after the initial notetaking session, the likelihood of the notes helping you is slim. Research on this topic concludes that without active engagement after taking notes, most students forget 60–75 percent of material over which they took the notes—within two days! That sort of defeats the purpose, don't you think? This information about memory loss was first brought to light by 19th-century German psychologist Hermann Ebbinghaus. Fortunately, you do have the power to thwart what is sometimes called the Ebbinghaus Forgetting Curve by reinforcing what you learned through review at intervals shortly after you take in the material and frequently thereafter.

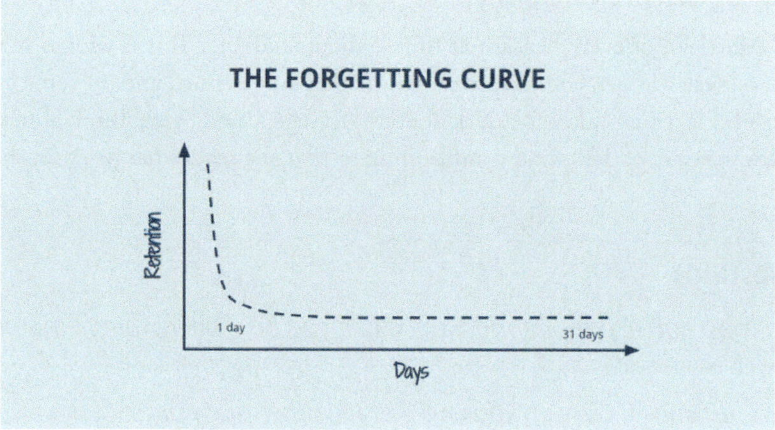

Figure 6.5 Ebbinghaus Forgetting Curve

The very best notes are the ones you take in an organized manner that encourages frequent review and use as you progress through a topic or course of study. For this reason, you need to develop a way to organize all your notes for each class so they remain together and organized. As old-fashioned as it sounds, a clunky three-ring binder is an excellent organizational container for class notes. You can easily add to previous notes, insert handouts you may receive in class, and maintain a running collection of materials for each separate course. If the idea of carrying around a heavy binder has you rolling your eyes, then transfer that same structure into your computer files. If you do not organize your many documents into some semblance of order on your computer, you will waste significant time searching for improperly named or saved files.

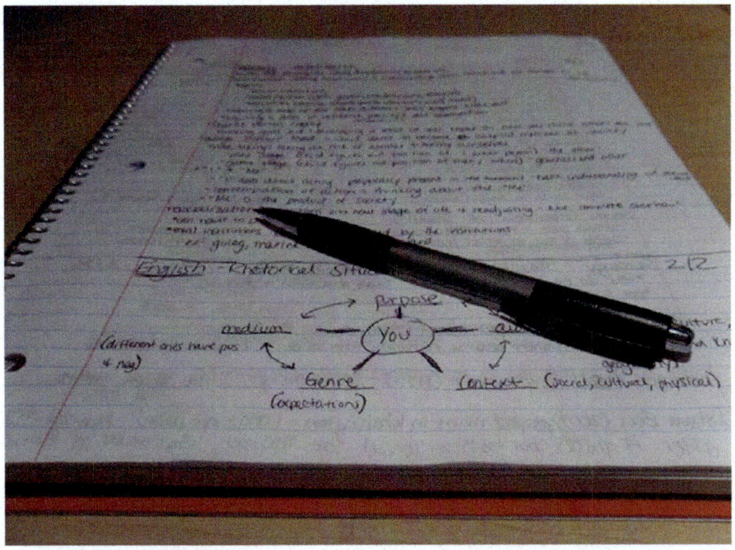

Figure 6.6 The best notes are the ones you take in an organized manner. Frequent review and further annotation are important to build a deep and useful understanding of the material.
(Credit: English106/Flickr/Attribution 2.0 Generic (CC-BY 2.0))

Notetaking Strategies

You may have a standard way you take all your notes for all your classes. When you were in high school, this one-size-fits-all approach may have worked. Now that you are in college, reading and studying more advanced topics, your general method may still work some of the time, but you should have some different strategies in place if you find that your method is not working as well with college content. You probably will need to adopt different notetaking strategies for different subjects. The strategies in this section represent various ways to take notes in such a way that you are able to study after the initial notetaking session.

Cornell Method

One of the most recognizable notetaking systems is called the Cornell Method, a relatively simple way to take effective notes devised by Cornell University education professor Dr. Walter Pauk in the 1940s. In this system, you take a standard piece of note paper and divide it into three sections by drawing a horizontal line across your paper about one to two inches from the bottom of the page (the summary area) and then drawing a vertical line to separate the rest of the page above this bottom area, making the left side about two inches (the recall column) and leaving the biggest area to the right of your vertical line (the notes column). You may want to make one page and then copy as many pages as you think you will need for any particular class, but one advantage of this system is that you can generate the sections quickly. The Cornell Method provides you with a well-organized set of notes that will help you study and review your notes as you move through the course. If you are taking notes on your computer, you can still use the Cornell Method in Word or Excel by creating your own or by using a template. See Appendix 6 for a blank form.

Now that you have the notetaking format generated, the beauty of the Cornell Method is its organized simplicity. Just write on one side of the page (the right-hand notes column)—this will help later when you are reviewing and revising your notes. During your notetaking session, use the notes column to record information over the main points and concepts of the lecture; try to put the ideas into your own words, which will help you not transcribe the speaker's words verbatim. Skip lines between each idea in this column. Avoid writing in complete sentences.

As soon as possible after your notetaking session, preferably within eight hours but no more than twenty-four hours, read over your notes column and fill in any details you missed in class, including the places where you indicated you wanted to expand your notes. Then in the recall column, write any key ideas from the corresponding notes column—just add the one- or two-word main ideas. These words in the recall column serve as cues to help you remember the detailed information you recorded in the notes column.

Once you are satisfied with your notes, summarize this page of notes in two or three sentences using the summary area at the bottom of the sheet. Now, before you move onto something else, cover the large notes column, and quiz yourself over the key ideas. Repeat this step often as you go along, not just immediately before an exam, and you will help your memory make the connections between your notes, your textbook reading, your in-class work, and assignments that you need to succeed on any quizzes and exams.

Academic Essay Elements	
Topic	**Topic** - Establishes context - Limits scope of essay - Introduces Issue/Problem
Thesis	**Thesis** - Central argument or point of paper - Arrives early in paper—usually toward end of first paragraph (maybe a bit later in longer papers) - Focused, clear, and specific - Reflects writer's position on the topic/issue
Supporting Details	**Supporting Detail Paragraphs** - Each paragraph has a specific topic - Clarify, explain, illustrate, expand on topic - Provide EVIDENCE—quotes, data, references Cite everything properly!
Conclusion	**Conclusion** - Tie back to intro/thesis - Show how details supported the argument - Why is it important? - Point to implications/outcomes, but don't introduce entirely new ideas
Use the structure, but don't follow it too rigidly. The most important pieces are a strong thesis and good evidence to back it up. The conclusion should not just summarize—take it a little further.	

Figure 6.7 This sample set of notes in the Cornell Method is designed to make sense of a large amount of information. The process of organizing the notes can help you retain the information more effectively than less consistent methods.

Outlining

Other note organizing systems may help you in different disciplines. You can take notes in a formal outline if you prefer, using Roman numerals for each new topic, moving down a line to capital letters indented a few spaces to the right for concepts related to the previous topic, then adding details to support the concepts indented a few more spaces over and denoted by an Arabic numeral.

You do not absolutely have to use the formal numerals and letters, but you have to be careful to indent so you can tell when you move from a higher-level topic to the related concepts and then to the supporting information. The main benefit of an outline is how organized it is.

The following formal outline example shows the basic pattern:

- I. Dogs (main topic–usually general)
  - A. German Shepherd (concept related to main topic)
    - i. Protection (supporting info about the concept)
    - ii. Assertive
    - iii. Loyal
  - B. Weimaraner (concept related to main topic)
    - i. Family-friendly (supporting info about the concept)
    - ii. Active
    - iii. Healthy
- II. Cats (main topic)
  - A. Siamese

Chart or Table

Similar to creating an outline, you can develop a chart to compare or contrast main ideas in a notetaking session. Divide your paper into four or five columns with headings that include either the main topics covered in the lecture or categories such as How, What, When, Advantages/Pros, Disadvantages/Cons, or other divisions of the information. You write your notes into the appropriate columns as that information comes to light in the presentation.

Table 6.1 Example of the Chart Notetaking Method

Example of a Chart to Organize Ideas and Categories				
	Structure	Types	Functions in Body	Additional Notes
Carbohydrates				
Lipids				
Proteins				
Nucleic Acid				

This format helps you pull out the salient ideas and establishes an organized set of notes to study later. (If you have not noticed that this reviewing later idea is a constant across all notetaking systems, you should . . . take note of that.) Notes by themselves that you never reference again are little more than scribblings. That would be a bit like compiling an extensive grocery list so you stay on budget when you shop, work all week on it, and then just throw it away before you get to the store. You may be able to recall a few items, but likely will not be as efficient as you could be if you had the notes to reference. Just as you cannot read all the many books, articles, and documents you need to peruse for your college classes, you cannot remember the most important ideas of all the notes you will take as part of your courses, so you must review.

Concept Mapping and Visual Notetaking

One final notetaking method that appeals to learners who prefer a visual representation of notes is called mapping or sometimes mind mapping or concept mapping, although each of these names can have slightly different uses. Variations of this method abound, so you may want to look for more versions online, but the basic principles are that you are making connections between main ideas through a graphic depiction; some can get rather elaborate with colors and shapes, but a simple version may be more useful at least to begin. Main ideas can be circled or placed in a box with supporting concepts radiating off these ideas shown with a connecting line and possibly details of the support further radiating off the concepts.

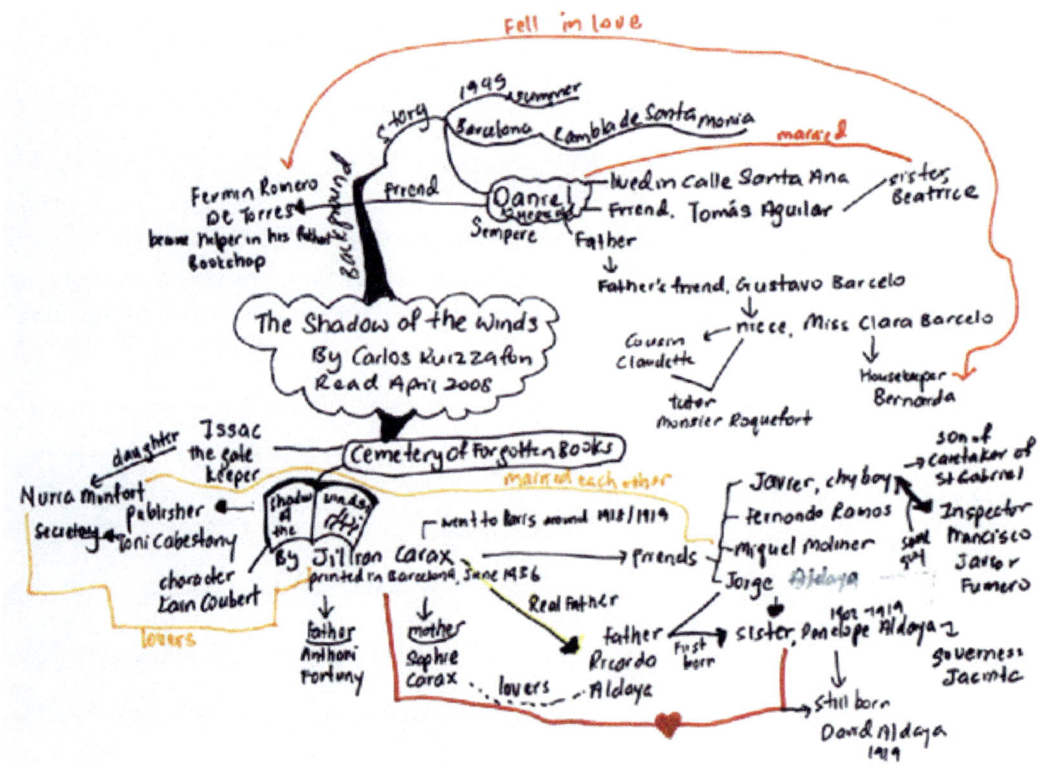

Figure 6.8 Concept mapping, sometimes referred to as mind mapping, can be an effective and very personalized approach to capturing information. (Credit: ArtistIvanChew/Flickr/Attribution 2.0 Generic (CC-BY 2.0))

You may be interested in trying visual notetaking or adding pictures to your notes for clarity. Sometimes when you cannot come up with the exact wording to explain something or you're trying to add information for complex ideas in your notes, sketching a rough image of the idea can help you remember. According to educator Sherrill Knezel in an article entitled "The Power of Visual Notetaking," this strategy is effective because "When students use images and text in notetaking, it gives them two different ways to pull up the information, doubling their chances of recall." Do not shy away from this creative approach to notetaking just because you believe you aren't an artist; the images do not need to be perfect. You may want to watch Rachel Smith's TEDx Talk called "Drawing in Class" to learn more about visual notetaking.

You can play with different types of notetaking suggestions and find the method(s) you like best, but once you find what works for you, stick with it. You will become more efficient with the method the more you use it, and your notetaking, review, and test prep will become, if not easier, certainly more organized, which can delete decrease your anxiety.

6.6 Memory

Questions to consider:

- How does working memory work, exactly?
- What is the difference between working and short-term memory?
- How does long-term memory function?
- What obstacles exist to remembering?

Memory is one of those cherished but mysterious elements in life. Everyone has memories, and some people are very good at rapid recall, which is an enviable skill for test takers. We know that we seem to lose the capacity to remember things as we age, and scientists continue to study how we remember some things but not others and what memory means, but we do not know that much about memory, really.

Nelson Cowan is one researcher who is working to explain what we do know about memory. His article "What Are the Differences between Long-Term, Short-Term, and Working Memory?" breaks down the different types of memory and what happens when we recall thoughts and ideas. When we remember something, we actually do quite a lot of thinking.[1]

We go through three basic steps when we remember ideas or images: we encode, store, and retrieve that information. Encoding is how we first perceive information through our senses, such as when we smell a lovely flower or a putrid trash bin. Both make an impression on our minds through our sense of smell and probably our vision. Our brains encode, or label, this content in short-term memory in case we want to think about it again.

If the information is important and we have frequent exposure to it, the brain will store it for us in case we need to use it in the future in our aptly named long-term memory. Later, the brain will allow us to recall or retrieve that image, feeling, or information so we can do something with it. This is what we call remembering.

Figure 6.9 Part of Memory Process.

1 NCBI. "What are the differences between long-term, short-term, and working memory?" https://www.ncbi.nlm.nih.gov/pmc/articles/PMC2657600/

Analysis Question

Take a few minutes to list ways you create memories on a daily basis. Do you think about how you make memories? Do you do anything that helps you keep track of your memories?

Foundations of Memory

William Sumrall et al. in the International Journal of Humanities and Social Science explain the foundation of memory by noting: "Memory is a term applied to numerous biological devices by which living organisms acquire, retain, and make use of skills and knowledge. It is present in all forms of higher order animals. The most evolutionary forms of memory have taken place in human beings. Despite much research and exploration, a complete understanding of human memory does not exist."[2]

Working Memory

Working memory is a type of short-term memory that we use when we are actively performing a task. For example, nursing student Marilyn needs to use her knowledge of chemical reactions to suggest appropriate prescriptions in various medical case studies. She does not have to recall every single fact she learned in years of chemistry classes, but she does need to have a working memory of certain chemicals and how they work with others. To ensure she can make these connections, Marilyn will have to review and study the relevant chemical details for the types of drug interactions she will recommend in the case studies.

In working memory, you have access to whatever information you have stored in your memory that helps you complete the task you are performing. For instance, when you begin to study an assignment, you certainly need to read the directions, but you must also remember that in class your professor reduced the number of problems the written instructions indicated you needed to finish. This was an oral addition to the written assignment. The change to the instructions is what you bring up in working memory when you complete the assignment.

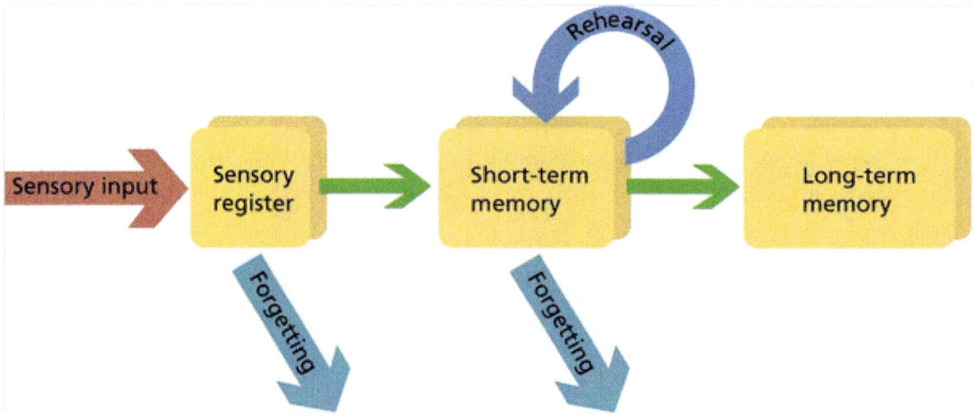

Figure 6.10 The Memory Process

2 Sumrall, William, et. al. "A Review of Memory Theory." *International Journal of Humanities and Social Science*, 2016. Vol. 6. No. 5.

Short-Term Memory

Short-term memory is a very handy thing. It helps us remember where we set our keys or where we left off on a project the day before. Think about all the aids we employ to help us with short-term memory: you may hang your keys in a particular place each evening, so you know exactly where they are supposed to be. When you go grocery shopping, do you ever choose a product because you recall an advertising jingle? If that memory causes you to buy that product, the advertising worked. We help our memory along all the time. In fact, we can modify these everyday examples of memory assistance for purposes of studying and test taking.

Activity 6.2

Consider this list of items. Look at the list for no more than 30 seconds. Then, cover up the list and use the spaces below to complete an activity.

Baseball	Picture frame	Tissue	Paper clip
Bread	Pair of dice	Fingernail polish	Spoon
Marble	Leaf	Doll	Scissors
Cup	Jar of sand	Deck of cards	Ring
Blanket	Ice	Marker	String

Without looking at the list, write down as many items as you can remember.

Now, look back at your list and make sure that you give yourself credit for any that you got right. Any items that you misremembered, meaning they were not in the original list, you won't count in your total. TOTAL ITEMS REMEMBERED ___________.

There were 20 total items. Did you remember between 5 and 9 items? If you did, then you have a typical short-term memory and you just participated in an experiment, of sorts, to prove it.

Harvard psychology professor George A. Miller in 1956 claimed humans can recall about five to nine (7 +/-2) bits of information in our short-term memory at any given time. Other research has come after this claim, but this concept is a popular one. Miller's article is entitled "The Magical Number Seven, Plus or Minus Two."[3]

Considering the vast amount of knowledge available to us, five to nine bits isn't very much to work with. To combat this limitation, we clump information together, making connections to help us stretch our capacity to remember. Many factors play into how much we can remember and how we do it, including the subject matter, how familiar we are with the ideas, and how interested we are in the topic, but we certainly cannot remember absolutely everything.

3 Miller, George A. "The Magical Number Seven, Plus or Minus Two: Some Limits on Our capacity for Processing Information." Psychological Review, 1956.

Activity 6.3

Now, let's revisit the items above. Go back to them and see if you can organize them in a way that you would have about five groups of items. See below for an example of how to group them.

Row 1: Items found in a kitchen

Row 2: Items that a child would play with

Row 3: Items of nature

Row 4: Items in a desk drawer/school supplies

Row 5: Items found in a bedroom

Cup	Spoon	Ice	Bread	
Baseball	Marble	Pair of dice	Doll	Deck of cards
Jar of sand	Leaf			
Marker	String	Scissors	Paper clip	
Ring	Picture frame	Fingernail polish	Tissue	Blanket

Now that you have grouped items into categories, also known as chunking, you can work on remembering the categories and the items that fit into those categories, which will result in remembering more items. Check it out below by covering up the list of items again and writing down what you can remember.

Look back at your list and make sure that you give yourself credit for any that you got right. Any items that you misremembered, meaning they were not in the original list, you won't count in your total. TOTAL ITEMS REMEMBERED ____________. Did you increase how many items you could remember?

Long-Term Memory

Long-term memory is exactly what it sounds like. These are things you recall from the past, such as the smell of your elementary school cafeteria or how to pop a wheelie on a bicycle. Our brain keeps a vast array of information, images, and sensory experiences in long-term memory. Whatever it is we are trying to keep in our memories, whether a beautiful song or a list of chemistry vocabulary terms, must first come into our brains in short-term memory. If we want these fleeting ideas to transfer into long-term memory, we must do some work, such as having frequent exposure to the information over time (such as studying the terms every day for a period or the repetition you performed to memorize multiplication tables or spelling rules).

According to Alison Preston of the University of Texas at Austin's Center for Learning and Memory, "A short-term memory's conversion to a long-term memory requires changes within the brain . . . and result[s] in changes to neurons (nerve cells) or sets of neurons. For example, new synapses—the connections between neurons through which they exchange information—can form to allow for communication between new networks of neurons. Alternatively, existing synapses can be strengthened to allow for increased sensitivity in the communication between two neurons."[4]

4 Preston, Alison. "Ask the Experts: How do short-term memories become long-term memories?" *Scientific American*, Dec. 2017. https://www.scientificamerican.com/article/how-do-short-term-memories-become-l/

We learn the lyrics of a favorite song by singing and/or playing the song over and over. That alone may not be enough to get that song into the coveted long-term memory area of our brain, but if we have an emotional connection to the song, such as a painful breakup or a life-changing proposal that occurred while we were listening to the song, this may help. Think of ways to make your study session memorable and create connections with the information you need to study. That way, you have a better chance of keeping your study material in your memory so you can access it whenever you need it.

Analysis Questions

What are some ways you convert short-term memories into long-term memories? Do your memorization strategies differ for specific courses (e.g., how you remember for math or history)?

Obstacles to Remembering

If remembering things we need to know for exams or for learning new disciplines were easy, no one would have problems with it, but students face several significant obstacles to remembering, including a persistent lack of sleep and an unrealistic reliance on cramming. Life is busy and stressful for all students, so you have to keep practicing strategies to help you study and remember successfully, but you also must be mindful of obstacles to remembering.

Lack of Sleep

Let's face it, sleep and college do not always go well together. You have so much to do! All that reading, all those papers, all those extra hours in the science lab or tutoring center or library! And then we have the social and emotional aspects of going to school. When you consider everything you need to attend to in college, you probably will not be surprised that sleep is often the first thing we give up as we search for more time to accomplish everything we are trying to do. That seems reasonable—just wake up an hour earlier or stay up a little later. But you may want to reconsider picking away at your precious sleep time.

If you cannot focus well because you did not get enough sleep, then you likely will not be able to remember whatever it is you need to recall for any sort of studying or test-taking situation. Most exams in a college setting go beyond simple memorization, but you still have a lot to remember for exams. For example, when Saanvi sits down to take an exam on introductory biology, she needs to recall all the subject-specific vocabulary she read in the textbook's opening chapters, the general connections she made between biological studies and other scientific fields, and any biology details introduced in the unit for which she is taking the exam.

Trying to make these mental connections on too little sleep will take a large mental toll because Saanvi has to concentrate even harder than she would with adequate sleep. She is not merely tired; her brain is not refreshed and primed to conduct difficult tasks. Although not an exact comparison, think about when you overtax a computer by opening too many programs simultaneously. Sometimes the programs are sluggish or slow to respond. Your body is a bit like that on too little sleep.

On the flip side, though, your brain on adequate sleep is amazing, and sleep can actually assist you in making connections, remembering difficult concepts, and studying for exams. The exact reasons for this are still a serious research project for scientists, but the results all point to a solid connection between sleep and cognitive performance.

Analysis Questions

How long do you sleep every night on average? Do you see a change in your ability to function when you haven't had enough sleep? What could you do to limit the number of nights with too little sleep?

Downside of Cramming

At least once in their college careers, most students will experience the well-known pastime called cramming. See if any of this is familiar: Shelley has lots of classes, works part-time at a popular restaurant, and is just amazingly busy, so she puts off serious study sessions day after day. She is not worried because she has set aside time she would have spent sleeping to cram just before the exam. That is the idea anyway. Originally, she planned to stay up a little late and study for four hours from 10 p.m. to 2 a.m. and still get several hours of refreshing sleep. But it is Dolphin Week or Beat State Day or whatever else comes up, and her study session does not start until midnight—she will pull an all-nighter. So, two hours after her original start time, she tries to cram all the lessons, problems, and information from the last two weeks of lessons into this one session. Shelley falls asleep around 3 a.m. with her notes and books still on her bed. After her late night, she does not sleep well and goes into the morning exam tired. Shelley does OK but not great on the exam, and she is not pleased with her results. More and more research indicate that the stress Shelley has put on her body doing this, combined with the way our brains work, makes cramming a seriously poor choice for learning.

Your brain simply refuses to cooperate with cramming—it sounds like a good idea, but it does not work. Cramming causes stress, which can lead to paralyzing test anxiety; it erroneously supposes you can remember and understand something fully after only minimal exposure; and it overloads your brain, which, however amazing it is, can only focus on one concept at a time and a limited number of concepts.

Leading neuroscientist John Medina claims that the brain begins to wander at about 10 minutes, at which point you need a new stimulus to spark interest.[5] That does not mean you cannot focus for longer than 10 minutes; you just need to switch gears a lot to keep your brain engaged. Have you ever heard a speaker drone on about one concept for, say, 30 minutes without somehow changing pace to engage the listeners? It does not take much to re-engage—pausing to ask the listeners questions or moving to a different location in the room will do it—but without these subtle attention markers, listeners start thinking of something else. The same thing happens to you if you try to cram all reading, problem-solving, and note reviewing into one long session; your brain will wander.

6.7 Strengthening Your Memory

Question to consider:

- What strategies help us remember and learn information best?

We have discussed the importance of zeroing in on the main concepts you learn in class and of transferring them from short-term to long-term memory. But how can you work to strengthen your overall memory?

5 Medina, John. *Brain Rules*. 2018, Pear Press.

Some people have stronger memories than others, but memorizing new information takes work for anyone. Below are some strategies that can aid memory.

Rehearsal

One strategy is rehearsal, or the conscious repetition of information to be remembered (Craik & Watkins, 1973). This strategy is linked to studying material frequently for shorter periods of time. You may not remember when or how you learned skills like riding a bike or tying your shoes. Mastery came with practice, and at some point, the skills became second nature. Academic learning is no different: if you spend enough time with important course concepts and practice them often, you will know them in the same way you know how to ride a bike, almost without thinking about them. For example, think about how you learned your multiplication tables. You may recall that 6 x 6 = 36, 6 x 7 = 42, and 6 x 8 = 48. Memorizing these facts is rehearsal.

Incorporate Visuals

Visual aids like note cards, concept maps, and highlighted text are ways of making information stand out. Because they are shorter and more concise, they have the advantage of making the information to be memorized seem more manageable and less daunting (than an entire textbook chapter, for example). Some students write key terms on note cards and hang them around their desk or mirror so that they routinely see them and study them without even trying.

Create Mnemonics

Memory devices known as mnemonics can help you retain information while only needing to remember a unique phrase or letter pattern that stands out. Mnemonic devices are memory aids that help us organize information for encoding. They are especially useful when we want to recall larger bits of information such as steps, stages, phases, and parts of a system (Bellezza, 1981).

There are different types of mnemonic devices, such as the acronym. An *acronym* is a word formed by the first letter of each of the words you want to remember. For example, even if you live near one, you might have difficulty recalling the names of all five Great Lakes. What if I told you to think of the word Homes? HOMES is an acronym that represents Huron, Ontario, Michigan, Erie, and Superior: the five Great Lakes.

Another type of mnemonic device is an *acrostic*: you make a phrase of all the first letters of the words. For example, if you are taking a math test and you are having difficulty remembering the order of operations, recalling the sentence "Please Excuse My Dear Aunt Sally" will help you, because the order of mathematical operations is Parentheses, Exponents, Multiplication, Division, Addition, Subtraction. There also are *jingles*, which are rhyming tunes that contain keywords related to the concept, such as "i before e, except after c."

Analysis Questions

Do you have other mnemonics that help you remember difficult material? What are they? How have they helped you with remembering important things?

Chunking

Another strategy is chunking, where you organize information into manageable bits or chunks (Bodie, Powers, & Fitch-Hauser, 2006). Chunking is useful when trying to remember information like dates and phone numbers. Instead of trying to remember 5205550467, you remember the number as 520-555-0467. So, if you met an interesting person at a party and you wanted to remember his phone number, you would naturally chunk it, and you could repeat the number over and over, combining the strategies of chunking and rehearsal.

Connect New Information to Old Information

Take stock of what you already know—information that is already stored in long-term memory—and use it as a foundation for learning newer information. It is easier to remember new information if you can connect it to old information or to a familiar frame of reference. For example, if you are taking a sociology class and are learning about different types of social groups, you may be able to think of examples from your own experiences that relate to the different types.

6.8 Test Taking and Test Anxiety

Questions to consider:

- What are the differences between test prep and taking the actual test?
- What can you do on test day to increase your confidence and success?
- What should you know about test anxiety?

Once you are practicing good study habits, you will be better prepared for actual test taking. Since studying and test taking are both part of learning, honing your skills in one will help you in the other.

Probably the most obvious differences between your preparation for an exam and the actual test itself are your level of urgency and the time constraints. A slight elevation in your stress level can be OK for testing—it keeps you focused and on your game when you need to bring up all the information, thinking, and studying to show what you have learned. Properly executed, test preparation mixed in with a bit of stress can significantly improve your actual test-taking experience.

Preparation versus Actual Test

You can replicate the effective sense of urgency an actual test produces by including timed writing into your study sessions. You don't need all of your study time to exactly replicate the test, but you would be well served to find out the format of the exam in advance and practice the skills you'll need to use for the various test components. On one early exam in history, Stuart learned the prof was going to include several short-answer essay questions—one for each year of the time period covered. Stuart set up practice times to write for about 15 to 20 minutes on significant events from his notes because he estimated that would be about how much time he could devote out of the hour-long testing session to write one or two required short-answer questions. He would write a prompt from his notes, set a timer, and start writing. If you are ready and you have practiced and know the material, 20 minutes is adequate to prepare, draft, and revise a short response.

Likewise, in a math exam, you will need to know what kinds of problems you will have to solve and to what extent you will need to show your computational work on the exam. If you are able to incorporate this sort of timed problem-solving into your study time, you will be more prepared and confident when you actually come to the exam. Making yourself adhere to a timed session during your study can help. It puts a sense of urgency on you, and it will help you to find out what types of problems you need to practice.

Leveraging Study Habits for Test Prep

In your mind, you probably know what you need to do to be prepared for tests. Occasionally, something may surprise you, like an emphasis on a concept you considered unimportant or a different presentation of a familiar problem. But those should be exceptions. You can take all your well-honed study habits to get ready for exams. Here is a checklist for study and test success for your consideration:

Figure 6.11 Study Habits for Test Preparation

Read this list with each separate class in mind and check off the items you already do. If you always take the success steps—congratulations! They are not a guarantee, but doing the steps mindfully will give you a nice head start.

Establishing Realistic Expectations for Test Situations

Would you expect to make a perfect pastry if you have never learned how to bake? Or paint a masterpiece if you've never tried to work with paints and brushes? Probably not. But often we expect ourselves to perform at much higher levels of achievement than that for which we have actually prepared.

Realistic continuous improvement is a better plan because people who repeatedly attempt challenges for which they have not adequately prepared and understandably fail often start moving toward the goal in frustration or they simply quit. This does not mean you settle for mediocre grades or refrain from your challenges. It means you become increasingly aware of yourself and your current state and potential future. Know yourself, know your strengths and weaknesses, and be honest with yourself about your expectations.

Prioritizing Time Surrounding Test Situations

Keep in mind that you do not have any more or less time than anyone else. You can only use the time everyone gets wisely and realistically. Exams in college classes are important, but they are not the only significant events you have in your classes. In fact, everything leading up to the exam, the exam itself, and the post-exam activities are all one large continuum.

If your instructor conducts some sort of pre-exam summary or prep session, make sure to attend. These can be invaluable. If this instructor does not provide that sort of formal exam prep, create your own with a group of classmates or on your own.

Strategies on Test Day and After

Test Day

Once you get to the exam session, try your best to focus on nothing but the exam. This can be very difficult with all the distractions in our lives.

Arriving to Class

Do not let yourself be sidetracked right at the end. Beyond the preparation we have discussed, give yourself some more advantages on the actual test day:

- Get to the testing location a few minutes early so you can settle into your place and take a few relaxing breaths.
- Do not let other classmates interrupt your calmness at this point.
- Just get to your designated place, take out whatever supplies and materials you are allowed to have, take a few deep breaths, and calm your mind.

Taking the Test

Once the instructor begins the test:

- Listen carefully for any last-minute oral directions that may have changed some detail on the exam, such as the timing or the content of the questions.
- As soon as you receive the exam sheet or packet, make a quick scan over the entire test.
- Do not spend a lot of time on this initial glance, but make sure you are familiar with the layout and what you need to do.

- Using this first review, decide how you will allocate your available time for each section.
- Then for each section be sure you read the section directions very carefully so you do not miss an important detail.
- Answer every required question on the exam. Even if you do not complete each one, you may receive some credit for partial answers.
- Read the entire question carefully if you think you know what the stem (the introduction of the choices) says and read all the choices.
- Skip really difficult questions or ones where your brain goes blank. Then you can go back and concentrate on those skipped ones later after you have answered the majority of the questions confidently. Sometimes a later question will trigger an idea in your mind that will help you answer the skipped questions.
- Allow yourself a few minutes at the end of the exam to review your answers. Make sure you have completed the entire test.

After the Test

As you leave the exam room, the last thing you may want to think about is the test. You probably have numerous other assignments, projects, and life obligations to attend to, especially if you pushed some of those off to study for this completed exam. Give yourself some space from this exam, but only for the duration of the time when your instructor is grading your exam. Once you have your results, study them—whether you did really well (Go, you!) or not as well as you had hoped (Keep your spirits up!). Both scenarios hold valuable information if you will use it.

When you receive your grade:

- Reflect upon what you did to get ready for the test.
- If you received a good grade, remember what you did to prepare for the test so that you can replicate your actions for future tests.
- If you were not satisfied with your test score, what do you need to change? Study strategies, effort, amount of time spent studying, etc.

Test Anxiety

Figure 6.12 Text anxiety can be a common occurrence, but you can use strategies to manage it.

Test anxiety is very real. You may know this firsthand. Almost everyone gets a little nervous before a major exam, in the same way most people get slightly anxious meeting a new potential date or undertaking an unfamiliar activity. And in most situations, testing included, that reasonable level of nervous anticipation can be a good thing—enhancing your focus and providing you with a bit of bravado to get you through a difficult time.

Test anxiety, however, can cause us to doubt ourselves so severely that we underperform or overcompensate to the point that we do not do well on the exam. Do not despair; you can still succeed if you suffer from test anxiety. The first step is to understand what it is and what it is not, and then to practice some simple strategies to cope with your anxious feelings relative to test taking. Whatever you do, do not use the label "test anxiety' to keep you from your dreams of completing your education and pursuing whatever career you have your eyes on. You are bigger than any anxiety.

Using Strategies to Manage Test Anxiety

You need to work hard to control test anxiety so it does not take an unhealthy hold on you every time you face a test situation. One of the best ways to control test anxiety is to be prepared for the exam. You can control that part. You can also learn effective relaxation techniques including controlled breathing, visualization, and meditation. Some of these practices work well even in the moment: at your test site, take a deep breath, close your eyes, and smile—just bringing positive thoughts into your mind can help you meet the challenges of taking an exam without anxiety taking over.

Summary

In this chapter, we learned that reading and notetaking are major elements of college studying and learning. The expectation in college is that you read considerable amounts of text for each subject. You may encounter reading situations, such as professional journal articles and long textbook chapters, that are more difficult to understand than texts you have read previously. As you progress through your college courses, you can employ reading strategies to help you complete your college reading assignments. Likewise, you will take notes in college that need to be complete so you can study and recall the information you learn in lectures and lab sessions. With so much significant information that you need to collect, study, and recall for your college courses, you need to be deliberate in your reading and notetaking. Also, studying and taking tests will always be a large part of college, so learning now to do these well can only help you be more successful. Experts provide us with many tools, techniques, and ideas to use when we determine how best to study, use our memories effectively, and prepare to take exams. You can help yourself by taking these guidelines seriously and tracking your progress. If one strategy works better for you in some classes and another is more suited to a different course, keep that in mind when you begin to study. Use all the resources available to you, and you will be well on your way to success in college.

References

Abel, M., and Bäuml, K.-H. T. (2013). Sleep can reduce proactive interference. *Memory, 22*(4), 332–339. doi:10.1080/09658211.2013.785570. Retrieved from http://www.psychologie.uni-regensburg.de/Baeuml/papers_in_press/sleepPI.pdf

Bellezza, F. S. (1981). Mnemonic devices: Classification, characteristics and criteria. *Review of Educational Research, 51*, 247–275.

Bodie, G. D., Powers, W. G., and Fitch-Hauser, M. (2006). Chunking, priming, and active learning: Toward an innovative approach to teaching communication-related skills. *Interactive Learning Environment, 14*(2), 119–135.

Craik, F. I. M., and Watkins, M. J. (1973). The role of rehearsal in short-term memory. *Journal of Verbal Learning and Verbal Behavior, 12*, 599–607.

Learning to Learn, https://www.oercommons.org/courseware/lesson/73880/overview?section=4

Chapter 7 Personal and Financial Wellness

Figure 7.1 Financial success depends on getting a good start and avoiding setbacks and wrong turns. It's a lifelong process, more like a marathon than a sprint. (Credit: Bengt Nyman/Flickr/Attribution 2.0 Generic (CC-BY 2.0))

Chapter Outline

Student Survey

How do you feel about health and wellness? How financially literate are you? These questions will help you determine how the chapter concepts relate to you right now. As we are introduced to new concepts and practices, it can be informative to reflect on how your understanding changes over time. Take this quick survey, ranking questions on a scale of 1–4, 1 meaning "least like me" and 4 meaning "most like me."

1. _____ I take the steps to eat healthily most days of the week.
2. _____ I get enough sleep.
3. _____ I feel like I know how to manage stress.
4. _____ I actively and regularly plan and/or monitor my finances.
5. _____ I understand the benefits and risks of credit.
6. _____ I regularly take steps to protect my identity and assets.

Chapter Outcomes

This chapter explores the many ways your health is impacted by your lifestyle choices. In this chapter, you also will learn to reach your personal life goals by implementing financial planning and strategies to protect yourself, manage your money today, and put yourself in a better position for tomorrow. How you act today impacts your tomorrow.

The goal of this material is to help you do the following:

- Describe actions you can take to improve your physical health.
- Identify ways to maintain and enhance your emotional health.
- Identify mental health risks and warning signs.
- Create a saving and spending plan and track your performance.
- Identify best practices and risks associated with credit cards and other debt.
- Determine the best opportunities for you to finance your college education.
- Articulate specific ways to secure your identity and accounts.

7.1 Taking Care of Your Physical Health

Questions to consider:

- What is healthy eating?
- Why is it important to stay hydrated?
- How important is exercise to a healthy body?
- Are you getting enough sleep to be healthy?
- What are toxins, and how can they affect your health?

You have one body. Treat it well so as to maximize our ability to serve you throughout your life. Often physical health gets moved to the bottom of the priority list when we are busy. Taking care of your physical health doesn't mean six-pack abs or training for a marathon. It means honoring your physical needs so your body can function properly, feeding your cells the nutrients that will keep your body working well your entire life, and minimizing exposure to toxins to reduce your risk of disease.

Healthy Eating

While it's not the only thing that contributes to great health, what you eat makes a huge difference. We have 37 trillion cells in our body. The only way they function optimally is with good nutrition. As a college student, you will be surrounded by temptations to eat poorly or even to overeat. It's now up to you to make wise choices in the face of these temptations. Your cafeteria is likely full of many healthy foods and just as many unhealthy foods. You may grab food on the run while racing to class or order a pizza at midnight while studying for a test. Lobby vending machines or a stash of snacks in your room should not turn into a substitute for real meals. The downside of fast food and easy access treats is that many are loaded with sugar, salt, or both.

There are five different food groups considered the building blocks for a healthy diet—vegetables, fruits, protein, grains, and dairy. It's also important to know what is not a healthy plate. A healthy plate is low in refined carbohydrates (donuts, pastries, pasta, cookies), low in sugar, and low in saturated fat (although we need healthy fats like avocado and nuts).

Nutritionists at Harvard created The Healthy Eating Plate, which is based on what they consider to be the best available science. Half the plate is vegetables and fruit. Aim for eight servings of veggies or fruits a day, more veggies than fruits.

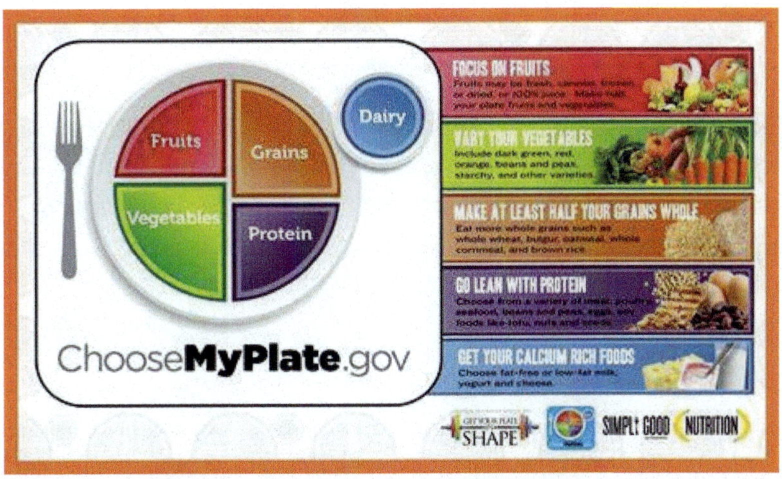

Figure 7.2 The USDA recommends that vegetables and fruits make up the largest portions of your diet, and dairy the smallest portion. (Credit: USDA / Public Domain)

What You Drink

What is your go-to drink when you are thirsty? Soda? Juice? Coffee? How about water? Most of your blood and every cell in your body is composed of water. In fact, water makes up 60 to 80 percent of our entire body mass, so when we don't consume enough water, all kinds of complications can occur. To function properly, all the cells and organs in our body need water. Just like plants need food and water to thrive, we need to be well-hydrated and nourished to feel our best. Proper hydration is key to overall health and well-being. By the time you feel thirsty, you are already dehydrated. Dehydration is when your body does not have as much water and fluids as it needs. Researchers at Virginia Polytechnic discovered that mild dehydration (as little as losing 1 to 2 percent of body water) can impair cognitive performance.[1] Water increases energy and relieves fatigue, promotes weight loss, flushes toxins, improves skin complexion, improves digestion, and is a natural headache remedy (your brain is 76 percent water). Headaches, migraines, and back pains are commonly caused by dehydration. Your body will also let you know it needs water by messaging through muscle cramps, achy joints, constipation, dry skin, and of course a dry mouth.

Staying hydrated is important to keep your body healthy, energized, and running properly. As a general guideline, aim to drink eight glasses of water a day, although a more helpful guide is to drink half your body weight in ounces (for example, if you weigh 150 lb, try to drink 75 oz of water a day). One of the best ways to remind yourself to drink throughout the day is to buy a reusable bottle and bring it everywhere you go.

Exercise

Many people exercise to maintain or lose weight, but weight loss is only one potential benefit of exercise. Regular exercise can improve the quality of your sleep, strengthen your bones, increase your energy levels, and reduce your risk of high blood pressure, diabetes, and even some forms of cancer.[2] Regular exercise is key to living a long, healthy life.

Generally, aim to do:

- 30 minutes of moderate-intensity cardio activity at least five days per week (150 minutes per week)
- At least 25 minutes of vigorous aerobic activity three days per week (75 minutes per week)[3]

Exercise also has many positive benefits for your mental health. It reduces your stress level and helps manage anxiety. Students at San Antonio College have access to the Candler Physical Education Building, which has open gym hours. Students can stay active by joining intramural sports or enrolling in kinesiology classes.

7.2 Sleep

Questions to consider:

- How much sleep is enough?
- What are the impacts of sleep deprivation?
- Which strategies and support can enhance sleep?

How often do you wake up filled with energy, eager to embrace the day? How often do you wake up still tired, with heavy eyes that just don't want to open? Your answer to these questions has a direct bearing on the quality of your decisions, your ability to use good judgment, the extent to which you can focus in the classroom, and ultimately your long-term health.

A great night's sleep begins the minute you wake up. The choices you make throughout the day impact how quickly you fall asleep, whether you sleep soundly, and whether your body can successfully complete the cycle of critical functions that only happen while you sleep.

---

1 University of Virginia https://www.ncbi.nlm.nih.gov/pmc/articles/PMC4207053/

2 7 Harvard Medical School https://www.health.harvard.edu/newsletter_article/Exercise_as_medicine

3 https://www.healthline.com/health/how-often-should-you-work-out

Sleep is the foundation of amazing health, yet almost 40 percent of adults struggle to get enough sleep.[4] Lack of sleep affects mental and physical performance and can make you more irritable. The diminished energy that results from too little sleep often leads us to make poor decisions about most things, including food. Think about the last time you were really tired. Did you crave pizza, donuts, and fries—or a healthy salad? Studies have shown that people who sleep less are more likely to eat fewer vegetables and eat more fats and refined carbohydrates, like donuts.[5]

With sufficient sleep it is easier to learn, to remember what you learned, and to have the necessary energy to make the most of your college experience. Without sufficient sleep it is harder to learn, to remember what you learned, and to have the energy to make the most of your college experience. It's that simple.

What Happens When We Sleep?

Sleep is a time when our bodies are quite busy repairing and detoxifying. While we sleep we fix damaged tissue, toxins are processed and eliminated, hormones essential for growth and appetite control are released and restocked, and energy is restored. Sleep is essential for a healthy immune system. How many colds do you catch a year? How often do you get the flu? If you are often sick, you do not have a healthy immune system, and sleep deprivation may be a key culprit.

A review of hundreds of sleep studies concluded that most adults need around eight hours of sleep to maintain good health. Some people may be able to function quite well on seven and others may need closer to nine, but as a general rule, most people need a solid eight hours of sleep each night. And when it comes to sleep, both quantity and quality are important. When sleep is cut short, the body doesn't have time to complete all the phases needed for the repair and detoxification.

If you are watching TV until the minute you go to bed and then sleep with the artificial light from smartphones and other devices, your brain is tricked into thinking it is still daylight. In addition, if the TV shows you watch before bed are violent or action-packed, your body will release cortisol (the stress hormone). Anything that creates stress close to bedtime will make it more difficult to fall asleep. A bedtime practice of quiet activities like reading, journaling, listening to music, or meditation will make it much easier to fall asleep.

What Happens If You Don't Get Enough Sleep?

Lack of sleep has a big impact on your overall state of health and well-being. Studies have linked poor sleep to a variety of health problems. The U.S. Centers for Disease Control and Prevention have identified sleep deprivation as a public health epidemic.

4 https://news.gallup.com/poll/166553/less-recommended-amount-sleep.aspx

5 Cleveland Clinic, https://health.clevelandclinic.org/lack-sleep-make-crave-junk-food/

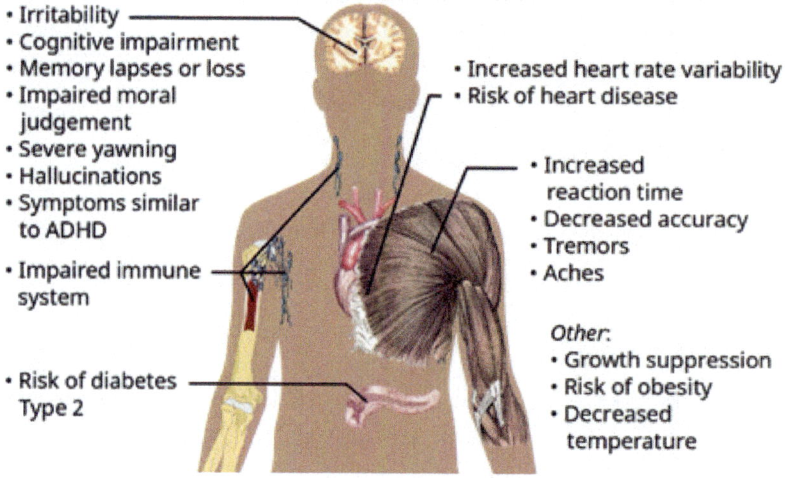

Figure 7.3 The Effects of Sleep Deprivation. This visual depicts many of the ways we are affected by insufficient sleep. (Credit: Häggström, Mikael (2014). "Medical gallery of Mikael Häggström 2014". WikiJournal of Medicine. Public Domain.)

Some of the health risks of insufficient sleep include the following:

- Increased risk of heart attack and stroke.[6]
- Impaired cognitive function: Even one night of sleeping less than six hours can impact your ability to think clearly the next day.
- Increased risk of accidents: Sleep deprivation slows your reaction time, which increases your risk of accidents. You are three times more likely to be in a car crash if you are tired. According to the American Sleep Foundation, 40 percent of people admitted to falling asleep behind the wheel at least once. A Governor's Highway Safety Association report estimates there are 6,400 fatal drowsy driving crashes each year. Fifty percent of these crashes involve drivers under the age of 25.[7]
- Weight gain/increased risk for obesity: Sleep helps balance your appetite by regulating hormones that play a role in helping you feel full after a meal. Also, cortisol is released during times of anxiety, and exhaustion causes your body to produce more cortisol. This can stimulate your appetite.
- Increased risk of cancer: Tumors grow up to three times faster in laboratory animals with severe sleep dysfunctions. Researchers believe this is because of disrupted melatonin production, as melatonin has both antioxidant and anticancer activity.
- Increased emotional intensity: The part of the brain responsible for emotional reactions, your amygdala, can be 60 percent more reactive when you've slept poorly, resulting in increased emotional intensity.

6 Matthew Walker, PhD Why We Sleep

7 Governors Highway Safety Association

Tips to Improve the Quality of Your Sleep

Now that you are more aware of the ways insufficient sleep harms your body, let's review some of the things you can do to enhance your sleep.

- Make sleep a priority. It can be challenging in college but try to get on a schedule where you sleep and wake at the same time every day to get your body accustomed to a routine.
- Sleep in a cool, quiet, dark room. Create a sleeping environment that is comfortable and conducive to sleep. If you can control the temperature in your room, keep it cool in the evening.
- Avoid eating late or drinking alcohol or caffeine close to bedtime. A 2013 Scientific Research study concluded that "energy drinks, other caffeinated beverages and alcoholic beverages are risk factors of poor sleep quality." It is important to finish eating hours before bedtime so your body can heal and detoxify so it is not spending the first few hours of sleep digesting a heavy meal.
- Start to wind down an hour before bed. There are great apps to help with relaxation, stress release, and falling asleep.
- Exercise for 30 minutes a day. One of the biggest benefits of exercise is its effect on sleep. Walking, yoga, swimming, strength training, jumping rope—whatever it is, find an exercise you like and make sure to move your body every day.
- Improve your diet. Low fiber and high saturated fat and sugar intake is associated with lighter, less restorative sleep with more wake time during the night. Processed food full of chemicals will make your body work extra hard during the night to remove the toxins and leave less time for healing and repair.

Sleep affects how we look, feel, and function on a daily basis and is vital to our health and quality of life. When you get the sleep your body needs, you look more vibrant, you feel more vibrant, and you have the energy to live your best life.

7.3 Taking Care of Your Emotional Health

Questions to consider:

- What are some of the ways to tell if you are holding onto stress?
- How do mindfulness and gratitude encourage emotional health?

Identifying and Managing Stress

According to a 2018 report from the American College Health Association, in a 12-month period 42 percent of college students reported that they have felt so depressed it was difficult to function, and 63 percent reported feeling overwhelming anxiety.[8] Your ability to manage stress, maintain loving relationships, and rise to the demands of school and work all impact your emotional health.

Stress is not always bad. In fact, some stress is helpful. Good stress is stress in amounts small enough to help you meet daily challenges. It's also a warning system that produces the fight-or-flight response, which increases blood pressure and your heart rate so you can avoid a potentially life-threatening situation. Feeling

---

8 American College Health Association 2018 report. https://www.acha.org/documents/ncha/NCHA-II_Spring_2018_Reference_Group_Executive_Summary.pdf

stressed can be perfectly normal, especially during exam time. It can motivate you to focus on your work, but it can also become so overwhelming you can't concentrate. It's when stress is chronic (meaning you always feel stressed) that it starts to damage your body.

What Chronic Stress Does to Your Body

Do you find it difficult to concentrate or complete your work? Are you frequently sick? Do you have regular headaches? Are you more anxious, angry, or irritable than usual? Do you have trouble falling asleep or staying awake? If you answered yes to any or all of these questions, you may be holding on to too much stress.

Stress that hangs around for weeks or months affects your ability to concentrate, makes you more accident-prone, increases your risk for heart disease, can weaken your immune system, disrupts your sleep, and can cause fatigue, depression, and anxiety.[9]

Some people refer to the time we are living in as the age of overload. It's easy to get worn down by social media and the constant news cycle, and to be overwhelmed by too many choices. We live in a fast-paced, always-on world with a lot of pressures.

You will have stress. Stress is inevitable. It's how you deal with it that can make all the difference. One of the most important things you can do is to keep perspective on your stressors. When feeling stressed, ask yourself, on a scale of 1 to 100, how stressful a situation is this? Will I even remember this three years from now? When facing potential stressors, the way you view what you're experiencing can intensify your stress or minimize it.

There are many ways to manage stress. Take a look at some of the ideas in the stress toolkit below. Which ones have you tried? Which ones do you want to try? It's helpful to have different tools for different situations—for example, a calming yoga pose in your dorm room and deep breathing in the classroom.

Mindfulness and Gratitude

Deep breathing, mindfulness, and practicing gratitude are some of the most effective ways to manage stress and take care of your emotional health.

Mindfulness

Mindfulness means being present with your thoughts, feelings, bodily sensations, and surrounding environment. Mindfulness is also without judgment—meaning there is no right or wrong way to think or feel in a given moment. When we practice mindfulness, our thoughts tune into what we're sensing in the present moment rather than rehashing the past or imagining the future.[10]

Anything that keeps you present in the moment and gives your prefrontal cortex (the reasoning and thinking part of your brain) a break is practicing mindfulness. Mindfulness can be a slow walk; looking intently at the grass, trees, flowers, or buildings; and being aware of what you are sensing and feeling. Mindfulness can be sitting quietly—even sitting still in a quiet place for as little as a few minutes can reduce heart rate and blood pressure.[11]

---

9 The University of Maryland Medical Center UMMC, https://www.umms.org/ummc

10 Moran, Joan; University of California at Los Angeles, http://newsroom.ucla.edu/stories/gratitude-249167

11 The Greater Good Science Center, UC Berkeley https://ggia.berkeley.edu/practice/

Developing a practice of mindfulness is easier than you may think:

- *Slow down.* From brushing your teeth, to washing your face, to shampooing your hair—can you take the speed out of getting ready in the morning? Focus on the activity, pay attention to what you are doing, stay present (this means don't think about what happened last night or what's in store for the day, just stay focused on the activity), and take your time.
- *Focus on your breath.* How fast are you breathing? Is your breath coming from your chest or your belly? Can you feel the air come through your nose on the inhale? Can you slow down the exhale? Can you feel your body relax when you slow the exhale?
- *Connect to your environment.* Walk for a few minutes, focused on the world around you—look at the leaves on the trees or the light at the corner, listen to the sounds around you, stay with your surroundings, and observe what you see and hear around you.

> "We can't change the world, at least not quickly, but we can change our brains. By practicing mindfulness all of us have the capacity to develop a deeper sense of calm."
>
> —Rick Hanson, author, Resilient

Gratitude

Too often people think it is the external factors that bring us joy and happiness, when really it's all related to internal work. According to UCLA's Mindfulness Awareness Research Center, "Having an attitude of gratitude changes the molecular structure of the brain, and makes us healthier and happier. When you feel happiness, the central nervous system is affected. You are more peaceful, less reactive and less resistant."[12]

Numerous studies show that people who count their blessings tend to be happier and less depressed. In a UC Berkeley study, researchers recruited 300 people who were experiencing emotional or mental health challenges and randomly divided them into three groups. All three groups received counseling services. The first group also wrote a letter of gratitude every week for three weeks. The second group wrote about their thoughts and feelings with negative experiences. The third group received only counseling. The people in the group who wrote gratitude letters reported significantly better mental health for up to 12 weeks after the writing exercise ended.

This would suggest that a healthy emotional self-care practice is to take note of good experiences or when you see something that makes you smile. Think about why the experience feels so good. According to Rick Hanson, author of Resilient, "Each day is strewn with little jewels. The idea is to see them and pick them up. When you notice something positive, stay with the feeling for 30 seconds. Feel the emotions in your whole body. Maybe your heart feels lighter or you're smiling. The more you can deepen and lengthen positive experiences the longer those positivity neurons in your brain are firing—and the longer they fire the stronger the underlying neural networks become. Repeat that process a half dozen times a day and you'll feel stronger, more stable, and calmer within a few weeks."

12 2016 Study Journal of PLoS One, https://journals.plos.org/plosmedicine/article?id=10.1371/journal.pmed.1000316

Build a Stress Toolkit	
Practice self- compassion	Laugh with friends
Eat clean food	Listen to music
Mindfulness Meditation Deep breathing (2-4-6-8) A walk in nature	Drink calming tea Watch a funny movie
Exercise/Movement Yoga, Tai chi Dance HIIT Run, Spin, Lift	Write in a gratitude journal Change phone screen to this picture Change passwords to calming words
Epsom salt baths Hugs	Keep something in your backpack that reminds you to take a deep breath every time you see it

Figure 7.4 Do you have a stress toolkit filled with a variety of stress-coping tools to help you navigate any stressful situation? (Credit: Modification of work by Robin Benzrihem)

Activity 7.1

Take a look at some of the suggested tools for your stress toolkit. Which ones have you tried? Have they been effective in helping you manage stress? Ask two friends or family members about their favorite stress-management strategies. What has worked for you and others that is not on this list? Identify two new tools you would like to explore and articulate how you will determine if they work for you, and then you can confidently add them to your stress toolkit.

7.4 Taking Care of Your Mental Health

Questions to consider:

- What is mental health?
- How can I take care of it?

The World Health Organization ranks mental health conditions as the leading cause of disability in the United States. One in four adults experience a diagnosable mental health disorder in any given year, yet more than half will not seek treatment. The primary reason people don't seek the help they need is shame and fear of judgment from friends, family, and coworkers. It is important to remove any stigma associated with mental health and encourage those who need help to seek support.

What Students Say

The graph below shows survey results of what college students feel are the most significant health issues they face.

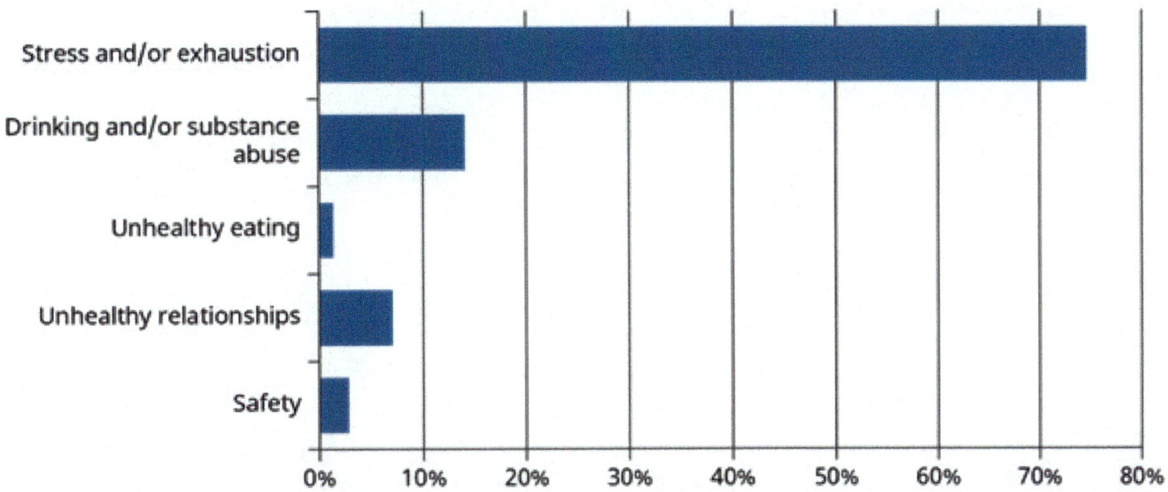

Figure 7.5 When you are facing an issue regarding your emotions, stress, mental health, or relationships, what do you typically do?

What is mental health?

Mental health is "the level of psychological well-being or an absence of mental illness. It is the state of someone who is functioning at a satisfactory level of emotional and behavioral adjustment."[13]

According to NAMI (National Alliance on Mental Illness), a mental illness is a condition that affects a person's thinking, feeling, or mood. The condition may affect a person's ability to relate to others and function throughout the day.

A mental health condition isn't the result of one event; it is most often the result of multiple overlapping causes. Environment, lifestyle, and genetic predisposition can all be factors in whether someone develops a mental health condition. Traumatic life events or stressful experiences may make some people more susceptible, and brain biochemistry may play a role as well. Mental health conditions show up in many ways. Anxiety, depression, and eating disorders are some of the most common.

Anxiety Disorders

We all experience the occasional feeling of anxiety, which is quite normal. New situations, meeting new people, driving in traffic, and public speaking are just a few of the common activities that can cause people to feel anxious. It is important to seek help when these feelings become overwhelming, cause fear, or keep us from doing everyday activities. Anxiety disorders are the most common mental health concern in the United States, and while there are many types of anxiety disorders, they all have one thing in common: "persistent, excessive fear or worry in situations that are not threatening."[14] Physically, your heart may race,

13 Wikipedia, https://en.wikipedia.org/wiki/Mental_health

14 NAMI, https://www.nami.org/NAMI/media/NAMI-Media/Images/FactSheets/Anxiety-Disorders-FS.pdf

and you may experience shortness of breath, nausea, or intense fatigue. Talk with a mental health care professional if you experience a level of anxiety that keeps you from your regular daily activities.

Eating Disorders

Eating disorders are not uncommon among students. Stress or anxiety may create a desire for some students to overeat, while others may develop a concern about body shape or weight and significantly reduce their food intake.

Anorexia nervosa is a potentially fatal illness marked by self-starvation. People with anorexia usually have an irrational concern about body shape or weight and eat a very restricted diet. They may also feel the need to exercise all the time, even when they are sick or exhausted.

Binge eating is the frequent consumption of large amounts of food in a short period of time. Bulimia involves cycles of excessive eating followed by eliminating food through vomiting or with laxatives. Eating disorders can lead to many complications, some of them very serious, like heart conditions and kidney failure. It is crucial for anyone with an eating disorder to stabilize their health, then continuing medical care and counseling to reach full recovery. Eating disorders can be treated successfully with medical care, psychotherapy, counseling, or coaching.

If you think you might have an eating disorder, visit a doctor or reach out to the Advocacy Center or Wellness 360 clinic on campus.

Depression

Most people feel sad at times. This is a normal reaction to loss or struggles we face. Being sad is not the same as having depression. When intense sadness lasts for several days or even weeks and you are no longer interested in activities you once enjoyed, it may be depression. Depression can lead to a variety of emotional and physical problems and can decrease a person's ability to function at work and at home.

Depression does not have a single cause. It can follow a life crisis or physical illness, but it can also occur spontaneously. Several factors including trauma, a significant life change, brain injury, and drug and alcohol misuse may contribute to depression. Depression is a treatable medical condition. Talk with a mental health care professional if you experience an ongoing level of sadness that keeps you from your regular daily activities.

Suicidal Behavior

People who contemplate suicide often experience a deep feeling of hopelessness. They often don't feel they can cope with challenging life events and are not able to see solutions to problems. In the moment, they are unable to see that the challenges are really only temporary. Most survivors of suicide attempts go on to live wonderful, full lives.

Depression is one risk factor for suicide, along with substance abuse, chronic debilitating pain, mental health disorders, and a family history of suicide.

These are some of the warning signs to help you determine if a friend or loved one is at risk for suicide, especially if the behavior is new, has increased, or seems related to a painful event:

- talking about wanting to die or to kill themselves
- looking for a way to kill themselves, like searching online or buying a gun
- talking about feeling hopeless or having no reason to live

- talking about feeling trapped or in unbearable pain
- talking about being a burden to others
- increasing the use of alcohol or drugs
- acting anxious or agitated; behaving recklessly
- sleeping too little or too much
- withdrawing or isolating themselves
- showing rage or talking about seeking revenge
- extreme mood swings[15]

If you or someone you know has warning signs of suicide, get help as soon as possible. Family and friends are often the first to recognize any warning signs and can help take the first step in finding treatment. If someone is telling you that they are going to kill themselves, do not leave them alone. The National Suicide Prevention Lifeline can be reached at 988 (call or text).

Additional Resources

Because entering college is such a big transition, it is important to know what health services are available on your campus. Remember the Student Advocacy Center and Wellness 360 are available at San Antonio College: 210-486-1111

7.5 Personal Financial Planning

Questions to consider:

- What simple steps do I take to create a financial plan?
- How do I use financial planning in everyday life?
- How is the financial planning process implemented for every purchase?

Honestly, practicing money management isn't that hard to figure out. In many ways it's similar to playing a video game. The first time you play a game, you may feel awkward or have the lowest score. Playing for a while can make you OK at the game. But if you learn the rules of the game, figure out how to best use each tool in the game, read strategy guides from experts, and practice, you can get really good at it.

Money management is the same. It's not enough to "figure it out as you go." If you want to get good at managing your money, you must treat money like you treat your favorite game. You have to come at it with a well-researched plan. Research has shown that people with stronger finances are healthier[16] and happier,[17] have better marriages,[18] and even have better cognitive functioning.[19]

---

15 https://suicidepreventionlifeline.org/how-we-can-all-prevent-suicide/; https://www.nimh.nih.gov/health/publications/suicide-faq/index.shtml

16 https://www.sciencedirect.com/science/article/pii/S0277953613002839

17 https://academic.oup.com/geronj/article-abstract/38/5/626/578092

18 https://onlinelibrary.wiley.com/doi/abs/10.1111/j.1741-3729.2012.00715.x and http://onlinelibrary.wiley.com/doi/10.1111/j.1741-3729.2012.00715.x/abstract

19 https://science.sciencemag.org/content/341/6149/976%20

Financial Planning Process

Personal goals and behaviors have a financial component or consequence. To make the most of your financial resources, you need to do some financial planning. The financial planning process consists of five distinct steps: goal setting, evaluating, planning, implementing, and monitoring.

Financial Planning in Five Steps

1. Develop Personal Goals
    - What do I want my life to look like?
2. Identify and Evaluate Alternatives for Achieving Goals for My Situation
    - What do my savings, debt, income, and expenses look like?
    - What creative ways are available to get the life I want?
3. Write My Financial Plan
    - What small steps can I take to start working toward my goals?
4. Implement the Plan
    - Begin taking those steps, even if I can only do a few small things each week.
5. Monitor and Adjust the Plan
    - Make sure I don't get distracted by life. Keep taking those small steps each week. Make adjustments when needed.

7.6 Savings, Expenses, and Budgeting

Questions to consider:

- How is the flow of money best measured?
- How do I keep things balanced?

Budgets

The term budget is unpleasant to some people because it just looks like work. But who will care more about your money than you? We all want to know if we have enough money to pay our bills, travel, get an education, buy a car, etc. Technically, a budget is a specific financial plan for a specified time. Budgets have three elements: income, saving and investing, and expenses. To help get started on a budget, you may want to use an app such as Mint, Mvelopes, Wally or Goodbudget.

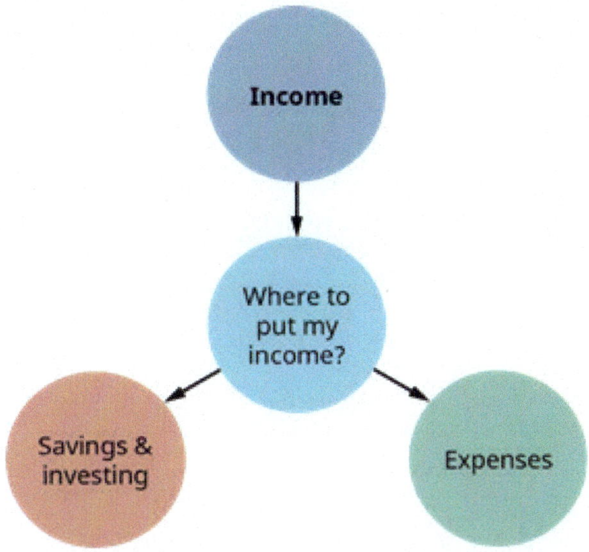

Figure 7.6 A budget is a specific financial plan for a finite amount of time. For example, you can set a budget for your family for a year.

Income

Income most often comes from our jobs in the form of a paper or electronic paycheck. When listing your income for your monthly budget, you should use your net pay, also called your disposable income. It is the only money you can use to pay bills. If you currently have a job, look at the pay stub or statement. You will find gross pay, then some money deducted for a variety of taxes, leaving a smaller amount—your net pay.

Some individuals receive disability income, social security income, investment income, alimony, child support, and other forms of payment on a regular basis. All of these go under income. During school, you may receive support from family that could be considered income. You may also receive scholarships, grants, or student loan money.

Saving and Investing

The first bill you should pay is to yourself. You owe yourself today and tomorrow. That means you should set aside a certain amount of money for savings and investments, before paying bills and making discretionary, or optional, purchases. Savings can be for an emergency fund or for short-term goals such as education, a wedding, travel, or a car. Investing, such as putting your money into stocks, bonds, or real estate, offers higher returns at a higher risk than money saved in a bank. Investments include retirement accounts that can be automatically funded with money deducted from your paycheck. Automatic payroll deductions are an effective way to save money before you can get your hands on it. Paying yourself first is a habit that pays off!

Expenses

Expenses are categorized in two ways. One method separates them into fixed expenses and variable expenses. Rent, insurance costs, and utilities (power, water) are fixed: they cost about the same every month and are predictable based on your arrangement with the provider. Variable expenses, on the other hand, change based on your priorities and available funds; they include groceries, restaurants, cell phone plans, gas, clothing, and so on. You have a good degree of control over your variable expenses. You can begin organizing your expenses by categorizing each one as either fixed or variable.

A second way to categorize expenses is to identify them as either needs or wants. Your needs come first: food, basic clothing, safe housing, medical care, and water. Your wants come afterward, if you can afford them while sticking to a savings plan. Wants may include meals at a restaurant, designer clothes, video games, other forms of entertainment, or a new car. After you identify an item as a need or want, you must exercise self-control to avoid caving to your desire for too many wants.

Activity 7.2

List the last ten purchases you made, and place each of them in the category you think is correct.

Item	Need Expense $	Want Expense $
Totals		

How do your total "need" expenses compare to your total "want" expenses? Should either of them change?

Balancing Your Budget

Would you take all your cash outside and throw it up in the air on a windy day? Probably not. We want to hold on to every cent and decide where we want it to go. Our budget allows us to find a place for each dollar. We should not regularly have money left over. If we do, we should consider increasing our saving and investing. We also should not have a negative balance, meaning we don't have enough to pay our bills. If we are short of money, we can look at all three categories of our budget: income, savings, and expenses.

We could increase our income by taking a second job or working overtime, although this is rarely advisable alongside college coursework. The time commitment quickly becomes overwhelming. Another option is to cut savings, or there's always the possibility of reducing expenses. Any of these options in combination can work.

Another, even less desirable option is to take on debt to make up the shortfall. This is usually only a short-term solution that makes future months and cash shortages worse as we pay off the debt. When we budget for each successive month, we can look at what we actually spent the month before and make adjustments.

Analysis Question

Can you identify areas in your life where you are losing money by paying fees on your checking account or interest on your loans? What actions could you take to stop giving away money and instead set yourself up to start earning money?

7.7 Credit Cards and Other Debt

Questions to consider:

- What do I need to know about student loans?
- How dangerous is debt?
- What should I think about when getting and using a credit card?

Yes, taking on too much debt can (and does) have disastrous effects on people's personal finances, but if used appropriately, debt can be a tool to help you build wealth. Debt is like fire. You can use it to keep yourself warm, cook food, and ward off animals—but if you don't know how to control it, it'll burn your house down.

The Danger of Debt

When you take out a loan, you take on an obligation to pay the money back, with interest, through a monthly payment. You will take this debt with you when you apply for auto loans or home loans, when you enter into a relationship with a partner in life, and so on. Effectively, you have committed your future income to the loan. While this can be a good idea with student loans, taking on too many loans and your future self will be poor, no matter how much money you make. Worse, you'll be transferring more and more of your money to the bank through interest payments.

Interest

Interest is the fee paid to use someone else's money. Compound interest is the interest you earn on interest. This can be illustrated by using basic math: if you have $100 and it earns 5% interest each year, you'll have $105 at the end of the first year. At the end of the second year, you'll have $110.25.

While compounding works to make you money when you are earning interest on savings or investments, it works against you when you are paying the interest on loans. To avoid compounding interest on loans, make sure your payments are at least enough to cover the interest charged each month. The good news is that the interest you are charged will be listed each month on the loan account statements you are sent by the bank or credit union, and fully amortized loans will always cover the interest costs plus enough principal to pay off what you owe by the end of the loan term.

The two most common loans on which people get stuck paying compounding interest are credit cards and student loans. Paying the minimum payment each month on a credit card will just barely cover the interest charged that month, while anything you buy with the credit card will begin to accrue interest on the day you make the purchase. Since credit cards charge interest daily, you'll begin paying interest on the interest immediately, starting the compound interest snowball working against you. When you get a credit card, always pay the credit card balance down to $0 each month to avoid the compound interest trap.

Student loans are another way you can be caught in the compound interest trap. When you have an unsubsidized student loan or put your loans into deferment, the interest continues to rack up on the loans. Again, you'll be charged interest on the interest, not just on the original loan amount, forcing you to pay compound interest on the loan.

Figure 7.7 Compound interest graphic

Sacrificing Your Future Fun

When you graduate college, you are most likely to graduate with student loan debt and credit card debt.[20] Many students use credit cards and student loans to allow them to pay for fun today, such as trips, clothing, and expensive meals.

Getting into debt while in college forces you to sacrifice your future fun. Say you take out $100,000 in student loans instead of the $50,000 you need, doubling your monthly payment. You are not just making an extra $338 payment; you are also sacrificing anything else you can do with that money. You sacrifice that extra $338 a month, every month, for the next twenty-five years. You can't use it to go to the movies, pay down other debt, save for a home, take a vacation, or throw a party. When you sign those papers, you sacrifice all those opportunities every month for decades. As a result, when you take out a loan, you should make sure it's a good loan.

Getting and Using a Credit Card

One of the most controversial aspects of personal finance is the use of credit cards. While credit cards can be an incredibly useful tool, their high interest rates, combined with how easily credit cards can bury you in debt, make them extremely dangerous if not managed correctly.

Benefits of a Credit Card

There are three main benefits of getting a credit card. The first is that credit cards offer a secure and convenient method of making purchases, similar to using a debit card. When you carry cash, you have the potential of having the money lost or stolen. A credit card or debit card, on the other hand, can be canceled and replaced at no cost to you.

Additionally, credit cards offer greater consumer protections than debit cards do. These consumer protections are written into law, and with credit cards you have a maximum liability of $50. With a debit card, you are responsible for transfers made up until the point you report the card stolen. In order to have the same

20 Debt.org. "Demographics of Debt." https://www.debt.org/faqs/americans-in-debt/demographics/

protections as with credit cards, you need to report the card lost or stolen within 48 hours. The longer you wait to report the loss of the card, or the longer it takes you to realize you lost your card, the more money you may be responsible for, up to an unlimited amount.[21]

The final benefit is that a credit card will allow you to build your credit score, which is helpful in many aspects of life. While most people associate a credit score with getting better rates on loans, credit scores are also important to getting a job, lowering car insurance rates, and finding an apartment.[22]

What is a good credit score?

Most credit scores have a 300–850 score range. The higher the score, the lower the risk to lenders. A "good" credit score is considered to be in the 670–739 score range.

Table 7.1 Ranges of Credit Scores

Credit Score Ranges	Rating	Description
<580	Poor	This credit score is well below the average score of US consumers and demonstrates to lenders that the borrower may be a risk.
580–669	Fair	This credit score is below the average score of US consumers, though many lenders will approve loans with this score.
670–739	Good	This credit score is near or slightly above the average of US consumers, and most lenders consider this a good score.
740–799	Very Good	This credit score is above the average of US consumers and demonstrates to lenders that the borrower is very dependable.
800+	Exceptional	This credit score is well above the average score of US consumers and clearly demonstrates to lenders that the borrower is an exceptionally low risk.

How to Improve Your Credit

The main action you can take to improve your credit score is to stop charging and pay all bills on time. Even if you cannot pay the full amount of the credit card balance, which is the best practice, pay the minimum on time. Paying more is better for your debt load but does not improve your score. Carrying a balance on a credit card does not improve your score. Your score will go down if you pay bills late and owe more than 30 percent of your credit available. Your credit score is a reflection of your willingness and ability to do what you say you will do—pay your debts on time.

How to Use a Credit Card

All the benefits of credit cards are destroyed if you carry credit card debt. Credit cards should be used as a method of paying for things you can afford, meaning you should only use a credit card if the money is already sitting in your bank account and is budgeted for the item you are buying. If you use credit cards as a loan, you are losing the game.

21 Federal Trade Commission. "Lost Or Stolen Credit, ATM, and Debit Cards." 2012.

22 Purposeful Finance. "Four Surprising Ways Your Credit Score Will Affect Your Life." https://www.purposefulfinance.org/home/Articles/2016/four-surprising-ways-your-credit-score-will-affect-your-life

Every month, you should pay your credit card off in full, meaning you will be bringing the loan amount down to $0. If your statement says you charged $432.56 that month, make sure you can pay off all $432.56. If you do this, you won't pay any interest on the credit card.

But what happens if you don't pay it off in full? If you are even one cent short on the payment, meaning you pay $432.55 instead, you must pay daily interest on the entire amount from the date you made the purchases. Your credit card company, of course, will be perfectly happy for you to make smaller payments—that's how they make money. It is not uncommon for people to pay twice as much as the amount purchased and take years to pay off a credit card when they only pay the minimum payment each month.

CapitalOne | SPARK BUSINESS

Payment Information

Payment Due Date
Mar. 28, 2020

For online and phone payments, the deadline is 8pm ET.

New Balance
$2,291.79

Minimum Payment Due
$22.00

LATE PAYMENT WARNING: If we do not receive your minimum payment by your due date, you may have to pay a $39.00 late fee and your APRs may be increased up to the Penalty APR of 30.90%.

MINIMUM PAYMENT WARNING: If you make only the minimum payment each period, you will pay more in interest and it will take you longer to pay off your balance. For example:

If you make no additional charges using this card and each month you pay...	You will pay off the balance shown on this statement in about...	And you will end up paying an estimated total of...
Minimum Payment	17 Years	$5,400
$83	3 Years	$3,003
Estimated savings if balance is paid off in about 3 years: $2,397		

If you would like information about credit counseling services, call 1-888-326-8055.

Figure 7.8 The cost of making minimum payments on your credit card. Source: https://www.allcards.com/credit-card-minimum-payment/

What to Look for in Your Initial Credit Card

1. Find a Low-Rate Credit Card
2. Avoid Cards with Annual Fees or Minimum Usage Requirements
3. Keep the Credit Limit Equal to Two Weeks' Take-Home Pay
4. Avoid Rewards Cards

7.8 Education Debt: Paying for College

Questions to consider:

- What are ways to pay for your college education?

- What choices should you consider when taking on student debt?
- What types of financial aid are available?
- How do you apply for financial aid?

As you progress through your college experience, the cost of college can add up rapidly. Worse, your anxiety about the cost of college may rise faster as you hear about the rising costs of college and horror stories regarding the "student loan crisis." It is important to remember that you are in control of your choices and the cost of your college experience, and you do not have to be a sad statistic.

Education Choices

Education is vital to living. Education starts at the beginning of our life, and as we grow, we learn language, sharing, and to look both ways before crossing the street. We also generally pursue a secular or public education that often ends at high school graduation. After that, we have many choices, including getting a job and stopping our education, working at a trade or business started by our parents and bypassing additional schooling, earning a certificate from a community college or four-year college or university, earning a two-year or associate degree from one of the same schools, and completing a bachelor's or advanced degree at a college or university. We can choose to attend a public or private school. We can live at home or on a campus.

According to US News & World Report, the average cost of college (including university) tuition and fees varies widely. In-state colleges average $9,716 while out-of-state students pay $21,629 for the same state college. Private colleges average $35,676. The local community college averages approximately $3,726. On-campus housing and meals, if available, can add approximately $10,000 per year.[23] See the table below, and create your own chart after you research.

Sample College Costs

Table 7.2 List of College Costs at 2-year, 4-year, Public, and Private Institutions

Type of School	Annual Tuition without Housing	Living on Campus Cost	Total Cost at Planned Completion
Community College (2 yr.)	$3,726	Live at Home	$7,452
Public University, In State (4 yr.)	$9,716	Live at Home	$38,864
Public University, In State (4 yr.)	$9,716	$10,000	$78,864
Public University, Out of State (4 yr.)	$21,629	$10,000	$126,516
Private College (4 yr.)	$35,676	$10,000	$182,704

You may need to adjust your college plan as circumstances change for you and in the job market. You can modify plans based on funding opportunities available to you (see next sections) and your location. You may prefer a community-college-only education, or you may complete two years at a community college and then

23 https://www.usnews.com/education/best-colleges/paying-for-college/articles/what-you-need-to-know-about-college-tuition-costs

transfer to a university to complete a bachelor's degree. Living at home for the first two years or all of your college education will save a lot of money if your circumstances allow. Be creative!

Types of Financial Aid: How to Pay for College

The true cost of college may be more than you expected, but you can make an effort to make the cost less than many might think. While the price tag for a school might say $40,000, the net cost of college may be significantly less. The net price for a college is the true cost a family will pay when grants, scholarships, and education tax benefits are factored in. The net cost for the average family at a public in-state school is only $3,980. And for a private school, free financial aid money reduces the cost to the average family from $32,410 per year to just $14,890.

If you haven't visited your college's financial aid office recently, it's probably worth it to talk with them. You must seek out opportunities, complete paperwork, and learn and meet criteria, but it can save you thousands of dollars.

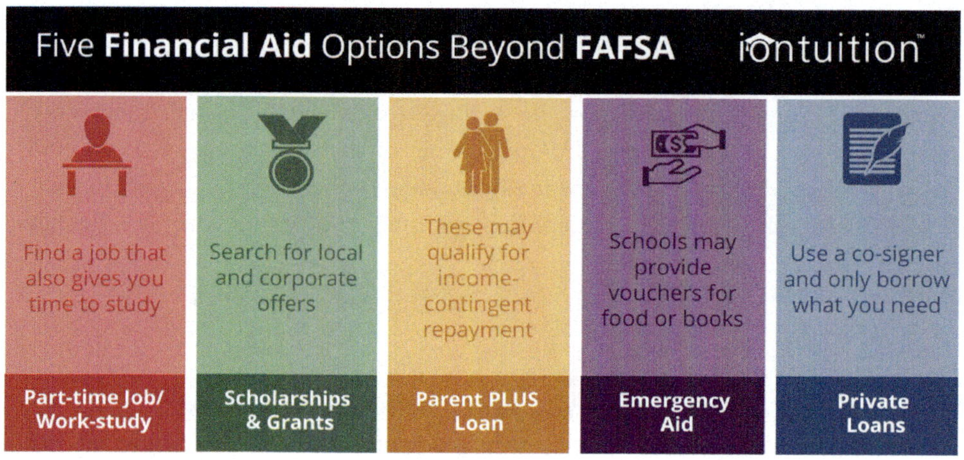

Figure 7.9 **Five financial aid options beyond FAFSA**

Grants and Scholarships

Grants and scholarships are free money you can use to pay for college. Unlike loans, you never have to pay back a grant or a scholarship. Students should be aware that many scholarships do require students to maintain Satisfactory Academic Progress (keeping overall GPA above a 2.0 and completing all courses). Alamo Colleges offers many scholarships to its students. Alamo Colleges' students submit one general scholarship application each academic year, and they are automatically considered for all Alamo Colleges Foundation scholarships and matched with eligible award opportunities.

Federal Grants

Federal Pell Grants are awarded to students based on financial need. The Pell Grant can give you more than $6,000 per year in free money toward tuition, fees, and living expenses.[24] If you qualify for a Pell Grant based on your financial need, you will automatically get the money.

---

24 https://studentaid.ed.gov/sa/types/grants-scholarships/pell

State Grants

Most states also have grant programs for their residents, often based on financial need. Eleven states have even implemented free college tuition programs for residents who plan to continue to live in the state. Even some medical schools are beginning to be tuition free. Check your school's financial aid office and your state's department of education for details.

Employer Tuition Reimbursement and Scholarships

Many employers also offer free money to help employees go to school. A common work benefit is a tuition reimbursement program, where employers will pay students extra money to cover the cost of tuition once they've earned a passing grade in a college class. And some companies are going even further, offering to pay 100 percent of college costs for employees. Check to see whether your employer offers any kind of educational support.

Federal Work-Study Program

The Federal Work-Study Program provides part-time jobs through colleges and universities to students who are enrolled in the school. The program offers students the opportunity to work in their field, for their school, or for a nonprofit or civic organization to help pay for the cost of college. If your school participates in the program, it will be offered through your school's financial aid office.

Student Loans

Federal student loans are offered through the US Department of Education and are designed to give easy and inexpensive access to loans for school. You don't have to make payments on the loans while you are in school, and the interest on the loans is tax deductible for most people. Direct Loans, also called Federal Stafford Loans, have a competitive fixed interest rate and don't require a credit check or cosigner.

- *Direct Subsidized Loans* - Direct Subsidized Loans are federal student loans on which the government pays the interest while you are in school.
- *Direct Unsubsidized Loans* - Direct Unsubsidized Loans are federal loans on which you are charged interest while you are in school. If you don't make interest payments while in school, the interest will be added to the loan amount each year and will result in a larger student loan balance when you graduate.
- *Direct PLUS Loans* - Direct PLUS Loans are additional loans a parent, grandparent, or graduate student can take out to help pay for additional costs of college. PLUS loans require a credit check and have higher interest rates, but the interest is still tax deductible. The maximum PLUS loan you can receive is the remaining cost of attending the school.
- *Private Loans* - Private loans are also available for students who need them from banks, credit unions, private investors, and even predatory lenders. But with all the other resources for paying for college, a private loan is generally unnecessary and unwise. Private loans will require a credit check and potentially a cosigner, they will likely have higher interest rates, and the interest is not tax deductible. As a general rule, you should be wary of private student loans or avoid them altogether.

Loan Repayment

Payments on student loans will begin shortly after you graduate or are no longer attending college. Most loans are paid off within 10 years. While many websites, financial "gurus," and talking heads in the media will encourage you to pay off your student loans as quickly as possible, you should give careful consideration to your repayment options and how they may impact your financial plans.

Financial Aid

Take this first step—you will need to do it. The federal government offers a standard form called the Free Application for Federal Student Aid (FAFSA), which qualifies you for federal financial aid and also opens the door for nearly all other financial aid. Most grants and scholarships require you to fill out the FAFSA, and they base their decisions on the information in the application.

The FAFSA only requests financial aid for the specific year you file your application. This means you will need to file a FAFSA for each year you are in college. Since your financial needs will change over time, you may qualify for financial aid even if you did not qualify before.

You can apply for the FAFSA through your college's financial aid office or at studentaid.gov if you don't have access to a financial aid office. Once you file a FAFSA, any college can gain access to the information (with your approval), so you can shop around for financial aid offers from colleges. Students can begin their FAFSA application in October for the following academic year.

Maintaining Financial Aid

To maintain your financial aid throughout your time in college, you need to make sure you meet the eligibility requirements for each year you are in school, not just the year of your initial application. The basic requirements include being a US citizen or eligible noncitizen, having a valid Social Security number, and registering for selective service if required. Undocumented residents may receive financial aid as well and should check with their school's financial aid office.

You also must meet satisfactory academic progress (SAP), including meeting a minimum grade-point average, taking and completing a minimum number of classes, and making progress toward graduation or a certificate. Your school will have a policy for satisfactory academic progress, which you can get from the financial aid office.

What to Do with Extra Financial Aid Money

One expensive mistake that students make with financial aid money is spending the money on noneducation expenses. Students often use financial aid, including student loans, to purchase clothing, take vacations, or dine out at restaurants. Nearly 3 percent spend student loan money on alcohol and drugs.[25] While this seems like fun now, these noneducation expenses are major contributors to student loan debt, which will make it harder for you to afford a home, take vacations, or save for your retirement after you graduate.

When you have extra student loan money, consider saving it for future education expenses. Just like you will need an emergency fund all your adult life, you will want an emergency fund for college when expensive books or travel abroad programs present unexpected costs. If you make it through your college years with extra money in your savings, you can use the money to help pay down debt.

25 https://studentloanhero.com/featured/smart-dumb-money-moves-students/

Chapter Summary

In this chapter you have been introduced to the wide range of factors that impact your health. Health is much more than keeping your physical body in good shape. Good health also includes your mental and emotional health.

The contributors to physical health include eating clean, non-processed food; staying hydrated; moving your body daily; and getting sufficient sleep. You now understand why it is necessary to prioritize sleep, and that quality sleep is also dependent on the way you eat and exercise. You have identified ways to improve what you eat and how you sleep. With these changes you should be able to fall asleep with ease, stay asleep all night, and wake up feeling energized. Your mind will be clear and sharp, and you'll get more done in less time, massively increasing your productivity and your success in college.

You now understand that a certain level of stress is to be expected. Chronic stress, however, is damaging to the body, so it's important to have a variety of tools to manage stress. Practicing mindfulness, deep breathing, and gratitude can have a powerful impact on your emotional, mental, and physical health.

Finally, we explored the aspects of financial literacy. There are a lot of benefits to good financial management. Primarily, it generally allows you to do more of what you want with your life. When you have poor financial habits, too much of your money goes into other people's pockets. But when you have good financial management habits, you can afford to do more because you have worked hard, separated needs from wants, saved and invested, and avoided credit card and debt pitfalls.

Chapter 8 Conclusion

Congratulations on finishing your first semester at San Antonio College!

You have committed time, energy and discipline to complete a challenging semester of coursework, and now it is time to celebrate your accomplishments. Your story is an important one. Take a moment to read the following SAC student bios. What similarities do you see between your story and theirs? What differences do you notice?

As you celebrate your accomplishments from this first semester, take a moment to write your own bio. Consider these questions as you write your own story:

- What is my background? Where am I from? What strengths do I gain from this?
- What are my goals for my education?
- What skills and strategies have I used this semester to be most successful?
- What piece of advice would I share with incoming students to help them succeed?

As you write your story, we hope you can see the commitment and dedication you have applied this semester. Now it is time to celebrate! Your journey has just begun, and we are so excited to see how much more you will achieve at San Antonio College!

Your Story

Student Highlights

My name is Jason and I am a passionate poet, budding entrepreneur, and aspiring community leader from San Antonio, Texas. As a proud Latino, I am deeply committed to activism, hoping to bring positive changes to my barrio and the broader community. Despite growing up in poverty, I overcame life's challenges with determination and resilience, focusing on empowering myself and others through education and opportunity.

As a freshman at San Antonio College, I have found solace and inspiration in my new academic environment. This close-knit campus feels like a family away from home, providing me with the encouragement, resources, and support I need to thrive academically and personally. I am majoring in Business Administration with a concentration in Data Analysis, and I am excited to learn more about how these skills can contribute to my future endeavors.

I have already become involved in various extracurricular activities on campus, including community service programs and Latino student organizations. These groups have allowed me to pursue my passion for poetry and activism and introduced me to like-minded individuals who share my commitment to making a difference.

My name is Gissel and I am 20 years old. I am a student at San Antonio College. I was born in Piedras Negras, Mexico in 2002 and moved to Eagle Pass, Texas within the day. I was raised in Eagle Pass and at age 11 found out that I was undocumented.

After graduating from high school, I moved to San Antonio for college. Now I am pursuing my education at San Antonio College and plan on transferring to a 4-year university to eventually get my master's degree in psychology. I was inspired by my Licensed Professional Counselor to change and save lives like he did with me to become one in the future.

My Professor for EDUC 1300 helped me become who I am today. She taught me how to learn, how to view life in a different perspective, and how to be a leader. Because I am an undocumented student, it is very difficult to find someone who understands and who is willing to hear me out in my life struggles. My Professor was always there when I needed her. She supported and pushed me to become the best version of myself. With this I created a Dreamers Club at SAC for undocumented students like myself, to have a safe place and to be excepted regardless of their status. I am thankful to have taken a course and to have an amazing Professor who has helped me grow as an individual and become who I am today.

My name is Dominique. I am a first-generation college student, I am a Veteran, I am a mother and I am a wife. San Antonio is a new life, it's the beginning of my legacy and it is the place I want to serve. I am studying Pre-nursing to become a Registered Nurse and treat veterans in my community.

Being at San Antonio College, I am supported with resources. For example, as a veteran we have the victory center to answer all questions related to us. I love the resources the advocacy center offers. I am invited to join clubs that challenge me to strive higher and raise the bar for myself. I can't shrink here because I belong here. As a student here at SAC I noticed the spirit this school has to help the students here succeed and follow their dreams.

I have a goal to graduate this year with my Associates in biology with hopes of starting a Bachelors program for nursing. My long-term goal is to become a Nurse Practitioner and specialize in mental health. Also, as a mother and as a non-traditional student, it is important to me to set a good example for my son. I want him to understand he can do anything he sets his mind to.

Legacy is not just what we achieve—it's the tools we pass to the next generation, and it's my responsibility as a mother to instill the benefit and importance of education into my son. It has been life changing and a pleasure to be a student here at San Antonio College, and I will carry my pride in being a student here for the rest of my life.

Appendix 1

ALAMO COLLEGES DISTRICT
San Antonio College

SAC Access-Friendly Campus Map

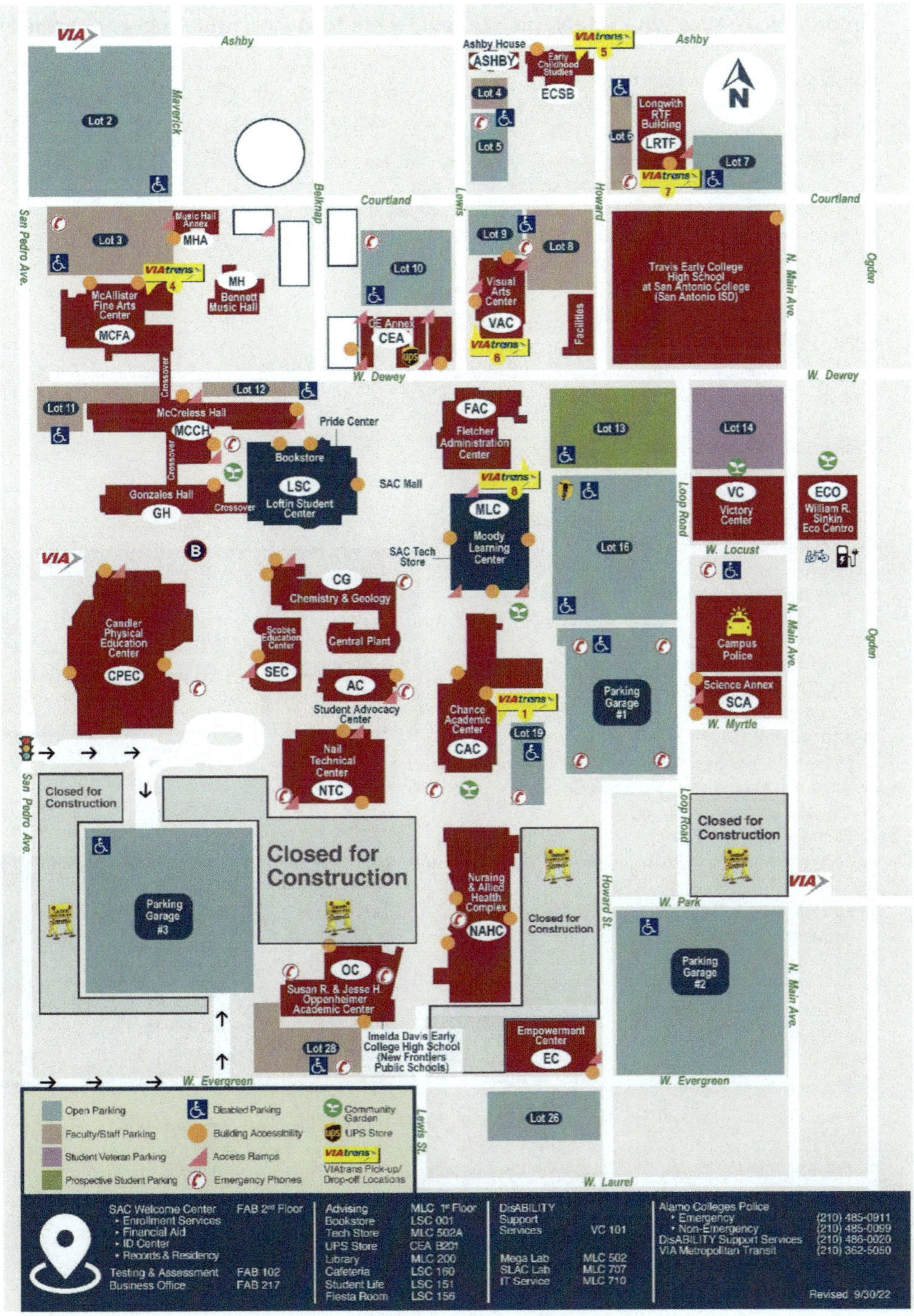

Appendix 2

Classroom Emergency/Safety Procedures Student Handout

In order to ensure your safety, please review the following material very carefully.

Safety/Emergency Information

- Location of nearest fire extinguisher and pull station
- Location of the nearest exit(s)
- At least two emergency exit routes out of building and assembly location
- Location of severe weather shelter space for building
- Location of nearest Automatic External Defibulator (AED) and first aid kit
- Personal Protective Equipment (PPE) needed for class if required
- Safety shower/eye wash station if applicable
- Sign up for Alamo Alerts in ACES

Door Lock Devices

- For your safety, new door lock devices have been installed in all classrooms for use during a Lockdown event. Practice using the new safety door locks.

Lockdown/Active Shooter

- Remember, **RUN, HIDE, FIGHT!**
- **RUN**: Escape the building or area if safe to do so
- **HIDE**: If you cannot get out of the building, identify the best place to hide (away from windows)
- Lock/Barricade the doors/windows
- Turn off lights
- Stay quiet and silence your cellphone
- Stay in place until "All Clear" is issued or police remove you from your location
- **FIGHT**: If the aggressor enters your room, FIGHT!
- Do not open doors for anyone

Evacuation/Fire

- In the event of a fire, evacuate the building and proceed to the assembly area
- If the Fire Alarm has not already been activated, pull the alarm at nearest pull station
- DO NOT use the elevators
- Follow ACPD and Building Action Team (BAT) instructions
- DO NOT return to the building until All Clear is issued

Shelter in Place/Severe Weather (Tornado)

- Move to the interior hallways or rooms of the building on lowest floor possible
- Stay away from all windows and doors
- Await further directions from ACPD or Building Action Team (BAT) member

Medical Emergencies

- Please remain calm and contact Alamo College Police Department or call 911
- Provide any assistance you are qualified to perform

ALAMO COLLEGES DISTRICT

Appendix 3

Peer Reviewed Journal Article Summary

Article Citation:

Research Objective - Why does this matter?

INTRODUCTION: What is the objective or purpose of the study? What key prior research was discussed or cited by the researchers? State the hypothesis.

Hypothesis Testing/Measurement - Is this reliable?

METHOD: How did the researchers test the hypothesis? Who were the participants in the study? What were they asked to do?

Key Research Findings - What was found?

RESULTS: What were the main findings of the study? What was the answer to the research question?

Importance & Conclusions - What did the researchers learn?

DISCUSSION: Provide the significant contributions of this research study. Did the researchers suggest any limitations or problems concerning the methods of the study? Discuss next steps or future directions for this research topic.

Application - What did you learn?

CRITICAL ANALYSIS: What did you learn from this research study? What questions do you have about this topic or research study? What did you learn that could be applied to your own experience?

Appendix 4

Week of Your Life Worksheet

(There are 168 hours in a week)

	Monday	Tuesday	Wednesday	Thursday	Friday	Saturday	Sunday
6:00 am							
7:00 am							
8:00 am							
9:00 am							
10:00 am							
11:00 am							
12:00 pm							
1:00 pm							
2:00 pm							
3:00 pm							
4:00 pm							
5:00 pm							
6:00 pm							
7:00 pm							
8:00 pm							
9:00 pm							
10:00 pm							
11:00 pm							
12:00 am							
1:00 am							
2:00 am							
3:00 am							
4:00 am							
5:00 am							

Note: make sure to include sleeping, getting ready, eating, travel, work, school, study, appointments, must-watch TV shows, family obligations, fun with friends, etc.

Appendix 5

Self-Regulation Questionnaire (SRQ)

The Self-Regulation Questionnaire (SRQ) is a tool that assesses an individual's ability to regulate their behavior, emotions, and thoughts in different situations. The SRQ can provide valuable insights into an individual's self-regulation skills and help guide interventions to improve these skills if necessary.

	Strongly Disagree	Disagree	Unsure	Agree	Strongly Agree
I usually keep track of my progress toward my goals	1	2	3	4	5
My behavior is not that different from other people's.	1	2	3	4	5
Others tell me that I keep on with things too long.	1	2	3	4	5
I doubt I could change even if I wanted to.	1	2	3	4	5
I have trouble making up my mind about things.	1	2	3	4	5
I get easily distracted from my plans.	1	2	3	4	5
I reward myself for progress toward my goals.	1	2	3	4	5
I don't notice the effects of my actions until it's too late.	1	2	3	4	5
My behavior is similar to that of my friends.	1	2	3	4	5
It's hard for me to see anything helpful about changing my ways.	1	2	3	4	5
I am able to accomplish goals I set for myself.	1	2	3	4	5
I put off making decisions.	1	2	3	4	5
I have so many plans that it's hard for me to focus on any one of them.	1	2	3	4	5
I change the way I do things when I see a problem with how things are going.	1	2	3	4	5
It's hard for me to notice when I've "had enough" (alcohol, food, sweets).	1	2	3	4	5
I think a lot about what other people think of me.	1	2	3	4	5
I am willing to consider other ways of doing things.	1	2	3	4	5
If I wanted to change, I am confident that I could do it.	1	2	3	4	5
When it comes to deciding about a change, I feel overwhelmed by the choices.	1	2	3	4	5
I have trouble following through with things once I've made up my mind to do something.	1	2	3	4	5
I don't seem to learn from my mistakes.	1	2	3	4	5
I'm usually careful not to overdo it when working, eating, drinking.	1	2	3	4	5
I tend to compare myself with other people.	1	2	3	4	5
I enjoy a routine, and like things to stay the same.	1	2	3	4	5
I have sought out advice or information about changing.	1	2	3	4	5

	Strongly Disagree	Disagree	Unsure	Agree	Strongly Agree
I can come up with lots of ways to change, but it's hard for me to decide which one to use.	1	2	3	4	5
I can stick to a plan that's working well.	1	2	3	4	5
I usually only have to make a mistake one time in order to learn from it.	1	2	3	4	5
I don't learn well from punishment.	1	2	3	4	5
I have personal standards, and try to live up to them.	1	2	3	4	5
I am set in my ways.	1	2	3	4	5
As soon as I see a problem or challenge, I start looking for possible solutions.	1	2	3	4	5
I have a hard time setting goals for myself.	1	2	3	4	5
I have a lot of willpower.	1	2	3	4	5
When I'm trying to change something, I pay a lot of attention to how I'm doing.	1	2	3	4	5
I usually judge what I'm doing by the consequences of my actions.	1	2	3	4	5
I don't care if I'm different from most people.	1	2	3	4	5
As soon as I see things aren't going right I want to do something about it.	1	2	3	4	5
There is usually more than one way to accomplish something.	1	2	3	4	5
I have trouble making plans to help me reach my goals.	1	2	3	4	5
I am able to resist temptation.	1	2	3	4	5
I set goals for myself and keep track of my progress.	1	2	3	4	5
Most of the time I don't pay attention to what I'm doing.	1	2	3	4	5
I try to be like people around me.	1	2	3	4	5
I tend to keep doing the same thing, even when it doesn't work.	1	2	3	4	5
I can usually find several different possibilities when I want to change something.	1	2	3	4	5
Once I have a goal, I can usually plan how to reach it.	1	2	3	4	5
I have rules that I stick by no matter what. If I make a resolution to change something, I pay a lot of attention to how I'm doing.	1	2	3	4	5
Often I don't notice what I'm doing until someone calls it to my attention.	1	2	3	4	5
I think a lot about how I'm doing.	1	2	3	4	5
Usually I see the need to change before others do.	1	2	3	4	5
I'm good at finding different ways to get what I want.	1	2	3	4	5
I usually think before I act.	1	2	3	4	5

	Strongly Disagree	Disagree	Unsure	Agree	Strongly Agree
Little problems or distractions throw me off course.	1	2	3	4	5
I feel bad when I don't meet my goals.	1	2	3	4	5
I learn from my mistakes.	1	2	3	4	5
I know how I want to be.	1	2	3	4	5
It bothers me when things aren't the way I want them. I call in others for help when I need it.	1	2	3	4	5
Before making a decision, I consider what is likely to happen if I do one thing or another.	1	2	3	4	5
I give up quickly.	1	2	3	4	5
I usually decide to change and hope for the best.	1	2	3	4	5
Total your column scores:					

Your Overall Score ____________________

Score Interpretation:

> 239 High (intact) self-regulation capacity (top quartile)

214–238 Intermediate (moderate) self-regulation capacity (middle quartiles)

< 213 Low (impaired) self-regulation capacity (bottom quartile)

Source: Adapted from Brown, Miller, & Lawendowski, 1999.

Appendix 6

Cornell Notes Template

Topic/Objective:		Name:
		Class/Period:
		Date:
Essential Question:		
Questions:	Notes:	
Summary:		

Appendix 7

Student Academic Outcomes After Completing a First-Year Seminar[1]

J. Klatt[2] and R. Ray[3]
University of Wisconsin-Madison
Madison, WI

Abstract: We examine the effects of a first-year seminar course on student academic outcomes in a college of agriculture and life sciences. Seven cohorts of students who had completed the seminar were compared to their peers who had not completed the seminar on several academic variables. Results indicate that students who completed the seminar had higher first-term grade point averages ($F = 3.23$, $p = .037$), shorter time to degree ($F = 3.713$, $p = .027$), higher retention in the college ($X^2 = 5.856$, $p = .016$), and were put on academic probation less often than their peers who had not completed the seminar ($X^2 = 5.028$, $p = .025$). Implications for teaching are discussed.

Keywords: first-year seminar, retention, time to graduation

Introduction

First-year seminars are widely believed to have positive effects on student success and are becoming common offerings in college and university curricula (Keup and Barefoot, 2005; Porter and Swing, 2006; Schnell et al., 2003). Educators have developed many types of first-year seminar courses to address a variety of student needs (Swing, 2002). First-year seminar courses may be particularly valuable to colleges of agriculture where, in recent years, enrollments have grown substantially as instructional resources have declined (Biemiller, 2012).

For example, in the College of Agricultural and Life Sciences at the University of Wisconsin-Madison, undergraduate enrollment rose 30% from 2009 to 2012 (Registrar's Enrollment Report, Fall 2012-2013) while instructional resources declined by more than 5% (Data Digest 2012–2013). Biemiller (2012) notes enrollment in Penn State's college of agriculture grew 48% since 2006 and its budget was cut by more than 18%. Biemiller (2012) indicates many other institutions are experiencing similar circumstances. Colleges of agriculture need new strategies for addressing student academic and career success as they have fewer resources to help greater numbers of students make a successful transition to university life.

Agricultural colleges are also adjusting to a new student population. The large growth in enrollment includes many students who have little direct experience in agriculture (Biemiller, 2012). Students who do not have agricultural backgrounds are interested in issues such as sustainability, local foods, bioenergy and health; they are drawn to majors such as: environmental science, food science, human nutrition, biological systems engineering, agricultural business and communications (Biemiller, 2012; Krogstad, 2012; Mihaljevich, 2010). In addition large numbers of students are interested in genetics, microbiology and biochemistry with intentions to pursue careers in research or veterinary and human medicine (Biemiller, 2012). Because many of these students lack agricultural

1 This study was deemed exempt by the University of Wisconsin-Madison Institutional Review Board.

2 Assistant Dean, Undergraduate Programs and Services, 116 Agriculture Hall, 1450 Linden Dr., Madison, WI 53706, 608-262-4618, jklatt@cals.wisc.edu

3 Professor Emeritus, Forest and Wildlife Ecology, Room 103b, 445 Henry Mall, Madison, WI 53706, 608-698-7517, roray@wisc.edu

literacy, they could benefit from exposure to the big issues colleges of agriculture and life sciences address through teaching, research and outreach. Students also need exposure to the wide range of academic disciplines they can study, the complex nature of the issues on which they are being trained to work and the ethical dilemmas these issues present.

Although attending to student success and student agricultural literacy are not new issues for agricultural colleges (Colbath and Morrish, 2010; Lancaster and Robinson, 2011), larger enrollments and fewer resources make these issues more challenging. First-year seminars are one approach to addressing these pressures.

First-Year Seminars

Researchers have reported positive academic and social benefits of first-year seminar courses (e.g. Keup and Barefoot, 2005; Porter and Swing, 2006). Schnell et al. (2003) examined whether college graduation rates of students taking a first-year seminar differed significantly from a comparison group. They found a significantly greater graduation rate for those enrolled in the seminar. In a survey of almost 20,000 first-year students at 45 four-year institutions, Porter and Swing (2006) examined how first-year seminars affect students' intentions to persist and found these seminars have a positive effect on persistence. Keup and Barefoot (2005) used regression analyses to evaluate a wide range of effects of first-year seminars. Participation in a first-year seminar was positively associated with many variables including studying with other students, speaking-up in class and discussing course content with students outside of class. Compared to students who did not take a first-year seminar course, students who enrolled in a first-year seminar also reported skipping fewer classes, developing more close friendships with other students, participating in more volunteer / community service work, participating in more intramural sports, attending more campus-sponsored events, and interacting more often with faculty outside of class or office hours.

Faculty and instructional staff members in agricultural colleges can create first-year seminars to address student retention, persistence and engagement. First-year seminars represent a promising instructional intervention for colleges adjusting to larger numbers of students and fewer resources to support student success.

Authors have identified several types of first-year seminars. Swing (2002) discussed four types: (a) college transition seminars which covered topics such as orientation to college, life transitions, and academic skills; (b) special academic seminars which focused on a specific topic that was often interdisciplinary; (c) discipline-based seminars which served as an introduction to a major or academic department and were usually housed in individual academic departments; and (d) remedial/study skills seminars which were closely focused on basic study skills. Smith et al. (2009) also discussed ways to differentiate first-year seminar courses. Some seminars served as an orientation to an institution and other seminars emphasized academic content which might be discipline-based. Other distinctions included whether or not the seminar was a requirement, or had credit associated with it. Seminars also differed in class size, length of the course and the components addressed in the course. Griffin et al. (2008) noted that despite differences, most of these courses shared common goals that included developing students' academic skills and orienting students to campus resources.

Teachers interested in developing first-year seminars can create courses based on the needs and educational goals of their departments or institutions. Faculty and instructional staff members can examine the needs rapid growth creates for their departments or the institution as a whole. Their assessment can then be used when considering the type of first-year seminar to create and implement. For example, a hybrid of an academic seminar and orientation seminar could help students with agricultural literacy and retention issues.

This Study

Our study examines the effects of a first-year seminar on a variety of academic variables. For more than a decade, the College of Agricultural and Life Sciences (CALS) at the University of Wisconsin-Madison has offered a first-year seminar. The seminar is a hybrid focusing on both academic content and transition issues. The course is designed to help students, particularly those in rapidly growing life science majors, not only learn about the big issues in agriculture, food, energy, and the environment, but also learn about resources and opportunities that support student success. The course has become an important part of the College as it has grown significantly in recent years.

CALS has 19 departments, 24 majors and about 3300 students. Students with interests relating to human, plant, or animal health; agriculture; energy; the environment; food; business; or community, find a home in CALS. Graduates work on challenging issues such as food safety and security for a global population, sustainable sources of energy, and health concerns such as diabetes and obesity.

The CALS curriculum has a strong focus on math and science. Most first-year students take math and general chemistry their first semester. The seminar provides a way for them to engage applied problems in agriculture and life sciences right away in their first term on campus. The seminar is a 1-credit course that has 14 sessions. The 14 sessions are divided in the following manner. The first two weeks are devoted to a class overview and presentation of ethical paradigms for assessing complex problems. The session on ethics serves as a base for the course because we want students to think about the topics in the course through various ethical paradigms. Ten sessions are devoted to significant topics CALS faculty address through teaching, research, and outreach such as bioenergy and genetically modified foods. Two sessions are devoted to transition issues, specifically advising and career planning. After the introductory session and ethics lecture, the seminar alternates between large lectures and small group discussions. There are five interdisciplinary topics addressed in the course. For example, water quality, bioenergy and food systems are common topics. One week, the students hear a lecture on one of these big complex issues. The next week they break into small groups of 8–10 students for a small group discussion of the topic. Faculty and staff from around the college convene and aid the small groups. Five faculty and staff also provide the lectures. During the class, all students have the opportunity to plan and lead a discussion, visit a faculty member, create an academic plan, and attend a public talk. They also choose four of eight additional activities such as exploring a research opportunity, or an international study opportunity.

With the rise of freshmen seminars and the widely held belief they benefit students; CALS started discussing the possibility of requiring all students to complete a first-year seminar. Therefore, it became important to know if the College's course had a benefit. In this study, we investigated the academic outcomes associated with the College's first-year seminar.

Methods

We used a quasi-experimental design with two groups to evaluate the success of the first-year seminar. The experimental group consisted of the students who completed the seminar and the control group consisted of the students who did not. We examined differences between the two groups on a variety of academic outcomes.

The course was implemented in 2002 and we only included students in the data set who had sufficient time to graduate after completing the seminar. Therefore the sample consisted of the seven cohorts of freshmen admitted between Fall 2002–Fall 2008. The sample included 2628 students, 607 (355 females and 252 males) completed the seminar and 2021 (1268 females and 751 males) did not. Table 1 contains additional details about the sample.

Table 1 Demographic Description of Sample

	Completed Seminar (n = 607)	Did Not Complete Seminar (n = 2021)	Percent of Sample Completing Seminar
Female Students	355	1268	58.5
International Students	31	121	5.1
First Generation College Students	108	259	17.8
Targeted Minority Students	28	141	4.6

All data were obtained from the university Registrar's student record database. We asked the Registrar to provide the following data elements for the students in our sample: high school cumulative grade point average, high school percentile rank, composite ACT scores, composite SAT scores, university grade point averages (first term, second term, degree term, and cumulative), time to degree, degree completion in the college, probation and dropped status, gender indicator, international student indicator, targeted minority student indicator, and first-generation student indicator. The high school academic information and demographic information were used to test the equivalency of the two groups. To investigate the effectiveness of the seminar, we used directional Multivariate Analysis of Variance to test for group differences on university GPA (first term, second term, degree term, cumulative) and time to degree. We used directional Chi Squared tests to investigate group differences on degree completion in the college, probation status, and dropped status.

Results and Discussion

To assess pre-existing differences between the students who completed the first-year seminar and those who did not, we compared the two groups on academic and demographic variables. The two groups did not differ on high school cumulative grade point average, high school percentile rank, composite ACT scores, and composite SAT scores. In addition, the gender distribution of the two groups and the percentage of international students in the two groups did not differ across those who completed the seminar and those who did not. There were differences on other demographic variables. The group that took the seminar had lower proportions of targeted minority and first generation students than the group that did not take the seminar. The groups did not have pre-existing differences on academic preparation and were comparable on some, but not all, demographic variables.

In this study, directional multivariate analysis of variance (MANOVA) was used to test between group differences on a variety of academic indicators of success. We used a directional test because previous theoretical and empirical work indicates first-year seminar courses promote academic success. Means and standard deviations for each outcome variable are presented in Table 2. The omnibus MANOVA test was significant, $F = 3.680$, $p = .002$, $r^2 = .011$. Follow-up analyses revealed several significant tests: first term GPA, $F = 3.23$, $p = .037$, $r^2 = .002$; degree term GPA, $F = 3.713$, $p = .027$, $r^2 = .002$; and time to degree in elapsed calendar years, $F = 4.382$, $p = .018$, $r^2 = .003$. Second term and cumulative grade point averages were not significant. These results indicate the seminar is associated with positive academic outcomes. However, the positive effect on grade point average is not maintained over time.

Table 2 Summary of Outcome Variables by Group – Means and Standard Deviations or Proportions

Group	First Term GPA	Second Term GPA	Degree Term GPA	Cumulative GPA	Time to Degree	Probation Status	Dropped Status	Earned Degree
Completed Seminar	3.21 (0.59)	3.10 (0.68)	3.47 (0.50)	3.28 (0.42)	3.91 (0.51)	191 / 607	28 / 607	319 / 607
Did not Complete Seminar	3.10 (0.71)	3.08 (0.74)	3.40 (0.60)	3.28 (0.43)	3.98 (0.58)	742 / 2021	120 / 2021	949 / 2021

We used Chi squared analyses to investigate group differences in the proportions of students placed on academic probation and dropped status. Placing students on academic probation is the first action taken when students are struggling in the classroom. Placing students on dropped status is a second, and more serious, action taken when students have sustained academic struggles. Fewer students who completed the first-year seminar were placed on academic probation than students who did not complete the seminar, $X^2 = 5.028$, $p = .025$, phi = .070, however, there were no group differences on dropped status. These findings suggest the seminar helps students who have less significant academic struggles succeed, but does not make a difference for those with more serious academic problems. The group difference observed for academic probation could be due to the personal connections students in the seminar develop. It is possible connections to the College faculty and staff members provide students with people to turn to when they need help. The difference could also be that students in the seminar are exposed to campus resources such as the MathLab, Chemistry Learning Center, and other tutoring options that can help them before they experience academic difficulty.

Finally, we investigated retention in CALS. It is important to note that we did not test retention for a degree at the university, just retention for a degree within CALS. We found group differences in the proportion of students retained for a degree in the college. A higher proportion of students in the first-year seminar earned a degree from CALS than those who did not take the seminar, $X^2 = 5.856$, $p = .016$, phi = .047. Students who did not complete the seminar were more likely than those who did to leave CALS for disciplines outside the College or to leave the university entirely. There are at least three possible explanations for this finding. First, students taking the seminar are aware of academic resources to help them succeed in the CALS curriculum that includes challenging math and science courses. Second, from both the topic lectures and course assignments, students see how the College's curricular options lead to careers of interest to them. Third, assignments that require the students to learn about co-curricular and extracurricular opportunities in CALS might connect them to the College. For example, assignments such as exploring a student organization or a research opportunity could get students involved in CALS outside the classroom and allow them to find a home in the College.

Our study focused on academic outcomes. However, future studies of first-year seminar courses in colleges of agriculture could focus on other variables. For example, other authors have examined the need for agriculture literacy and the need for students to understand the complex food, energy, environmental, and health problems on which they could work (Colbath and Morrish, 2010). First-year seminars could be a way to address these issues. If teachers design seminars to cover these topics, then there is justification for having the seminars in the curriculum. The seminar tested in this study was designed to help students, particularly those who do not have an agricultural background, learn about important issues in agriculture and life sciences. A future study could compare the agricultural literacy among students who completed the seminar and those who did not complete the seminar.

Our first assessment focused on practical outcomes. A follow-up is needed that focuses on outcomes such as engagement. Kuh (2005) argues student engagement measures make valuable contributions to an institution's assessment program. When engagement data are combined with other information, the results can be used for: evaluating student performance associated with first-year seminars, assessing teaching and learning processes and meeting accreditation requirements. Future research could examine patterns in student engagement among those who take the first-year seminar course compared to those who do not. Given the nature of assignments in the seminar, students who complete this seminar could be more likely than those who do not to engage in high-impact practices (Kuh, 2008) such as undergraduate research and international experiences.

Future research could also examine outcomes of first-year seminar courses for specific groups of students. Do first-year seminars contribute to positive outcomes for targeted minority students, first-generation college students, and / or international students? It is possible that courses addressing transition to college (e.g. exploring campus resources, connecting to faculty and staff members, exploring co-curricular opportunities) are particularly beneficial for some groups of students.

Weissman and Magill (2008) noted there is limited research on the types of seminars that are most effective for specific types of students. They describe a study that used cluster analysis to develop a typology of student groups based on pre-college characteristics and examined the influence of two types of seminars on the academic performance of each student group. Their findings indicated the effects of the two types of seminars varied across the groups. The authors suggested that students' pre-college characteristics, such as grade point average, can be moderated by participation in the appropriate type of first-year seminar. Instructors should think carefully about their students' characteristics when developing first-year seminars. Additional research is needed to examine the effects of various types of first- year seminars for targeted minority, first-generation, and international students.

As we noted in the literature review, there are different types of first-year seminars. Educators who are considering implementing a first-year seminar can determine the best option for their department or college by asking themselves a few questions. For example, what academic disciplines are taught in their institutions? What qualities should students acquire before graduation? What are some of the goals of the curriculum? What does an ideal student look like at graduation? Should the seminar focus on academic content, transition issues, or both? Answers to these questions can help teachers identify the most important topics a seminar should address and the most appropriate assignments to include. Dooris and Blood (2001) provide a useful discussion of first-year seminar implementation and assessment which could help instructors who are developing a seminar.

There are two notable limitations of this study. First, we cannot generalize the results of this study to other seminars. We use a hybrid seminar that has academic and transition components. The seminar is designed to meet specific college needs. The uniqueness of the seminar limits the conclusions we can draw between our results and first-year seminars generally. Educators and institutions implementing first-year seminars should include assessment in their efforts. Assessment will allow them to investigate the effects their seminars have. Second, we cannot attribute a causal effect to the seminar. We did not have a true experimental design. Students were not randomly assigned to the seminar or no seminar conditions. In addition, students who did not take the seminar might have completed other campus academic programs, such as learning communities or first-year interest groups, which have similar goals. Self-selection or other unidentified factors may have influenced the results of this study.

Summary

Recent growth in colleges of agriculture pressures institutions to develop new ways of supporting student success and helping students learn about the careers they can enter. First-year seminar courses represent one way to address these issues. Our study investigated the academic outcomes of a first-year seminar course. The course was designed to introduce students to curricular themes in agricultural and life science, connect them to activities that would help with professional development, and orient them to the college. Although this study indicates the course is associated with positive outcomes, coping with rapid growth requires a multifaceted approach, not just a first-year seminar.

Literature Cited

Academic Planning and Institutional Research. 2013. Data Digest 2012–2013. (http://apir.wisc.edu/datadigest/201213Digest/digest_13_web.pdf). APIR Reports (accessed 11/25/2013).

Biemiller, L. 2012. As land-grant law turns 150, students crowd into agriculture colleges. *Chronicle of Higher Education* 58(39): A1–A11.

Colbath, S.A. and D.G. Morrish. 2010. What do college freshmen know about agriculture? An evaluation of agricultural literacy. *NACTA Jour* 54(3): 14–17.

Dooris, M.J. and I.M. Blood. 2001. Implementing and assessing first-year seminars. Assessment Update 13(4): 1–4.

Griffin, A., J. Romm and B.F. Tobolowsky. 2008. The first-year seminar characteristics. In B.F. Tobolowsky and Associates (eds.). *2006 National Survey of First-Year Seminars: Continuing innovations in the collegiate curriculum* (Monograph No. 51, pp. 11–62). Columbia, SC: University of South Carolina, National Resource Center for the First-Year Experience and Students in Transition.

Keup, J.R. and B.O. Barefoot. 2005. Learning how to be a successful student: Exploring the impact of first-year seminars on student outcomes. *Jour. of the First-Year Experience & Students in Transition* 17(1): 11–47.

Krogstad, J.M. 2012. Colleges see higher demand for degrees in agriculture. (http://usatoday30.usatoday. com/money/industries/food/story/2012-08-01/ agriculture-industry-studies-surge/56809406/1). *USA Today* (accessed 10/5/2013).

Kuh, G.D. 2005. Putting student engagement results to use: Lessons from the field. Assessment Update 17(1): 12–13.

Kuh, G.D. 2008. High-impact educational practices: What they are, who has access to them, and why they matter. Washington, DC: Association of American Colleges and Universities.

Lancaster, S.H. and J.S. Robinson. 2011. Factors associated with student success in an introductory Plant Sciences Course. *NACTA Jour.* 55(2): 26–31.

Mihaljevich, M.F. 2010. College enrollment attests interest in ag is on the rise. (http://www.farmworldonline.com/News/NewsArticle.asp?newsid=11348). *Farm World* (accessed 10/5/2013).

Porter, S. and R. Swing. 2006. Understanding how first-year seminars affect persistence. *Research in Higher Education*, 47(1): 89–109. DOI: 10.1007/s11162-005-8153-6

Office of the Registrar. 2012. Registrar's enrollment report: As of the end of the sixth week of instruction. (http://registrar.wisc.edu/documents/Stats_all_ 2012-2013Fall.pdf). Registrar's Enrollment Reports (accessed 10/5/2013).

Schnell, C.A., K.S. Louis and C.D. Doetkott. 2003. The first-year seminar as a means of improving college graduation rates. *Jour. of the First-Year Experience and Students in Transition* 15(1): 53–75.

Smith, D.N., R. Goldfine and M. Windham, 2009. Comparing student learning outcomes in an independent section of a first-year seminar to a first- year seminar embedded in a learning community. *Jour. of the First-Year Experience and Students in Transition* 21(2): 47–63.

Swing, R.L. 2002.What type of seminar is best? Brevard, NC: Policy Center on the First Year of College. (http://www.brevard.edu/fye/fyi/essays/essay4.pdf). Brevard College (accessed 10/5/2006).

Weissman, J. and B.A. Magill. 2008. Developing a student typology to examine the effectiveness of first- year seminars. *Jour. of the First-Year Experience and Students in Transition* 20(2): 65–90.

Appendix 8

Self-Discipline Outdoes IQ in Predicting Academic Performance of Adolescents

Angela L. Duckworth[1] and Martin E.P. Seligman
Positive Psychology Center, University of Pennsylvania

Abstract: In a longitudinal study of 140 eighth grade students, self-discipline measured by self-report, parent report, teacher report, and monetary choice questionnaires in the fall predicted final grades, school attendance, standardized achievement-test scores, and selection into a competitive high school program the following spring. In a replication with 164 eighth graders, a behavioral delay-of-gratification task, a questionnaire on study habits, and a group-administered IQ test were added. Self-discipline measured in the fall accounted for more than twice as much variance as IQ in final grades, high school selection, school attendance, hours spent doing homework, hours spent watching television (inversely), and the time of day students began their homework. The effect of self-discipline on final grades held even when controlling for first-marking-period grades, achievement-test scores, and measured IQ. These findings suggest a major reason for students falling short of their intellectual potential: their failure to exercise self-discipline.

What distinguishes top students from others? Are they simply smarter? If so, what explains the wide range of performance among children of equal IQ?

Intellectual strengths (e.g., long-term memory, ability to think abstractly) and nonintellectual strengths (e.g., motivation, self-discipline) surely both contribute to a student's academic performance. Valid measures of IQ have been available since the early 1900s, making possible serious research into the correlates and consequences of intellectual ability. In contrast, nonintellectual strengths, including self-discipline, have lagged behind as objects of empirical investigation. For every article on academic achievement and self-discipline in the PsycInfo database, there are more than 10 articles on academic achievement and intelligence.

Reliable and stable measures of self-discipline for children and adolescents exist. However, reported correlations among different measures are moderate and often inconsistent in magnitude (e.g., White, Moffitt, Caspi, & Bartusch, 1994), suggesting that a valid measure of self-discipline for this age group requires a multimethod, multisource approach. In this investigation, we included self-report, parent report, teacher report, and both hypothetical and behavioral delay-of-gratification measures.

Studies exploring individual differences in self-discipline within nonclinical populations are rare and, unlike the current investigation, have focused on either college students or very young children. Most notably, Mischel and his colleagues showed that greater ability to delay gratification measured at age 4 predicted higher academic and social functioning more than a decade later (H.N. Mischel & Mischel, 1983; W Mischel, Shoda, & Peake, 1988; Shoda, Mischel, & Peake, 1990). More recently, Wolfe and Johnson (1995) found self-discipline to be the only one among 32 measured personality variables (e.g., self-esteem, extraversion, energy level) that predicted college grade point average (GPA) more robustly than SAT scores did. Similarly, Hogan and Weiss (1974) found that high self-discipline distinguished Phi Beta Kappa undergraduates from nonPhi Beta Kappa students of equal intellectual ability. In two large samples of undergraduates, Tangney, Baumeister, and Boone (2004) found that

1 Address correspondence to Angela L. Duckworth, Positive Psychology Center, University of Pennsylvania, 3701 Madcet St., Suite 200, Philalelphia, PA 19104; e-mail: angela_,luckworth@yahoo.com.

self-discipline correlated positively with self-reported grades, as well as a broad array of personal and interpersonal strengths.

In the current investigation, we used a multimethod, multisource approach and a longitudinal, prospective design to test three hypotheses:

- Self-discipline measured in the fall will predict academic performance the following spring. Specifically, compared with their less impulsive counterparts, highly self-disciplined students will earn higher final GPAs and achievement-test scores, come to school more often, watch less television, start their homework earlier, and more likely gain admission to a competitive high school program.
- Self-discipline measured in the fall will account for more variance in academic-performance outcomes than will IQ measured in the fall.
- Self-discipline measured in the fall will predict final GPA, controlling for IQ and first-marking-period GPA.

Our investigation proceeded in two stages. For Study 1, we recruited eighth graders and measured self-discipline and academic performance in the fall and spring. In Study 2, we replicated this study, adding a behavioral delay-of-gratification task of our own design, a group-administered IQ test, and a questionnaire about study and lifestyle habits.

Method

Research Participants

The participants were two consecutive cohorts of eighth-grade students recruited from a socioeconomically and ethnically diverse magnet public school in a city in the Northeast. Fifth-grade students are admitted to this school on the basis of their grades and standardized test scores. At the end of the eighth grade, roughly 70% of these students are selected for a more competitive high school program.

In Study 1, 71% of the school's 198 eighth-grade students ($N = 140$) elected to participate. In mid-November 2002, when the self-discipline measures were administered, the mean age of the participants was 13.4 years ($SD = 0.37$). Fifty-five percent of the participants were Caucasian, 32.1% were Black, 8.6% were Asian, 3.6% were Latino, and 0.7% were American Indian. Fifty-six percent of the participants were female.

In Study 2, 83% of the students ($N = 164$) elected to participate. In mid-October 2003, when the self-discipline measures were administered, the mean age of the participants was 13.8 years ($SD = 0.51$). Fifty-two percent of the participants were Caucasian, 31.1% were Black, 12.2% were Asian, 4.3% were Latino, and 0.6% were American Indian. Fifty-four percent of the participants were female.

Procedure

With the intent of creating a composite self-discipline score for each participant, we recorded questionnaire data from students, parents, and teachers, as well as delay-of-gratification data, in the fall of 2002 for Study 1. We collected the same data and, additionally, administered an IQ test in the fall of 2003 for Study 2. Academic-performance data for each study were recorded approximately 7 months following the collection of the self-discipline data. With the exception of the parent and teacher questionnaires used in Study 2, we confirmed 7-month test-retest reliability for all self-discipline measures by administering them again in the spring.

Measures for Study 1

We employed two widely used self-report measures of self-discipline. The Eysenck I.6 Junior Impulsiveness Subscale (EJI; Eysenck, Easting, & Pearson, 1984) was designed exclusively for children and includes 23 yes/no questions about doing and saying things impulsively. The Brief Self-Control Scale (BSCS; Tangney et al., 2004) is a 13-item questionnaire that is face valid for adolescents but has previously been used only with adult subjects to measure self-regulatory behavior in four domains: thoughts, emotions, impulses, and performance.

Simultaneously, we asked parents and teachers to complete the Self-Control Rating Scale (SCRS; Kendall & Wilcox, 1979). This 33-item questionnaire asks the rater to assess the child using a scale from 1 to 7, where 4 represents "the average child," 7 represents "maximally impulsive," and 1 represents "maximally self-controlled." Items tap the ability to inhibit behavior, follow rules, and control impulsive reactions. To avoid confounding teachers' ratings and teacher-determined grades, we asked students' homeroom advisors rather than subject teachers to complete the questionnaires. To accommodate different interpretations of "average child," we standardized each teacher's scores about his or her own mean prior to all statistical analyses. To assess the ability to delay gratification, we used the Kirby Delay-Discounting Rate Monetary Choice Questionnaire (Kirby, Petry, & Bickel, 1999). This questionnaire, originally designed for adults but face valid for adolescents, contains 27 questions. Each question asks the respondent to choose either a smaller, immediate reward or a larger, delayed reward. From these responses, we calculated a discounting rate (*k*), a parameter that reflects the degree to which future rewards are diminished in value as a function of the delay that must be endured to receive them. As a measure of internal reliability, a consistency value was calculated for each subject as the proportion of responses that were consistent with that subject's *k* value. To normalize the distribution of scores, we used a natural-log transformation of k for all statistical analyses.

We recorded data for a variety of academic-performance variables from school records. These variables included reportcard grades, TerraNova Second Edition Achievement Test Normal Curve Equivalent (NCE) scores from April 2003, attendance, and selection into the school's high school program, a decision made by a committee of eighth-grade teachers and administrators on the basis of the student's likelihood of success in that more rigorous academic program.

Measures for Study 2

For self-reported self-discipline, we again used the EJI and BSCS. However, because several teachers and parents in Study 1 had complained that the format of the SCRS questionnaire confused them, we omitted it from Study 2. Instead, we adapted Lhe Brief Self-Conlrol Scale for parenls and leachers with permission of the authors (R.F. Baumeister, personal communication, July 1, 2003).

In addition to the Kirby Monetary Choice Questionnaire, which taps the ability to delay hypothetical gratification, we included a behavioral measure of the same ability. In a task we designed and called the Delay Choice Task, we gave each participant an envelope that held a $1 bill. We then asked the student to either take the dollar at that moment or return it to us in exchange for $2 dollars a week later, coding the choice to take the dollar immediately as "O" and the choice to wait as "l." We administered the same task again in the spring of 2004 to assess 7-month test-retest reliability.

We also added a measure of intelligence: the Otis-Lennon School Ability Test Seventh Edition (OLSAT7) Level G. This 40-min group-administered intelligence test measures verbal, quantitative, and figural reasoning skills most important to academic learning. The OLSAT 7 School Ability Index (SAI) is a standard score normalized according to the student's age in months, with a mean of 100 and a standard deviation of 16. SAis were converted to percentile ranks, which show standing relative to students of the same age, and then finally to NCE scores for use in all parametric statistical analyses.

We recorded the same academic-performance variables as in Study I. In addition, we asked students in spring 2004 to answer questions about their study and lifestyle habits (e.g., "What time do you usually start your homework'?").

Results

Highly self-disciplined adolescents outperformed their more impulsive peers on every academic-performance variable, including report-card grades, standardized achievement-test scores, admission to a competitive high school, and attendance. Self-discipline measured in the fall predicted more variance in each of these outcomes than did TQ, and unlike TQ, self-discipline predicted gains in academic performance over the school year.

Reliability and Validity of the Self-Discipline Measures

The measures of self-discipline demonstrated satisfactory internal reliability and 7-month test-retest stability. Summary statistics are given in Table 1.

Intercorrelations (rs) between single measures of self-discipline in Study 1 ranged from .12 to .66, with an average of .31. Intercorrelations between single measures of self-discipline in Study 2 ranged from .06 to .73, with an average of .32. To increase validity and reduce multicollinearity, we created composite measures of self-discipline. Scores for some variables were recoded so that for all variables, the larger the score, the higher the level of measured self-discipline. First, we created a composite self-reported self-discipline score for each student as the mean of standardized scores for the EJI and BSCS. Next, we standardized this score and averaged il with standardized scores for the teacher, parent, and delay-of-gratification measures. We calculated the internal reliability of these linear combinations using a formula specific to linear combinations of standardized scores (Nunnally, 1978). The reliability (*r*) of the composite self-discipline score was .96 for Study 1 and .90 for Study 2. We give correlations between single measures of self-discipline and the composite measure in Table 1. Composite self-discipline in Study 2 did not correlate significantly with IQ (r = .13, p = .10).

Self-Discipline Predicts Academic Performance More Robustly Than IQ Does

As shown in Table 2, compared with their more impulsive peers, highly self-disciplined eighth graders earned higher GPAs and achievement-test scores, were more likely to gain admission to a selective high school, had fewer school absences, spent more time on their homework, watched less television, and started their homework earlier in the day. Most correlations between self-discipline and academic-performance variables ranged from medium to large in effect size (Cohen, 1992), and all were statistically significant. In contrast, correlations between IQ and academic-performance variables were at most medium in magnitude, and only half were statistically significant in the predicted direction. For example, in Study 2, the correlation between self-discipline and final GPA (r = .67) was twice the size of the correlation between IQ and final GPA (r = .32). A comparison of these correlation coefficients following the approach of Meng, Rosenthal, and Rubin (1992) showed that self-discipline predicted six of eight academic-performance variables significantly better than did IQ (see Table 2).

When IQ and self-discipline were entered simultaneously in a multiple regression analysis, self-discipline accounted for more than twice as much variance in final GPA (P = .65, $p < .001$) as IQ did (P = .25, $p < .001$). These findings are consistent with Figure 1, which shows that final GPA varied more steeply as a function of self-discipline than as a function of IQ.

Self-Discipline and Changes in GPA Over the School Year

To test the effect of self-discipline on grades controlling for past academic achievement in Study 1, we conducted a simultaneous multiple regression analysis with final GPA as the dependent variable and first-marking-period GPA and self-discipline measured in the fall as predictors. The overall regression was significant, $R^2 = .85$, $F(2, 135) = 386.73$, $p < .001$. Self-discipline predicted final GPA, controlling for first-marking-period GPA (P = .10, p = .02; see Table 3).

In Study 2, we tested the effect of self-discipline on grades controlling for both past academic achievement and IQ. We conducted a simultaneous multiple regression analysis with final GPA as the dependent variable and first-marking-period GPA, April achievement-test scores, self-discipline measured in the fall, and IQ as predictor variables. The overall regression was significant, $R^2 = .90$, F(3, 151) = 4,51.49, $p < .001$. Self-discipline predicted final GPA, even when controlling for IQ and first-marking-period GPA (ß = .08, p = .02; see Table 3).

Table 1 Summary Statistic for the Self-Discipline Measures

Measure	Observed range	Internal reliability	Test-retest stability	Mean	SD	*r* with composite self-discipline
Brief Self-Control Scale (1-5)						
Study l	1–5	.83	.75	3.10	0.74	.66
Study 2	1–5	.86	.76	3.26	0.73	.68
Eysenck l.6 Junior Impulsiveness Subscale* (0-23)						
Study 1	1–22	.80		11.48	4.71	.56
Study 2	1–22	.83	.58	11.06	5.02	.66
Self-Control Rating Scale-parent* (33 231)						
Study 1	42–179	.96	.76	89.55	30.57	.74
Study 2	—	—	—	—	—	—
Self-Control Rating Scale-teacher* (33-231)						
Study 1	33–210	.99	.83	80.21	43.35	.78
Study 2	—	—	—	—	—	—
Kirby Monetary Choice Questionnaire* (.0002–.2485)						
Study 1	.0004–.2485	.98	.60	.03	0.05	.57
Study 2	.0002–.2485	.98	—	.02	0.04	.67
Brief Self-Control Scale-parent (1–5)						
Study 1	—	—	—	—	—	—
Study 2	1–5	.91	—	3.91	0.75	.71
Brief Self-Control Scale-teacher (1–5)						
Study 1	—	—	—	—	—	—
Study 2	1–5	.97	—	4.12	0.99	.71
Delay Choice Task (0–1)						
Study 1	—	—	—	—	—	—
Study 2	0–1	Not applicable	.41	.82	0.39	.51

Note. We report scores in a manner consistent with the originally published scoring protocols; asterisks indicate those measures for which higher scores indicate lower self-discipline. For correlations with the composite measure of self-discipline, these scores were recorded such that higher scores indicate higher self-discipline.

Discussion

We found that self-discipline predicted academic performance more robustly than did IQ. Self-discipline also predicted which students would improve their grades over the course of the school year, whereas IQ did not.

The multimethod, multisource approach to measuring self-discipline employed in this study provided a sounder measure of trait self-discipline than used in most prior studies of this age group. There was high test-retest stability for the measures; the ratings of parents, teachers, and students concurred (average $r = .41$ in Study 1 and .47 in Study 2); preferences for deferred rather than immediate hypothetical monetary rewards correlated positively with these personality measures {average $r = .12$ in Study 1 and .33 in Study 2); and preference for deferred rather than immediate real monetary awards correlated positively with all other types of self-discipline measures {average $r = .14$ in Study 2). Thus, adolescents reliably differed in their ability Lo choose successfully between conflicting desires and impulses, and when we measured self-discipline by a composite measure rather than by a single measure, we found that self-discipline substantially influenced academic performance.

When it comes to predicting student achievement, does self-discipline outdo IQ? In Study 2, we found that correlation coefficients between self-discipline and most achievement indicators were significantly higher than and at least twice the size of correlations between IQ and the same outcomes. Also, the standardized regression coefficient of self-discipline was more than twice that of TQ in a simultaneous multiple regression predicting final GPA. These results suggest that, indeed, self-discipline has a bigger effect on academic performance than does intellectual talent.

Table 2 Intercorrelations Between Academic-Performance Indicators and Composite Self-Discipline Score and IQ

	Study 1 (*N* = 140)	Study 2 (*N* = 164)		Two-tailed *p* of difference between the IQ and self-discipline correlations
Academic-performance variable	Self discipline	Self-discipline	IQ	
First-marking-period GPA	.52***	.66***	.34***	<.001
Final GPA	.55***	.67***	.32***	<.001
Spring achievement test	.29***	.43***	.36***	n.s.
Selection to high school	.42***	.56***	.26***	<.001
School absences	–.17*	–.26**	–.07	.06
Homework hours	—	.35***	–.09	<.001
Television hours	—	–.33***	–.06	.01
Time of day homework is begun	—	–.26**	.18*	<.001

Note. GPA = grade point average.
$^{*}p < .05$. $^{**}p < .01$ $^{***}p < .001$.

We see three possible objections to this conclusion. First, it can be argued that self-discipline in this study was measured with greater reliability than IQ, and that this alone accounts for its higher correlation with GPA. However, an argument against this hypothesis is the accuracy and precision of the Otis-Lennon test. This widely used measure has a Kuder-Richardson internal reliability coefficient of .9 and a standard error of measurement of 5.7 SAI units on a scale from 0 to 160 (Otis & Lennon, 1997). Moreover, correlations (*rs*) between the single self-discipline measures and final GPA ranged from .33 to .57, whereas the correlation between IQ and final GPA was only .32.

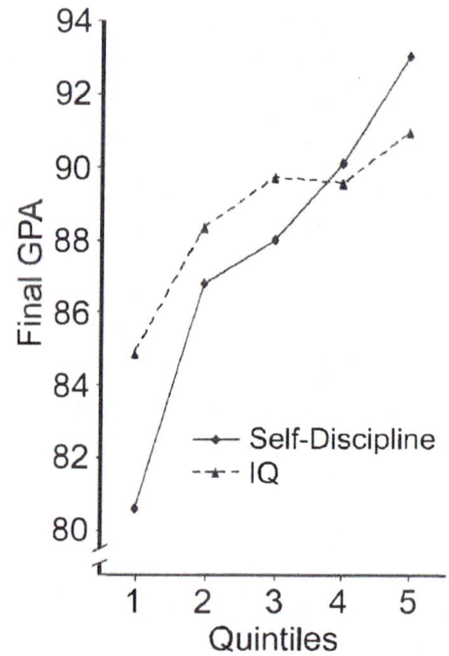

Fig. 1 Final grade point average (GPA) as a function of ranked quintiles of IQ and self-discipline in Study 2.

A second objection to the claim that discipline outdoes talent in predicting academic performance is that in the studied population, there was restriction of range for IQ, but not for self-discipline. Indeed, whereas the standard deviation for the Otis-Lennon is 16 for a normative population, in the current study of magnet-school students, the standard deviation for the Otis-Lennon was just under 10. In contrast, for the only self-discipline measure for which normative data for the same age group are available-the EJI-the variance in the present study was typical of a normative population. According to classical test theory (Lord & Novick, 1968), the unattenuated population correlation (p) between IQ and final GPA in the current study is estimated as .49, still smaller than the observed correlation between self-discipline and GPA (r = .67). Moreover, the fact that students from this school were admitted on the basis of their past academic success and the finding that academic success and self-discipline were highly correlated suggest that there was likely some restriction on range for self-discipline, as well as for IQ. To address this limitation, we plan to replicate these studies with more heterogeneous populations of adolescents.

Table 3 Summary of Simultaneous Multiple Regression for Variables Predicting Final Grade Point Average (GPA) in Study 1 (*N* = 137) and in Study 2 (*N* = 1.54)

Variable	*B*	*SE B*	ß
Study 1			
First-marking-period GPA	0.96	0.04	.87***
Self-discipline	0.95	0.39	.10*
Study 2			
IQ	0.01	0.01	.01
First-marking-period GPA	0.84	0.04	.89***
Self-discipline	0.76	0.33	.08*

$^{*}p < .05$. $^{***}p < .001$.

Finally, the claim that discipline influences achievement more than talent does is weakened if one puts more stock in standardized achievement-test scores than in report-card grades: In Study 2, the correlation between self-discipline and achievement-test scores (r = .43) was nonsignificantly higher than that between IQ and achievement-test scores (r = .36). However, we believe that insofar as GPA reflects performance on hundreds of exams, papers, class discussions, and homework assignments assessed by multiple teachers over the course of a school year, GPA is a more valid indicator of academic achievement than a standardized test that samples a student's knowledge and skills over the course of a few hours. We also suspect that some of the common variance between IQ and achievement-test scores is due to shared method variance. It may be that independently of what they know or can do, some students excel at both kinds of multiple-choice tests taken under strict time limits.

Underachievement among American youth is often blamed on inadequate teachers, boring textbooks, and large class sizes. We suggest another reason for students falling short of their intellectual potential: their failure to exercise self-discipline. As McClure (1986) has speculated, "Our society's emphasis on instant gratification may mean that young students are unable to delay gratification long enough to achieve academic competence" (p. 20). We believe that many of America's children have trouble making choices that require them to sacrifice short-term pleasure for long-term gain, and that programs that build self-discipline may be the royal road to building academic achievement.

Acknowledgments: This research was supported by a National Science Foundation Graduate Fellowship and by National Institute of Mental Health Grants MH-52270 and MH-63430 (both to M.E.P.S.). For helpful comments on this manuscript, we thank Dianne Chambless, Sara Jaffee, Christopher Peterson, John Sabini, and Joseph Strayhorn. For assistance in gathering F and processing data, we gratefully acknowledge the efforts of Alan Carniol, Daphnee Jean-Francois, Derek Freres, Kelly Li, Alex McCauley, and Jennifer Yu.

References

Cohen, J. (1992). A power primer. *Psychological Bulletin, 112,* 155–159.

Eysenck, S.B., Easting, G., and Pearson, P. (1984). Age norms for impulsiveness, venturesomeness and empathy in children. *Personality and Individual Differences, 5,* 315–321.

Hogan, R., and Weiss, D.S. (1974). Personality correlates of superior academic achievement. *Journal of Counseling; Psychology, 21,* 144–149.

Kendall, P.C., and Wilcox, L.E. (1979). Self-control in children: Development of a rating scale. *Journal of Consulting and Clinical Psychology, 47,* 1020–1029.

Kirby, K.N., Petry, N.M., and Bickel, W.K. (1999). Heroin addicts have higher <discount rates for delayed rewards than non-drug-using controls. *Journal of Experimental Psychology: General, 128,* 78–87.

Lord, F.M., and Novick, M.R. (1968). *Statistical theories of mental test scores.* Reading, MA: Addison-Wesley.

McClure, H.F. (1986). Self control and achievement motivation in young and old subjects. *Psychology: A Journal of Human Behavior, 23(1),* 20–22.

Meng, X.-L., Rosenthal, R., and Rubin, D.B. (1992). Comparing correlated correlation coefficients. *Psychological Bulletin, 111,* 172–175.

Mischel, H.N., and Mischel, W. (1983). The development of children's knowledge of self-control strategies. *Child Development, 54,* 603–619.

Mischel, W., Shoda, Y., and Peake, P.K. (1988). The nature of adolescent competencies predicted by preschool delay of gratification. *Journal of Personality and Social Psychology, 54,* 687–696.

Nunnally, J. (1978). *Psychometric theory.* New York: McGraw-Hill.

Otis, A.S., and Lennon, R.T. (1997). *Otis-Lennon School Ability Test (OLSAT) technical manual.* San Antonio, TX: Harcourt Brace Educational Measurement.

Shoda, Y., Mischel, W., and Peake, P.K. (1990). Predicting adolescent cognitive and self-regulatory competencies from preschool delay of gratification: Identifying diagnostic conditions. *Developmental Psychology, 26,* 978–986.

Tangney, J.P., Baumeister, R.F., and Boone, A.L. (2004). High self-control predicts good adjustment, less pathology, better grades, and interpersonal success. *Journal of Personality, 72,* 271–322.

White, J.L., Moffitt, T.E., Caspi, A., and Bartusch, DJ. (1994). Measuring impulsivity and examining its relationship to delinquency. *Journal of Abnormal Psychology, 103,* 192–205.

Wolfe, R.N., and Johnson, S.D. (1995). Personality as a predictor of college performance. *Educational and Psychological Measurement, 55,* 177–185.

(Received 10/20/04: Revision accepted 12/01/04; Final materials received 12/21/04)

Appendix 9

General Health of Students

General health of students of medical sciences and its relation to sleep quality, cell phone overuse, social networks and internet addiction

Rasool Kawyannejad[a], Maryam Mirzaei[b], Ali Valinejadi[c], Behzad Hemmatpour[d], Hasan Ali Karimpour[d], Javad AminiSaman[d], Ebrahim Ezzati[a], Siavash Vaziri[e], Mojgan Safaeepour[a] and Saeed Mohammadi[1,d]

(Full list of author information is available at the end of the article)

Abstract

Background: In recent years, the phenomena of access to the cell phone and addiction to the Internet have been developed among students due to their many applications and attractiveness. Therefore, the present study was conducted with the aim of evaluating general health status and also determining the predictive role of variables such as cell phone usage, sleep quality, internet addiction and social networks addiction in students.

Methods: This cross-sectional study was conducted on 321 students of Kermanshah University of Medical Sciences in an analytical approach. Data collection tools were: Goldberg's General Health Questionnaire, Pittburgh Sleep Quality Index, Young Internet Addiction Test, Social Network Addiction Questionnaire, and Cell Phone Overuse Scale. Data analysis was done using SPSS version 21 and general linear model.

Results: Based on the results, the mean (SD) score of the general health was 21.27 (9.49). Variables of gender, sleep quality, and levels of cell phone usage were independent predictors of student's health. Male students (β (95% CI) = -0.28 (-0.49 to -0.01) and students with favorable sleep quality (β (95% CI) = -0.22 (-0.44 to -0.02) had lower total health score than the reference category (female students and students with unfavorable sleep quality, respectively). In addition, students with cell phone overuse (β (95% CI) = 0.39 (0.08 to 0.69) had a higher general health score than the reference category (students with cell phone little use).

In general, this group of students had lower general health status (Low or high scores of general health indicate a higher and lower general health status for subjects, respectively).

Conclusion: Variables of gender, sleep quality and cell phone use were the most important variables associating the general health of medical students.

Keywords: General health, Sleep quality, Internet addiction, Student

Background

General health as a substantial basis of the health system consists of overarching social activities and actions that are mainly based on the prevention strategy [1]. Since the health of the students guarantees the level of science and development of each community, attention to promoting the general health of students of medical sciences as human resources and responsible persons for the health of community and also identifying the factors

1 Correspondence: dr.saidmohamadi@gmail.com

affecting this variable seems necessary [2–4]. In Iran, numerous studies have been conducted on the general health of students, and the results of these studies can provide valuable information about educational planning to the authorities. According to Jahanbani et al., 11.8% of students did not have good general health [5]. According to a review and meta-analysis study that combined the results of 77 studies in 2016, the prevalence of mental disorders among Iranian universities based on the general health questionnaire was estimated to be 33% (95% CI = 0.29–0.37) [6]. Technology and its daily communication are among the most influential factors on health [3, 7]; On the other hand, in recent years, the phenomenon of access and addiction to the Internet and social networks has been developed among students due to its various applications and attractiveness [7]. Since educational environments such as universities are the places of Internet addiction development, by cell phone overuse and spending lots of time on the Internet students can be exposed to abnormal patterns of sleep, lifestyle changes and weak academic performance [8, 9].

The lifestyle changes of students can threaten the general health of students as a result of using Internet and cell phone, and may cause a loss in active human resources [6, 8]. Surveys on general health of students have shown that variables such as gender, cell phone overuse, addiction to social networks, sleep quality, etc. affected the general health. In a research conducted in 2009 on students of Zahedan University of Medical Sciences, reported the association of the general health of participants with the level of Internet addiction; in the other word, general health and its dimensions were more threatened among the Internet addicts compared to normal users [10]. In the study of Bahri et al. [11] the general health score has shown a significant and negative statistical relationship with addiction to the Internet. Other studies have reported a significant positive correlation between general health dimensions and cell phone overuse in students; besides, the disturbance of students' sleeping patterns due to cell phone overuse, as well as psychological demands and pressures of academic environments were common among students [12–14].

Therefore, it seems that sleep quality, Internet addiction, and cell phone overuse and their relationship with general health in the students need to be examined.

To date, In Iran, few studies have investigated the relationship between general health and variables such as Internet and cell phone addiction, but in interpreting the results cultural differences and other factors such as different usage rate of Internet and cell phone should have been considered for the students of different universities [11, 12, 15].

Until now, however, general health and the factors associating the general health among medical students in Iran have received minimal attention and little is known about the factors associating the general health in this group. As mentioned above, according to the serious concerns about the association of cell phone overuse, Internet and social networks on health, the present study was conducted to determine better understand the students' general health status and its relationship with cell phone overuse, Internet and social networks, as well as the sleep quality (as one of the key indicators of general health) on the students of Kermanshah University of Medical Sciences. The results of this study can be useful to identify the factors associating general health and preventative actions to eliminate these factors in medical students.

Methods

Participants

After obtaining ethical permission from Ethics Committee of Kermanshah University of Medical Sciences in 2016, this cross-sectional study was conducted on 321 students of medical sciences in Kermanshah University of Medical Sciences through random cluster sampling. In the first semester of 2016 in Kermanshah University of Medical Sciences, a sample size of 350 out of 5000 students was randomly selected using Morgan table with a 95% confidence interval and 5% error. They were selected from all levels (bachelor, master, G.P.) and disciplines (paramedical, medical, nursing, dentistry, health, and pharmacy) (out of 350 samples, 29 did not return the questionnaire). The inclusion criteria included being a second year student or above, using smartphone and social networks applications, and being an indigenous student of Kermanshah and not living in dormitories. Before the commencement of the study, participants were informed of the objectives and importance of the survey. All the subjects were also assured that the data were confidential and they were collected just for the current research.

Instruments

In the present study, the main variables included general health, sleep quality, cell phone overuse, social networks addiction, age, and gender. The data collection tools were General Health Questionnaire (GHQ28), Pittsburg Sleep Quality Index, Social Network Addiction Questionnaire, and Cell Phone Overuse Scale.

General Health Questionnaire (GHQ-28) is a psychometric screening tool to examine the mental health in the recent month. It comprises 28 questions, each with a four-point Likert scale for responses. It was developed by Goldberg and Hillier. GHQ-28 is divided into four components ((1) somatic symptoms, (2) social dysfunction, (3) anxiety and insomnia and (4) severe depression); and each subscale comprises 7 items. The scoring range is from 0 to 84. After scoring, the total score of general health is calculated from the total score of the questions. Based on the study of Norbala et al. [15] the cut-off point for the general health score was determined 23. Less and more scores below this cut-off point, respectively, indicated a higher and lower general health status for subjects. Validity and reliability of the original questionnaire as well as the Persian version have been confirmed in various studies [15, 16].

Pittburgh Sleep Quality Index investigates the attitude towards sleep quality in the last 4 weeks. It has seven component scores including subjective sleep quality, sleep latency, sleep duration, habitual sleep efficiency, sleep disturbances, use of sleeping medication, and daytime dysfunction. Each item is scored on a 0–3 Likert scale. The total score is calculated, ranging from 0 to 21. Higher score denotes a lower quality sleep. The total score above 5 indicates a significant sleep disorder. Validity and reliability of this questionnaire in Iran were confirmed by Cronbach's alpha (0.77) in the study of Moghaddam et al. [17].

Cell Phone Overuse Scale is designed based on the psychological index of the Diagnostic and Statistical Manual of Mental Disorders. It has 23 items and scoring is based on a 6-point Likert scale. The score above 75 shows overuse, the score between 25 and 75 demonstrates normal use, and the score below 25 shows low usage [18]. Validity and reliability of this questionnaire in Iran were confirmed by Cronbach's alpha (0.90) in the study of Golmohammadian et al. [12].

Young Internet Addiction Test (YIAT) is a reliable and valid questionnaire including 20 items being assessed through a five-point Likert scale [7]. The minimum score is 20 and the maximum is 100. Based on the participants' scores, three groups were classified as following: no Internet addiction (score 20–49), exposed to the Internet addiction (50–79), and Internet addiction (80–100) [7].

Social Network Addiction Questionnaire is a researcher-made questionnaire, which comprises 15 questions about knowing social networks (Facebook, Orkut, MySpace, Viber, Line, Tango, WeChat, Telegram, Whatsapp, Instagram, Twitter, LinkedIn, YouTube, Status, etc.) and using them. The scoring is based on a five-point Likert scale (from 5 = always to 1 = rarely). For developing this researcher-made questionnaire various authentic scientific texts, similar studies, and experts' opinions in this field were used. Its validity was confirmed by five faculty members and its reliability was confirmed by Cronbach's alpha (0.83). Assessing and scoring were as following: total score from 1 to 25 assumed as a normal user; the scores from 26 to 49 suggested that the user was exposed to get addicted to social networks and it was better to prevent it; and scores from 50 to 75 considered that the user was addicted to social networks and the user should think about the treatment as soon as possible [19].

In the present study, the reliability of all the used questionnaires was confirmed by the alpha coefficient of 0.7.

Statistical tests

The descriptive statistics of mean (standard deviation (SD)) and frequency (percentage) were used to describe the variables.

The probability of normal distributions of data was confirmed by Kolmogorov-Smirnov test for quantitative variables ($P > 0.05$). Pearson correlation analysis was used to assess the association between the quality of sleep and general health subscale.

General linear model (GLM) was used to determine the relationship between the variables including gender, age, internet addiction cell phone overuse, sleep quality and general health's total score, as well as to determine the proportion of each variable in the general health score. Qualitative variables were introduced into the analysis as dummy variables; first, each unadjusted variable was entered into the GLM, then based on single-variable tests the variables with $P < 0.05$ by the adjustment of other variables entered the GLM. Data analysis was performed by SPSS version 21 (SPSS Inc. Chicago, II, USA); and the significance level was determined less than 0.05.

Results

The mean (SD) age of the students participating in the survey was 22.03(1.81) years; and 39.9% of them were male students. The amount of real sleep in the participants was 6.58 (1.05) hours; and the ranging score was from 0 to 21. Besides, 53.9% of students had poor sleep quality. The duration of daily cell phone use was 3.32 (1.42) hours; and the duration of daily activity in social networks was 3.87 (2.87) hours, as 31 subjects (9.7%) had social networks addiction (Table 1). The mean (SD) total score of general health in students was 21.27 (9.04), while the minimum score was 5 and the maximum was 66. Total score of general health by the studied variables is shown in Table 2. The highest scores of general health were seen in students who had cell phone overuse and addiction to the Internet and social networks, as well as in the female students.

Table 1 Frequency distribution and percentage of students according to the variables ($n = 321$)

Variable	Categories	Frequency (percentage)
Gender	Male	128 (39.9)
	Female	193 (60.1)
Social networks addiction	No social networks addiction	116 (36.1)
	Exposed to the social networks addiction	174 (54.2)
	Social networks addiction	31 (9.7)
Internet addiction levels	No Internet addiction	215 (67)
	Exposed to the Internet addiction	83 (25.9)
	Internet addiction	23 (7.2)
Cell phone overuse	Overuse	29 (9)
	Normal use	241 (75.4)
	Little use	50 (15.6)
Sleep quality	Favorable	167 (52)
	Unfavorable	154 (48)
Age (years)[a]		22.03 (1.82)

[a]Mean (SD)

Table 2 The mean (SD) total score of general health in the students according to the variables ($n = 321$)

Variables	Categories	Mean (SD)
Gender	Male	19.93 (8.42)
	Female	22.16 (9.38)
Social networks addiction	No social networks addiction	19.95 (9.12)
	Exposed to the social networks addiction	21.89 (8.88)
	Social networks addiction	22.71 (9.26)
Internet addiction levels	No Internet addiction	21.17 (9.39)
	Exposed to the Internet addiction	20.81 (7.96)
	Internet addiction	23.91 (9.26)
Cell phone overuse	Little use	20.51 (8.97)
	Normal use	22.06 (8.33)
	Overuse	24.50 (9.19)
Sleep quality	Favorable	20.07 (8.66)
	Unfavorable	22.17 (9.22)

Furthermore, there were significant moderate correlations between quality of sleep and the total score of general health (r = 0.506, p < 001) and its four components (somatic symptoms (r = 0.381) social dysfunction (r = 0.301) anxiety and insomnia (r = 0.325) and severe depression (0.341); all p value < 0.001).

The relationship between the variables and the general health of students is shown in Table 3.

Based on the univariate analysis, there was a significant relationship between the mean total score of general health, gender, cell phone overuse, and sleep quality levels (p < 0.05). Then, based on the multivariate analysis and by adjusting other variables, the gender, cell phone overuse and sleep quality found a significant relationship with general health score; these variables predicted 20% of general health variance in medical students (Table 3). Overall, male students (β (95%CI) = −0.28 (−0.49 to −0.01) and students with favorable sleep quality (β (95%CI) = −0.22 (−0.44 to −0.02) had lower general health scores than the reference category (female students and students with unfavorable sleep quality, respectively).

Moreover, students with over use (β (95%CI) = 0.39 (0.08 to 0.69) of cell phone had higher general health scores. In the other words, students with over use of cell phone are less healthy than the reference category (students with cell phone little use).

Discussion

In the present study the mean score of general health was at a favorable level. There was a significant relationship between sleep quality and general health. In addition to the level of sleep quality, the gender and cell phone overuse were also other associate factors of general health in students.

The mean total score of general health in the students was 21.27 (9.04) (the scores ≤ 23 in health were considered as favorable scores). According to other national studies, the mean (SD) general health in students of Gonabad University of Medical Sciences, Rasht Midwifery School, and Urmia University of Medical Sciences were respectively 25.84 (11.97), 22.54 (11.22), 23.42 (22.09) [11, 20, 21].

Table 3 Comparison of general health's total score with variables based on univariate and multivariate general linear model (*n* = 321) (depended variable: General health)

Variables	β (95%CI)	Unadjusted *P*-Value	β (95%CI)	Adjusted *P*-Value
Gender	Female (reference)			
	Male −0.25 (−0.48 to −0.03)	0.031	−0.28 (−0.49 to −0.01)	0.019
Social networks addiction	Social networks addiction (reference)			
	No Internet addiction 0.31 (−0.09 to 0.71)	0.131	—	—
	Exposed to the social networks addiction 0.10 (−0.47 to 0.29)	0.644	—	—
Internet addiction levels	Internet addiction (reference)			
	No Internet addiction 0.32 (−0.13 to 0.73)	0.913	—	—
	Exposed to the Internet addiction 0.35 (−0.12 to 0.81)	0.254	—	—
Cell phone overuse	Little use (reference)			
	Normal use 0.27 (−0.19 to 0.73)	0.245	0.23 (−0.71 to 0.25)	0.354
	Overuse 0.44 (0.13 to 0.75)	0.044	0.39 (0.08 to 0.69)	0.014
Sleep quality	Unfavorable (reference)			
	Favorable −0.24 (−0.46 to- 0.02)	0.039	−0.22 (−0.44 to −0.02)	0.041
Age (years)	0.06 (−0.17 to 0.06)	0.230	—	—

In the current study, one of the associate factors was the gender variable. It is seen that general health's total score in male students was less than in the reference category (female students); and the general health in male students was more favorable than in female students ($P < 0.05$). Various studies have reported significant relationship between the general health's total score and the student's gender; these results were consistent with results of the current study [22–24]. On the contrary, this significant relationship between the general health's total score and the student's gender was not seen in the studies of Hashemi et al., Mosalanejad et al., and Sotodeh et al. [5, 25, 26]. Lower quality of general health in female students can be attributed to issues such as the discrimination and cultural differences existing in the society of Iran between men and women (e.g. constraints, lack of sports facilities, and unreasonable prejudice towards women), which negatively affects women's general health [23, 24].

In the present study, based on the variable of cell phone, the highest mean scores for general health were seen in students with overuse of cell phone. This indicates that students who had over use of cell phone had lower general health status than the reference category (students with cell phone little use). These findings are consistent with the results of similar studies in this field [10, 12, 27, 28].

The Yaseminejad et al. indicated that general health score was significantly associated with cell-phone over use in students [12]. Similar results can be attributed to the fact that students who have overuse and unnecessary use of cell phone may neglect many of their daily activities. Besides, cell phone overuse results in improper behavior patterns, such as staying awake at night and exchanging messages; this results in disturbances in sleep patterns and, consequently, weakening their general health [29]. In sum, these findings support the negative impact of cell phone overuse on students' physical and psychological health [30].

In this study, GHQ_total score in subjects with poor sleep quality was higher than those with good sleep quality. So that the group with favorable sleep level had higher level of general health than the reference category (students who had unfavorable sleep level). Previous studies have shown that the variable of sleep quality has played an important role in the general health of students, and the increase of favorable sleep level could improve the general health, and as a result it could improve the quality of life and academic performance of students. Mohammadi et al., in their study in 2012, found a positive and significant relationship between the sleep quality and general health [31]. Likewise Chegini et al. in their research stated that the scores of sleep quality had strong and significant correlation with the general health's total score [32]. According to the results of the present study that indicate the positive relationship between general health and cell phone overuse, there is a presumption that cell phone addiction affects the quality of medical students' sleep, and consequently abnormal sleeping pattern in students negatively affects their general health [29, 33].

Findings of the present study showed no significant relationship between age, levels of Internet and social networks addiction and the general health score. These findings are consistent with other studies in this field, for instance, Heravi et al.'s study on Tehran's nursing students indicated that there was no significant correlation between age and general health score [23].

On the other hand, regarding the lack of significant relationship between the levels of Internet and social networks addiction and the general health's total score, the results of the current study were not consistent with the results of some similar studies in this regard [10, 11, 34]. This inconsistency of results can be due to some issues such as the difference in nature of populations, the difference in the evaluation methods and reporting the studied variables, cultural and social differences, and universities' welfare facilities.

As the main strengths of the study we can mention the appropriate sample size and the use of valid and reliable questionnaires. The current study has some limitations. First, due to the cross-sectional nature of the present study, it is not possible to deduce the causal relationship. Moreover, since the study subjects were limited to medical sciences students and they are not represent the general population of young adults, results of the present study cannot be generalized to the general population of young adults. Along with the consideration of more variables in the future, conducting prospective studies is recommended to confirm the causal relationship of the variables.

Conclusion

The present study reviewed the general health and some of its predictive factors in students of Kermanshah University of Medical Sciences. The mean score of general health was moderate. Variables such as gender, sleep quality, and cell phone overuse were associated of general health. Since general health affects many aspects of students' life, including their academic achievement, identifying health-related factors can be fruitful in planning for enhancing factors of general health in medical students.

Abbreviations

GHQ-28: General Health Questionnaire; GLM: General linear model; SD: Standard deviation; YIAT: Young Internet Addiction Test

Acknowledgments

We would like to extend our sincere gratitude and appreciation to the Research Deputy of Kermanshah University of Medical Sciences and all the students who greatly assisted the research.

Funding

This study was granted by Kermanshah University of medical sciences (grant number 95313). The funder had no role in the study design, the collection, analysis and interpretation of the data, the writing of the report, and the decision to submit the article for publication.

Availability of data and materials

The data set supporting the conclusions of this publication is included within the article.

Authors' contributions

RK designed the original idea, designed the research and methodology, conducted the data acquisition and wrote the initial drafts of the manuscripts. MM developed all statistical analyses, co-wrote the manuscript, and made substantial contributions to each section of the manuscript through the final version of the article. AV, BH, HK and JA helped in designing, conducting the study, and revise the manuscript. EE and SV helped in designing the study, interpret the data and writing the manuscript. MS helped in designing the study and collecting the data. SM helped in designing and conducting the study and writing the manuscript. All authors read and approved the final manuscript.

Ethics approval and consent to participate

The study was approved by the ethics committee of Kermanshah University of medical sciences, Kermanshah, Iran. Individual participate consent was not required.

Consent for publication

Not applicable.

Competing interests

The authors declare that they have no competing interests.

Publisher's Note

Springer Nature remains neutral with regard to jurisdictional claims in published maps and institutional affiliations.

Author details

[a]Department of Anesthesia, School of Allied Medical Sciences, Kermanshah University of Medical Sciences, Kermanshah, Iran. [b]Department of Rehabilitation and Sports Medicine, School of Allied Medical Sciences, Kermanshah University of Medical Sciences, Kermanshah, Iran. [c]Department of Health Information Technology, School of Allied Medical Sciences, Semnan University of Medical Sciences, Semnan, Iran. [d]Department of Anesthesia, School of Medicine, Kermanshah University of Medical Sciences, Kermanshah, Iran. [e]Department of Infectious Disease, School of Medicine, Kermanshah University of Medical Sciences, Kermanshah, Iran.

Received: 2 February 2019 Accepted: 21 April 2019

Published online: 14 May 2019

References

1. World Health Organisation. Mental health: concepts, emerging evidence, practice. Geneva: University of Melbourne; 2010.
2. Jackson SF, Cole DC. Graduate global public health education: activities and outcomes in relation to student prior experience. *Global J Health Sci.* 2013;5:54.
3. Mirzaeean B, Baezzat F. Internet addiction among students and its impact on mental health. *J Inf Commun Technol Educ.* 2006;3:185–206.
4. Block RC, Duron V, Creigh P, McIntosh S. International service and public health learning objectives for medical students. *Health Educ J.* 2013;72:530–6.
5. Jahani Hashemi H, Rahimzadeh Mirmahalleh S, Ghafelehbashy H, Sarichloo M. Investigating the mental health of the first- and last-year students of QUMS (2005). *J Qazvin Univ Med Sci.* 2008;7:30–8.
6. Zare N, Parvareh M, NOURI B, Namdari M. Mental health status of Iranian university students using the GHQ-28: a meta-analysis. *Sci J Kurdistan Univ Med Sci.* 2016;21:1–16.
7. Alavi SS, Jannatifard F, Eslami M, Rezapour H. Survey on validity and reliability of diagnostic questionnaire of internet addiction disorder in students users. *ZJRMS.* 2011;13:34–8.
8. Yang SC, Tung C-J. Comparison of internet addicts and non-addicts in Taiwanese high school. *Comput Hum Behav.* 2007;23:79–96.
9. Vizeshfar F. Assessment of the internet addiction between Iranian net users. *J Fundam Mental Health.* 2005;7:27–33.
10. Nastiezaie N. The relationship between general health and internet addiction. *Zahedan J Res Med Sci.* 2009;11:57–63.
11. Bahri N, SadeghMoghadam L, Khodadost L, Mohammadzade J, Banafsheh E. Internet addiction status and its relation with students' general health at Gonabad Medical University. *Mod Care Sci Q Birjand Nurs Midwifery Fac.* 2012;8:166–73.
12. Yaseminejad P, Golmohammadian M, Yoosefi N. The study of the relationship between cell-phone use and general heath in students. *Knowl Res Appl Psychol.* 2012;13:62–72.
13. Toda M, Monden K, Kubo K, Morimoto K. Mobile phone dependence and health-related lifestyle of university students. *Soc Behav Personal Int J.* 2006; 34:1277–84.
14. Beranuy M, Oberst U, Carbonell X, Chamarro A. Problematic internet and mobile phone use and clinical symptoms in college students: the role of emotional intelligence. *Comput Hum Behav.* 2009;25:1182–7.
15. Noorbala A, Mohammad K. The validation of general health questionnaire- 28 as a psychiatric screening tool. *Hakim Res J.* 2009;11:47–53.
16. Sterling M. General health questionnaire–28 (GHQ-28). *J Phys.* 2011;57:259.
17. Moghaddam JF, Nakhaee N, Sheibani V, Garrusi B, Amirkafi A. Reliability and validity of the Persian version of the Pittsburgh sleep quality index (PSQI-P). *Sleep Breathing.* 2012;16:79–82.
18. Jenaro C, Flores N, Gómez-Vela M, González-Gil F, Caballo C. Problematic internet and cell-phone use: psychological, behavioral, and health correlates. *Addict Res Theory.* 2007;15:309–20.
19. Barat Dastjerdi N, Sayasi S. Relationship between using social networks and internet addiction and depression among students. *J Res Behav Sci.* 2013; 10:332–41.
20. Namazi A, Alizadeh S, S K-T. The correlation between general health, emotional intelligence and academic achievement together on midwifery students. *J Clin Nurs Midwifery.* 2015;4:20–8.
21. Tofighi A, Babaei S, Eloon Kashkuli F, R B. The relationship between the amount of physical activity and general health in Urmia Medical University students. *J Urmia Nurs Midwifery Fac.* 2014;12:168.
22. Zare N, Daneshpajooh F, Amini M, Razeghi M, Fallahzadeh MH. The relationship between self-esteem, general health and academic achievement in students of Shiraz University of Medical Sciences. *Iran J Med Educ.* 2007;7:59–67.
23. Heravi-Karimooi M, Rejeh N, Sharif Nia H. The relationship between nursing students' spiritual intelligence and their general health in Tehran, 2012. *Iran J Med Educ.* 2014;14:1–14.
24. Samimi R, Rodsary DM, Hosseini F, Tamadonfar M. Correlation between lifestyle and general health in university students. *Iran J Nurs.* 2007;19:83–93.
25. Mosalanejad L, Mitra A. The effect of education on mental vulnerability and the last two groups of first year students of Medical Sciences. *Q J Fundam Mental Health.* 2004;6(21–22):71–6 [Persian].
26. Sotodeh N, Rezaei H, Nazari M, Ghanbari F. Comparison of health status among junior and senior students of nursing and medicine in Semnan University of medical sciences in 2011-2012 academic years. *Iran J Med Educ.* 2014;14:232–40.

27. Santini R, Santini P, Danze JM, LeRuz P, Seigne M. Study of the health of people living in the vicinity of mobile phone base stations: I. influences of distance and sex. *Pathol Biol.* 2002;50:369–73.

28. Raskauskas J. Associations with traditional bullying and depression among New Zealand adolescents. *J Sch Violence.* 2010;9:74–97.

29. Morsy AA, NS S. The use of technology by university adolescent students and its relation to attention, sleep, and academic achievement. *J Am Sci.* 2012;8:264–70.

30. Kamibeppu K, Sugiura H. Impact of the mobile phone on junior high school students' friends hips in the Tokyo metropolitan area. *Cyber psychol Behav.* 2005;8:121–30.

31. Mohammadi Farrokhran E, Mokhayer Y, Tavakkol Z, Mansouri A. Relationship between quality of sleep and medical health among students living in dormitories. *Knowl Health.* 2012;7:112–7.

32. Chegini A, GhaleBandi MF, K A. Sleep quality in medical residents and its relationship with general health. *Iran J Psychiatry Clin Psychol* 2015;22:50–57.

33. Ahn SY, YJ K. The influence of smart phone use and stress on quality of sleep among nursing students. *Indian J Sci Technol. 2015;8:1–6.*

34. Pirzadeh A. The relation between general health and internet addiction in medical students, Isfahan, Iran. *J Health Syst Res.* 2012;8:52–8.

Index

R

S

T

U

V

W